Human Immortality
and the Redemption of Death

Human Immortality and the Redemption of Death

Simon Tugwell, O.P.

Templegate Publishers
Springfield, Illinois

First published in 1990 by
Darton, Longman & Todd Ltd
89 Lillie Road, London SW6 1UD

First published in the United States in 1991 by
Templegate Publishers
302 East Adams Street / P.O. Box 5152
Springfield, Illinois 62705

ISBN 0-87243-181-9

Other books by Simon Tugwell:

The Beatitudes
Ways of Imperfection
New Heaven? New Earth?
Prayer: Living with God
Prayer in Practice
Did You Receive the Spirit?

This book is based on ten lectures given in the University of Bristol in 1988, when the author was invited to be the Read-Tuckwell lecturer for that year. The Read-Tuckwell lectureship was established by a residual bequest to the University of Bristol made by Alice Read-Tuckwell, who directed in her will that income deriving from the trust funds should be used to establish and maintain the lectureship and that the lecturer should deliver a course of lectures on Human Immortality and related matters, the course of lectures to be printed and published.

Contents

Preface

'Pale death' may indeed kick, sooner or later, at everybody's door,[1] but this does not mean that we find it easy to know what to make of death. And it seems to be almost impossible to stop the human race wondering what lies beyond death and what it is like being dead. Embarrassment about the silliness of the questions we want to ask drives us, as likely as not, to talk with a confidence it would be hard to justify, asserting boldly that being dead cannot mean anything to the dead precisely because they are dead, or perhaps that death is but the gateway to a brighter life, or at least to a comfortable and well-earned rest. Philosophers of all sorts and in all ages have discoursed eloquently about immortality, devising ingenious arguments for and against the claim that in some sense or other we are immortal, or that some aspect of us, such as the soul, is immortal. Christian theologians have not been slow to join in the fun, but a study of christian tradition suggests that perhaps, at the end, we have achieved little real clarity about just what it is we are to look forward to. For some time now there has been a conventional 'orthodoxy' (which is far from being the same thing as that orthodoxy which can properly be expected of all believers); this 'orthodoxy' has settled for the apparently clear conclusion that we have an immortal soul which, as such, survives death by right, and that we look forward, beyond that, to the resurrection of the body at some point in the future, when this world is brought to an end. But, even apart from the more rigorous philosophical difficulties which have been raised about this scenario, it appears that, whatever appeal it may once have had, it no longer satisfies some of our contemporaries, whether because they dislike talk of 'souls' or object to any kind of dissecting of the human person into body and soul, or because they find the idea of the resurrection of the body implausible or unattractive. In any case it must be said that the credentials of the conventional orthodoxy are not all that impressive, if one takes a broader view of the development of christian thinking on such subjects.

This book is based essentially on ten lectures I gave at Bristol University in 1988, when I was invited to deliver the annual Read-Tuckwell lectures on Human Immortality. The lectures were divided into two series and the book accordingly falls into two parts.

When I embarked on the lectures I knew little more than the audience did where they were going to lead me, and I have left the basic shape unchanged in the hope that the reader will be able to share something of the fun and excitement of my own voyage of discovery. This means, I am aware, that the connection between the two parts of the book is neither as rigorous nor as obvious as it might be. When I gave the first five lectures, I had only the vaguest idea of how the second series was going to take shape. Nor, when I started, did I foresee that so much of the first series was going to be devoted to pre-christian classical texts. I set off with little more than an undeveloped hunch that immortality might prove a rather costly notion, both in terms of conceptual puzzles and in terms of human values. I then found that it was possible to explore and cultivate this hunch with the help of far more classical literature than I had originally dreamed of using, and that my suspicions were far more deeply embedded in the christian tradition than I had dared to hope.

It would, I am sure, be possible to conduct a similar inquiry on the basis of literary and philosophical texts quite different from those that I have used; but there is a certain advantage in taking classical texts, both because they are safe from any suspicion of christian influence and because of their status in the early development of the culture which is still, to some extent, ours. What emerges from my study of them, I think, is a somewhat clearer picture of the human, as well as the conceptual and philosophical, issues involved in any attempt to breach the limits imposed on us by mortality. The first two chapters look at the obvious conceptual and linguistic problems inherent in claiming that a creature so manifestly mortal as ourselves is immortal; the problem can be located fairly precisely in the claim that the boundary between life and death can be fudged, which usually goes with the ascription to 'soul' of some life of its own, distinct from the psychosomatic life of the human person. The next two chapters look at various Greek attitudes to mortality, leading to the suggestion that there is a high human price to be paid for trying to evade mortality, either by denying it or by depriving it of its sting. The first half of the book then concludes on this basis by introducing the claims of christian theology, with the provisional intimation that christianity does, in principle, contain the wherewithal to make some sense of life and death, without falling foul of the human requirements that have emerged from the discussion of classical texts.

The second part is devoted chiefly to a study of the evolution of christian eschatology from its beginnings up to the end of the Middle Ages, by which time the conventional 'orthodoxy' was well established. One of my concerns was to try and discover something of the dynamics of the discussion which led to the formulation of this 'orthodoxy', and in the process I came to the conclusion that any tendency to insist heavily either on the immortality of the soul or the resurrection of the body is the product of an essentially false problematic.

The concluding chapter is not really a conclusion. In some ways it represents the beginning of a further inquiry, rather than the satisfying tying up of all the issues raised so far. But I do suggest there some rather hesitant steps which, I think, can be taken in the direction of clarifying the substance of the traditional christian eschatological hope.

I have deliberately not concerned myself very much with philosophical arguments for or against either the immortality of the soul or the resurrection of the body. Such arguments are brought in only where they can serve my own purpose, which is to try to interpret traditional christian doctrine and to suggest that this doctrine does make human and speculative sense, even if it falls short of answering all the questions we might like to raise.

Neither the original lectures nor this book which has resulted from them can claim to provide a systematic treatise on 'the Last Things'. But I hope that these avowedly selective probings into the history of classical and christian thought do add up to a suggestive pattern. I doubt if more can be expected. As the Sacred Congregation for the Doctrine of the Faith reminded us in 1979, 'Neither the Bible nor the theologians supply us with enough light to be able to describe properly the life that is to come after death.'[2]

To assist readers who, like me, find it easy to lose their chronological bearings, I have appended a list of sources, with minimal biographical information including dates, and some bibliographical matter, as well as a bibliography of modern works that I have used.

It remains only to thank all the people who have contributed to the making of this book. First and foremost, obviously, I am deeply indebted to the electors in Bristol University who gave me the incentive and the occasion to undertake what proved to be a fascinating intellectual and historical exercise. I must also express my profound appreciation of the kindness shown to me by members of several Departments in the university, whose fidelity to the lectures and the accompanying seminars and whose friendly attentions made my weekly visits extremely enjoyable; in particular I must mention Dr Denys Turner and Professor John Burrow. I am grateful to the librarians of the Biblioteca Apostolica Vaticana and the Cambridge University Library for their willingness to let me have microfilms of manuscripts which were important to this study. I am, finally, happy to acknowledge the help I have received from friends and colleagues who have read and commented on all or part of my typescript, notably (and in non-hierarchical alphabetical order) Brian Davies OP, Marcus Hodges OP, Fergus Kerr OP, Herbert McCabe OP and J. O. Urmson.

SIMON TUGWELL OP
18 MAY 1989

NOTES

1 Horace, *Odes* I 4.13–14.
2 *Acta Apostolicae Sedis* 71 (1979) p. 942.

Part I

Happily Ever After?

1

On the face of it the whole topic of human immortality looks most unpromising. A very little research in the Oxford English Dictionary reveals, not surprisingly, that 'immortal' means 'not liable or subject to death,' and that 'death' means 'the end of life, the final cessation of the vital functions of an animal or plant.' Even less research is needed to discover that it is rather characteristic of that particular kind of animal which we ourselves are that its vital functions do generally cease sooner or later, and cease finally. As Seneca drily remarks, it would be absurd to cite instances of human mortalilty to prove the point.[1] It is self-evident that human beings are liable or subject to death and are therefore not plausible candidates for immortality, unless we are willing to envisage a being which is simultaneously mortal and immortal. The New Testament seems to be on much more solid ground in claiming that God alone possesses immortality (1 Tim. 6:16).

Nevertheless from Plato onwards, and indeed even before Plato, philosophers have often not been shy of affirming immortality of human beings or at least of their souls, and the immortality of the soul has for centuries been regarded as an essental item of christian belief. To cite but two, fairly formal, texts, the Catechism of the Council of Trent, somewhat perversely, interprets the credal doctrine of the resurrection of the flesh as meaning primarily to teach the immortality of the soul;[2] and John Wesley, in the inaugural discourse which he preached on being appointed chaplain to the dowager Countess of Buchan, apparently on the recommendation of the famous Countess of Huntingdon, says without further ado 'that God has entrusted us with our soul, an immortal spirit made in the image of God.'[3]

In view of the plain fact that human beings die, and are therefore mortal, it is clear that some kind of conceptual jiggery-pokery must be involved in the contention that they are immortal, and our first task must be to try to pin down exactly where this jiggery-pokery lies. Fascinating arguments have been proposed for and against belief in human immortality, but it is not my intention here to pay much attention to them. My concern is the simpler and perhaps more primary one of trying to interpret what such belief means, and to see what human and speculative sense can be made of it.

Since, at least in our culture, it was the Greeks who started the whole discussion, let us begin with them.

As we might have expected, the old 'riddler' Heraclitus[4] throws us straight into the deep end, with the unabashed claim that mortality and immortality, and indeed that life and death, do coincide. Hippolytus quotes him as saying, 'Immortals are mortals, mortals immortals, living their death, having died their life.'[5] As with everything else that Heraclitus said, the interpretation of this fragment has been much disputed, but at least the syntax of it can be clarified fairly confidently. 'Having died their life' is a phrase which left its mark on subsequent Greek literature. In a fragment of some play, possibly by Menander, an unidentified character tells the audience in confidence that he has undergone a drastic change of life, perhaps owing to a conversion to philosophy. The darkness has gone, and he has come back to life. 'Gentlemen,' he says, 'I have entirely died the other life that I was living.'[6] Even though the text is corrupt in the only surviving papyrus, it is clear that this is what he is saying, and it seems likely that he is echoing Heraclitus. Later the Alexandrian Jewish philosopher Philo refers explicitly to our fragment of Heraclitus to support his contention that there is a kind of moral death that occurs 'when the soul dies the life of virtue and only lives the life of wickedness.'[7] Evidently Greek readers understood 'having died their life' as being modelled on the phrase 'to live such and such a life', and it is reasonable to presume that this is correct. To 'die' a particular kind of life is to stop living that kind of life. Similarly 'living their death' must be modelled on such phrases as 'living the life of a lord', and it must mean something like living the kind of life that can only be lived when one has stopped living 'their life'. The whole sentence must then mean that immortals and mortals are essentially the same beings;[8] qua mortals, they live a life which is, from the immortal point of view, death. They have ceased living the life of immortals, having 'died their life', and live as mortals, living the death of what they were as immortals.[9]

Since Hippolytus is our only direct source for this fragment, it is worth considering briefly what he makes of it. He presents it as a typical instance of the way in which Heraclitus identifies things which would normally be regarded as opposite to one another. It is quoted in connection with other remarks of the same kind, such as 'The way up and the way down are one and the same'[10] and 'Sea is both the purest water and the most foul.'[11] Hippolytus' interest in all this is to show that Noetus was a disciple of Heraclitus rather than of Christ, in line with his general strategy of trying to prove that the doctrines of the various christian heretics antedate the coming of Christ and so cannot be ascribed to christian revelation.[12] Noetus' refusal to distinguish the person of God the Son from that of God the Father is presented as a typically Heraclitean coincidence of opposites: the Father is the same as the Son, the Son being not one person born of another, but the same person being born of himself and in due course giving the Spirit to himself, dying and not dying and raising himself up on the third day.[13]

Hippolytus' own Christology is somewhat undeveloped,[14] but he could ill afford to treat Noetus' 'Heraclitean' paradoxes as mere nonsense, and in the *Contra Noetum*, assuming that it too is by Hippolytus or at least a report of his teaching,[15] he treats Noetus as posing a serious theological challenge calling for a serious theological answer. Certainly no orthodox Christology can dispose of the problem of Christ both dying and not dying, being both mortal and immortal, by appealing to the distinction of persons in the Trinity.[16] The *Contra Noetum* avoids the stark paradoxes which Hippolytus foists on Noetus, but the difficulty is still there: 'Although he is God made manifest, he does not deny what is human about him,' so he who is Life dies, but to show that 'being Life, he was not mastered by death,' he said, 'I have power to lay down my life and I have power to take it up again.' 'He who raises the dead is laid in the tomb, and he who is the resurrection and the life is raised on the third day by the Father.'[17] Pointing out that it is in his humanity that he is mortal and dies, while it is in his Godhead that he is immortal and does not die, does not eliminate the awkwardness of the doctrine that it is one and the same person who is thus both mortal and immortal, and dies while remaining alive.

To what extent christianity is simply echoing the Heraclitean paradox is a question we must return to later. For the moment our business is with Heraclitus, who was certainly not concerned with Christology or with the doctrine of the Trinity. Indeed for our present purposes it is not even very important to discover what he was concerned with, when he declared that 'immortals are mortals, mortals immortals.' It will suffice to consider how this startling proposition is related to other things that the Greeks said.

That mortals and immortals are essentially the same kind of being, only differently circumstanced, is a doctrine not peculiar to Heraclitus. There is a formal statement of it in Pindar, for example: 'The race of men, the race of God, is one; from one mother we both have breath. But we are separated by a complete distinction of power, so that the one is nothing, while on the other hand the bronze heaven endures always as a secure abode.'[18] For Pindar, however, at least in most of his poems, the separation between mortals and immortals is absolute:

> We must seek from the gods of fortune (πὰρ δαιμόνων) things which are fitting for mortal minds, knowing what is at our feet, of what estate we are. My soul, do not aspire to an immortal life, but make the most of what is practicable.[19]

This warning not to infringe the prerogatives of the gods is typical of Greek morality.[20]

All the same, Greek mythology was familiar with the idea of some mortals becoming immortal. Thus Ganymede was famously taken to dwell with the immortals as Zeus' cupbearer,[21] and the Homeric *Hymn to Aphrodite* draws the obvious conclusion and makes Hermes reassure Ganymede's father that he is now 'immortal and unageing like the gods.'[22] Similarly Zeus is said, in what is probably an interpolated addition to Hesiod's *Theogony*, to have made Dionysus' wife Ariadne 'immortal and unageing.'[23]

If we assume that there is no radical difference between the nature of mortals and that of the immortals, there is no particular problem about cases like these, where someone is said to have become immortal instead of dying. Precisely because they did not die, but were rescued before having to face death, they can straightforwardly be called 'immortal' (ἀθάνατοι, deathless), once their status is changed so as to guarantee that they will never have to face death in the future.

The situation is rather more delicate when people do die and are then divinised. The author of the *Iliad* scrupulously avoids this situation. For him, even Heracles and the Dioscouroi (Castor and Polydeuces) are simply dead.[24] In the *Odyssey* though, the position is rather more complicated. In the famous book XI one of the people Odysseus meets in Hades is Heracles; but, at least in the text as we now have it, the poet goes on to specify that what Odysseus actually met was only an 'image' (εἴδωλον), a word used several times to describe the dead in Hades, while 'he himself (Heracles) is with the immortal gods, enjoying their festivities.'[25] So Heracles, in the form of his εἴδωλον, is in Hades, like all the other dead, but at the same time he is also enjoying himself with the immortals – though it is worth noticing perhaps, that he is not actually said to be immortal himself or even, for that matter, alive. The situation is not totally different, though it is obviously very different, from that of the heroes who are left lying on the battlefield while their souls depart to Hades.[26]

The later story, found in the mythographer Apollodorus, has a cloud descend while Heracles is on his pyre, apparently still alive, and carry him up to heaven with a thunderclap, and in heaven he receives immortality and marries Hebe, after being reconciled with Hera.[27] This version of the story is presumably intended to eliminate the awkwardness of having him die, so that there will be no further question of his being simultaneously both dead and immortal.

Lucian, with the benefit of later speculation, cites Heracles' passing as an analogy for the way in which philosophy purges people: when he was burned on Mount Oeta he became a god, casting off whatever was human and so detaching what was divine in him and ascending with it to the gods.[28] Once again it looks as if this purging out of what is mortal is intended to be a way of letting him off dying so that he can become a god, an immortal, without the complication of being also dead. But Lucian's terminology suggests that all along there was something in Heracles which was divine, and so presumably immortal, by right. Until the human, mortal element was purged out he was therefore a kind of hybrid, like the unfortunate Strephon in *Iolanthe*, whose predicament caricatures nicely all such 'hybrid' views of human immortality: 'My upper half is immortal, but my lower half grows older every day, and some day or other must die of old age. What's to become of my upper half when I've buried my lower half I really don't know.'[29]

In principle, however, stories of people being made immortal by fire are quite independent of any 'hybrid' theory. They are found as early as the Homeric *Hymn to Demeter*, which its recent editor dates to the seventh century BC.[30] Demeter there takes a purely human baby, Demophon, and sets about making it immortal by putting it in the fire every night, and she claims she would have succeeded in making him 'immortal and unageing', had she not been interrupted.[31]

The unexplicitated presupposition of stories like this is that mortality is not an essential attribute of human beings, it is more like a virus which can be expelled, if the right procedure for doing so can be discovered. But it has to be discovered in time: immortality is an alternative to dying. There is something profoundly unsatisfactory about the Homeric Heracles who is both in Hades and with the immortals.

Dionysus' mother, Semele, posed a similar problem. According to the traditional story, found in Apollodorus, Zeus loved Semele, but Hera, in a fit of jealousy, persuaded her to ask her lover to appear to her in the same form as when he wooed Hera. The result so terrified the poor lady that she died. Later on her son Dionysus sought her in Hades and rescued her and took her with him to heaven.[32] This means that she too was strictly both dead and divine, a paradox clearly relished by Pindar, who yokes life and death together in a deliberately shocking manner in his comment on her: 'She lives in Olympus, having died from the thunder's roaring' (ζώει μὲν ἐν'Ολυμπίοις ἀποθανοῖσα).[33] As in the case of Heracles, this paradox was found offensive to some people. Pausanias, after reporting the traditional story, comments, 'I am not persuaded that Semele, being Zeus' wife, ever died in the first place.'[34]

The most intractable case was that of the Dioscouroi. In the *Iliad* they are simply presented as being dead, 'held in the earth;'[35] but in the *Odyssey* they are held *alive* in the earth, having honour from Zeus, being alive and dead on alternate days (ἄλλοτε μὲν ζώουσ' ἑτερήμεροι, ἄλλοτε δ'αὖτε τεθνᾶσιν),[36] and this curious arrangement was reported in the non-Homeric *Cypria* in such a way that Proclus could sum it up as 'immortality on alternate days' (ἑτερήμερον ἀθανασίαν).[37]

Pindar fills out the story. Polydeuces and Castor have the same human mother, but Castor has a mortal father while Polydeuces' father is Zeus. When Castor gets killed in battle Polydeuces prays, 'Father Zeus, what release will there be from sorrows? Command death for me too with him, Lord.'[38] Zeus then offers him the chance to escape death and old age if he wants, by coming with him to Olympus. 'But if you strive for your brother and intend to share everything equally, then for half the time you can breathe beneath the earth and for half the time you can breathe in the golden home of heaven.' Polydeuces opts to go equal shares with his brother, so Castor is retored to life,[39] and thereafter they spend one day with Zeus and one day in the recesses of the earth.[40] This is clearly a refusal of immortality on Polydeuces' part, as Apollodorus explicitly says,[41] which makes the story more sophisticated than the one apparently told in the *Cypria*, which simply calls Polydeuces 'immortal'.[42] Instead of by-passing death, as he could have done if he had accepted Zeus' offer, he prefers to share both life and death with his brother, spending one day alive and one day dead (or at least in the earth, like the dead).

When we get to Lucian the story is retold for comic purposes. In the *Dialogues of the Gods* Apollo asks why Castor and Polydeuces are never seen in heaven together, why there is always one of them dead, while the other is a god. Hermes explains that 'they do this out of brotherly love. When one of Leda's sons was due to die and one to be immortal, this is how they divided up immortality.' Apollo comments that it is a stupid arrangement,[43] which of course it is, and Lucian wants us to enjoy the absurdity of it. And not the least part of the absurdity is this idea of having a half-share in immortality, so that both parties spend half their time deathless and half their time dead.

Although Lucian was not the first person to employ the word 'immortality' in connection with the Dioscouroi, it is clear that he can get much more comic mileage out of this bizarre kind of on-and-off immortality than he could have done with the more cautious version of the tale in which Polydeuces refuses immortality. And his obvious relishing of the absurdity of combining death and immortality like this confirms the presence of an instinct to keep death and immortality rigorously apart.

What seems to be much less worrying to the Greeks is the combination of death and continued existence. Hesiod's account of the successive ages of mankind is interesting in this regard.[44] He prefaces it with the announcement that he is going to tell us 'how both gods and mortal men came into being from the same source' (ὁμόθεν) and then launches into a description of the 'golden race of men' which was the first to be made by the mortals. These people lived without any ills to disturb them, free from old age, and they died as easily as going to sleep. 'But since the earth covered this race, they are *daimones*, by the counsel of great Zeus, good guardians on earth of mortal men.' It apparently does not matter that they are both on earth and covered by the earth, or that they continue to function even though they are dead. But they are quite certainly not to be identified with the 'immortal guardians' of men referred to elsewhere in the poem, even though the interpolation of some lines about these latter into the passage on the dead of the golden age shows that they were confused in antiquity.[45] The function of the two sets of guardians is quite distinct: the first are givers of wealth, while the second are supervisors of human morality. There is no suggestion in Hesiod that the former are immortal, nor does he even say they are alive. They continue to operate, and indeed operate in a new way, but they are dead for all that.

After the golden race comes the silver race, and they lived shorter and more wretched lives than their predecessors, and then they too were covered by the earth. There 'they are called blessed mortals, beneath the earth.' Although they merit the epithet 'blessed', like the gods, they are explicitly contrasted with the immortals; and, inasmuch as they are more straightforwardly 'beneath the earth', without being in any sense still 'on' it, they seem to be more completely subject to death than the more fortunate men of the golden race.

Next comes the bronze race, and they were rather a bad lot. They died at each other's hands and went down to Hades 'unnamed, and dark death took them, mighty though they were, and they left the bright light of the sun.' This is the first race explicitly consigned to Hades, and it is apparently even more dead than either of the two preceding races.

Then comes a vastly superior race, a 'divine race of hero-men, who are called demigods.' They were all overtaken by death and Zeus gave them a place at the ends of the earth, where they dwell, free from care, in the Isles of the Blessed. An interpolator adds that this residence of theirs is quite separate from that of the immortals, and it is clear that Hesiod himself would not have wanted us to confuse these privileged mortals in any way with the immortals.

As far as Hesiod is concerned, then, the dead are dead, whatever may happen to them after death. Some are perhaps more dead than others, and they may all continue to exist after they are dead, but Hesiod does not say that any of them is still alive, let alone that they are immortal. Even if mortals and immortals all derive from the same ultimate origin, their paths are kept rigorously distinct.

There may be puzzling cases then, of people who are both dead and divine, even dead and alive, like the Homeric Heracles, like Semele, like the Dioscouroi, but on the whole, judging from the evidence we have looked at so far, the Greeks seem to have retained an instinctive sense that death and life do not mix. If the dead continue to exist, this does not mean that they are, after all, still living; they continue to exist precisely as dead people.

The bearer of post mortem existence is, in Homeric language, generally called ψυχή, conventionally translated 'soul'. And, as has been pointed out often enough, ψυχή does not, for Homer, denote the seat of personal identity for the living.[46] Achilles sent 'many souls of heroes to Hades, making the heroes themselves (αὐτούς) the prey of dogs.'[47] This distinction between the person and his 'soul' is typical. When the soul departs the person is dead. And it is only superficially confusing that you can say either that the soul goes to Hades or that the person goes there.[48] And, since a person dies when he loses his soul, it is quite intelligible, even if mildly illogical, for Odysseus to say to the Cyclops, 'I wish I could send you to the house of Hades, bereft of soul and life,'[49] or for Aeschylus to refer to the dead in Hades as being 'without soul' (ἄψυχοι).[50] Being without soul means being dead, even if, in Hades, soul takes over, so to speak, as the dead equivalent of the person. In Hades therefore soul can be readily identified as the person, but the person precisely as dead. So it is quite natural that the soul of a masculine dead person can be treated sometimes as feminine, in accordance with the gender of ψυχή, and sometimes as masculine, as when the soul of Teiresias is said to come having (ἔχων, masculine) a golden sceptre, and then 'he' drinks of the sacrificial blood.[51]

Although Homer's dead are presented as having some interests in continuity with their previous life, it is clear that their souls, at least from the point of view of the living, do not represent a genuine continuation of personal life. As the soul of Achilles says to Odysseus, Hades is the place 'where the mindless dead dwell, images (εἴδωλα) of mortals who have been overcome.' Teiresias alone has the unique privilege of retaining his mind (νόος) in Hades.[52] In a moving passage in *Iliad* XXIII the dead Patroclus appears to Achilles, who bursts out in grief: 'So there is, even in the halls of Hades, a soul and image, but there is no mind there at all (ἀτὰρ φρένες οὐκ ἔνι πάμπαν). All night long the soul of poor Patroclus has stood over me, groaning and lamenting, and gave me detailed instructions, and it was marvellously like him.'[53]

In Homer Hades is emphatically the realm of the dead; so much so that Odysseus and his companions, on their return from visiting Hades, are addressed by Circe as 'twice-dying.'[54] And the souls which make up the population of Hades seem to have no function at all before death, except to get lost at death. If the presence of soul is essential for life, this appears to mean only that the continuation of life requires that there should not be any presence of the person's soul elsewhere.

However a fragment of Pindar preserved in the pseudo-Plutarch collection of consolatory commonplaces, known as the *Consolatio ad Apollonium*, appears to tell a rather different story and brings us back to the 'hybrid' view of human beings:

> The body of everyone follows mighty death, but there remains alive (ζωόν) an image (εἴδωλον) of life, for it alone is from the gods. And it sleeps when the limbs are active, but to people who are asleep it shows in many dreams an impending judgment of things pleasant and unpleasant.[55]

The 'image' here is obviously the same as the Homeric 'soul', and a similar doctrine of ψυχή occurs also in the Hippocratic treatise on dreams: the soul is awake when the body is asleep and vice versa.[56]

In spite of his normal strictures on daydreams of immortality, Pindar certainly gives the impression, in the fragment just cited, of crediting the soul with an immortality that it possesses by right. And at least occasionally he seems to envisage a glorious post mortem life for this immortal soul, if it is worthy of it.[57]

This doctrine looks so different from that of Homer that Dodds famously conjectured an influx of shamanistic beliefs to account for it;[58] but the novelty should not be exaggerated and needs to be identified more precisely. Bremmer may well be right to connect much of what Pindar says with widespread primitive beliefs, and to suggest that the non-appearance of such beliefs in Homer is due to the requirements of Homer's own narrative.[59]

What is new in Pindar, by comparison with Homer and Hesiod, is the ascription of *life* to the soul in its own right, with the consequence that the distinction between the living person and the dead person becomes a distinction between the mortal body and the (apparently) immortal soul. Pindar's way of talking allows us to say that the soul goes on living when the body dies, whereas for Homer it is more a matter of the whole person dying, so that soul is not a principle of post mortem life, it is rather the representative of the dead person in the place of death, Hades. Death introduces a dichotomy, not primarily between body and soul as two separable entities, but between the dead person left on the battlefield or wherever and the dead person in Hades.[60]

However for both Pindar and Homer the essential thing is that soul, ψυχή, represents an alternative mode of existence to what we ordinarily call life, and there is no normal contact between the activities (if any) of soul and the consciousness of the living. In Homer, as in Pindar and the Hippocratic treatise on dreams, soul seemingly comes into its own, not only in death but also on other occasions on which waking consciousness is suspended. Soul is explicitly said to depart when someone swoons,[61] and there is a definite parallelism between death and sleep: not only are both 'poured over' people,[62] they are declared to be 'twin brothers',[63] and in the *Odyssey* there is a reference to sleep as 'most closely resembling death.'[64] So there is no radical division between what happens in sleep or swooning and what happens in death. As Odysseus' mother explains to him in Hades, the law which governs mortals when anyone dies is that flesh and bones are consumed by fire, but the soul 'flits away like a dream.'[65] From the point of view of the living (or the waking), soul is no more than a dream, a semblance of life. From a different point of view, which does not concern Homer or which he perhaps rejected, but which was not necessarily unthinkable in his culture, this 'dream' existence might have considerable value.

Between Homer and Pindar then, there is not necessarily any fundamental disagreement about the relationship between soul and human life. The chief point at issue is whether soul, in itself, can be regarded as alive and capable of having an interesting and significant life on its own, or whether soul is simply that whose presence ensures life and whose absence denotes death. Hesiod, as we have seen, is prepared to allow at least some of the dead a post mortem existence every bit as pleasant as that which Pindar describes; only he never calls it 'life'. If Homer, on the whole, presents a much more gloomy view of what it is like being dead, it was probably his own choice to do so, not something inherited from his culture.

Even the poet of the *Odyssey* stresses a very negative assessment of what it is like being dead. When Odysseus tries to cheer up the soul of Achilles by pointing out that in Hades he is a powerful ruler among the dead, Achilles refuses the consolation: 'Do not assuage death for me; I would rather be on earth as someone's serf . . . than rule all the dead.'[66] But there are at least some hints that the picture need not have been painted in such bleak colours. During his visit to the underworld Odysseus sees Minos judging the dead, and this surely means that he is determining their postumous fate, not, as Garland suggests, that he is dealing with lawsuits between the dead.[67] Even the *Iliad* refers to post mortem punishment of perjurers by the Furies.[68] If neither poem actually alludes to any outcome of this infernal judgment except punishment, the sheer fact of judgment implies the possibility of a more benign verdict in some cases. And at the end of the *Odyssey*, though this may be due to a later interpolator, we learn that the souls of the slain suitors are escorted by Hermes to 'the asphodel meadow where souls dwell,'[69] which does not sound too dreadful.

What does not seem to be allowed in the Homeric poems or in Hesiod, and was perhaps genuinely unthinkable, was the idea of *life* after death. When the poet of the *Odyssey* wants to give someone a happier final destiny, he sends him to bliss as an alternative to dying, not as a consequence of dying. It would apparently not be right for Menelaus to die, so instead the immortals intend to despatch him to the Elysian plains, we are told, where there is the easiest possible way of life (βιοτή) for human beings.[70] There is no question of *soul* being thus transported to posthumous delights, as there is in Pindar, because for Homer 'soul' always connotes death, not life. Pindar's living soul, however rooted in tradition, does seem to be an innovation. Because it is alive it can be immortal; Homeric 'soul' cannot be immortal because it was never really alive in itself.

So far then, we have found little sign, except in Pindar, of any context which would diminish the paradoxical effect of Heraclitus' combination of mortality and immortality, life and death. Mortals die, and when they are dead they are dead, whatever may befall them thereafter; they are therefore not deathless, ἀθάνατοι.

Conversely it is self-evident that immortals do not die. Although St Anselm bids us, in rather dramatic terms, consider whence we have fallen, 'from the delightfulness of immortality into the bitterness and horror of death,'[71] it does not, on the face of it, make sense to imagine that any really immortal being could ever fall from immortality to death. It is intelligible to postulate that Adam *need* not have died, but as long as he *could* die he was not immortal, or he was immortal only in the utterly trivial sense in which any living creature that has not yet died and is not immediately at risk is 'deathless'.

In Greek literature we find reasons both of common sense and of theology for insisting on the inamissibility of immortality. This is the point of the joke in Aristophanes' *Birds:* Iris, the messenger of the gods, is caught trying to fly through the airspace of Cloud-cuckoo-land by Peisthetairos, who assures her that, if she had got what she deserved, she would have been put to death. She protests that she is immortal, but he, stern immigration official that he is, will have none of this: even if she is immortal, she would still have been put to death.[72]

More seriously Aristotle cites Xenophanes as arguing that to ascribe birth to the gods is as impious as ascribing death to them,[73] which implies, as Kahn points out, that everyone would agree about the impropriety of ascribing death to the gods.[74] It is on this basis that Callimachus disposes very brusquely of the Cretan claim to possess the birthplace of Zeus: 'Cretans are always liars, for the Cretans have made a tomb for you, Lord; but you do not die, for you are for ever.'[75]

Essentially then, mortals are mortals and immortals are immortals. Even people with mixed mortal and immortal parentage do not end up, like Strephon in *Iolanthe*, half mortal and half immortal. Thetis, we are told, wanted to make Achilles immortal by burning off whatever was mortal in him.[76] Since she failed, he remained entirely mortal and in due course died. If she had succeeded he would have become entirely immortal and would not have died. Traditional Greek mythology can envisage changes of status of this kind, such that someone who was mortal becomes immortal instead of dying. But otherwise the boundary between the two categories is secure.

What traditional Greek usage does allow for is that the dead go on existing and, at least in some cases, go on functioning, but only as 'souls', that is, precisely as people who are dead. There is an evident undertow of resistance to the idea that souls are alive or immortal in their own right or that the dead in some sense continue to live.

The ascription of life and immortality to the soul seems to derive from a quite different source, which the Greeks themselves regarded as foreign or at least esoteric. Herodotus asserts that it was the Egyptians who first maintained that the human soul is immortal and, when the body perishes, migrates into other animal forms until it eventually returns to a human body, the whole cycle taking three thousand years. 'And,' he goes on, 'some Greeks have made use of this account as it if were their own, some earlier, some later. I know their names, but do not write them here.'[77] It is far from certain that the Egyptians ever did develop a fully-fledged theory of metempsychosis,[78] but it is still significant that Herodotus thought that it was originally a non-Greek belief. And if his unnamed Greeks include Pythagoras, as seems likely, his allegation of plagiarism is supported by Heraclitus, who makes the same accusation, though without specifying that Pythagoras' source was a foreign one.[79] Plato too introduces the idea of the immortality of the soul as being an esoteric religious doctrine,[80] clearly not part of the everyday beliefs of the Greeks.

The idea that the soul is alive and indeed immortal in its own right was perhaps facilitated by, or perhaps it was a cause of, a change in the use of the word ψυχή, making it denote the conscious personality of the living, not just the bearer of the alternative mode of existence which takes over when waking life goes into abeyance or ceases entirely. This new usage is found as early as Anacreon, as Hermann Fränkel points out.[81] In one of his poems the sixth-century poet says:

O boy with the girlish look,
I pursue you and you take no notice,
not knowing that you hold the reins
of my soul (ψυχή).[82]

If soul is immortal and alive and conscious in its own right, somewhat bizarre linguistic puzzles ensue. Witness Herodotus' account of the Getae, who claim immortality for themselves: 'They think that they do not die, but that the person who perishes (τὸν ἀπολλυμένον) goes to the daimon Salmoxis.' Every five years they choose someone by lot to go to Salmoxis as a messenger to tell him of their needs. The chosen party is thrown in the air on to three spears being held nearby. If he 'dies', this is a sign that the god has accepted their embassy. If he does not die, they blame the intended messenger and find someone else to go instead. They give him his marching orders while he is 'still alive.'[83]

Judging from the cursing tablets which have been found in graves all over the Greek world, dating from the late fifth century onwards, the Greeks themselves adopted the practice of using the dead as messengers to the chthonic deities; but there is no evidence of such a practice in earlier times, and it may be regarded as a foreign importation.[84]

In any case it is clear that we are now embroiled in considerable jiggery-pokery. Precisely because the soul is alive and goes on living after death, death becomes a significant and potentially useful part of life. It is not the simply living or the simply dead who can be used as messengers to the gods, it is the living dead.

If we annexe this idea of the immortality and personality of the soul to the traditional notion of the departed ψυχή as the bearer of an existence which is an alternative to life, we get into an even knottier linguistic perplexity, as we can see from a passage in Plato's *Gorgias*. Socrates suggests that it is people who need nothing who are happy, which prompts Callicles to exclaim that in that case 'stones and dead people would be the happiest.' Socrates retorts that Callicles' policy of indulging all desires would make for a dreadful life, and he would not be surprised if Euripides was right to say, 'Who knows if life isn't death and death life?' 'Perhaps we are really dead,' Socrates goes on, alleging the authority of 'the wise' for the belief that in this life we are dead and our bodies are our tombs.[85]

This sort of language brings us much closer to Heraclitus, and indeed Heraclitus is explicitly interpreted in the light of just such a belief by Philo: 'Heraclitus says, "We live their death, we have died their life;" that is, now, while we are alive, the soul is dead and buried in the body as in a tomb, but, if we die, the soul lives its own life, freed from evil and the dead bond of the body.'[86] A similar doctrine became part of Neoplatonist orthodoxy, as we can see from Damascius' commentary on the *Phaedo*, which points out that there are two kinds of death for the soul, one which buries it in the body, and one which delivers it from the body.[87]

A doctrine like this presupposes the traditional view that it is not possible to have life (in the ordinary sense) and an existence as soul simultaneously, but, contrary to the more fundamental Greek tradition, it ascribes life and immortality to the soul. Therefore soul, precisely because it is alive in its own right, has to die if ordinary mortal life is to ensue, to resume its own life only when this mortal life dies. And if soul is immortal, with all the glamorous associations that go with this word, then clearly the life of the soul must be a much more real and worthwhile life than anything we enjoy as mortals. So long as we are living this mortal life therefore, we are really dead, and it is only when we are dead that we are really alive.

As is suggested by Harder in his study of Cicero's *De Somnio Scipionis*,[88] the contention that this life is really death grows out of the conventional Greek pessimism which is expressed, for instance, in these lines of Theognis:

> The best thing of all for people on earth is never to have been born nor to see the rays of the sharp sun, but, once one has been born, the best thing is to go as quickly as possible to the gates of Hades and lie with a great heap of earth over one.[89]

According to Aristotle it is on everyone's lips that 'not being born is best of all, and being dead is better than being alive.'[90]

There are, of course, perfectly ordinary ways of talking about life which at least make it somewhat easier to raise the question whether this earthly life is really life at all. When Catullus says, *Vivamus mea Lesbia atque amemus* ('Let us live, let us love, my Lesbia'),[91] we all know what he means; nor is Seneca being opaque, when he says that 'we live only the smallest part of life, the rest is not life, but time.'[92] Mere biological life is not what we mean by 'life', and the Greeks could say that as easily as we can. Xenophon, for instance, refers to 'the fine things which make up what we mean by "life",'[93] and Euripides alludes to a life which 'is not life, but disaster.'[94] All the same it is going a long way beyond ordinary parlance to suggest that we are only really alive when we are dead.

It is not surprising that Aristophanes could have great fun playing around with Euripides' question whether life is not really death. In the *Frogs* he has Aeschylus fuming over the way his rival brought on women in his plays claiming that 'living is not living,'[95] and when, later on, Dionysus announces that Aeschylus has won the competition so that he, not Euripides, is to be brought back to life, and Euripides complains that he is being neglected now that he is dead, Dionysus blithely comments, 'Who knows whether life isn't death and breath isn't broth and sleep a fleece?'[96] In everyday language it must always be the case that life and death are radically opposed to one another, so that where a living character would say, 'Strike me dead!', Aristophanes can make one of the dead characters in the *Frogs* use the corresponding oath, 'Strike me alive!'[97]

Once we bring in a living and personal soul, though, endowed with immortality by right, it is difficult to see how we can avoid some sort of paradoxical compounding of life and death, and a 'hybrid' view of man, allocating endless life to the soul and mortality and death to the body, yields only a specious clarification of this paradox and generates further paradoxes of its own.

Human beings have probably always told stories about privileged instances of people abandoning their mortality and becoming gods, and they have probably always told stories about the dead and about what it is like being dead. But the problems become much more acute when different kinds of story begin to merge with each other, and they become devastatingly difficult once we attempt to shed philosophical light on them. One of the first to undertake this attempt among the Greeks was Plato, and it is to him that we must now turn.

NOTES

1 *Consol. ad Marciam* 12.5.
2 *Catechismus Romanus* I xii 2.
3 Sermon 51.1.2, in A. C. Outler, ed., *The Works of John Wesley*, vol. II, Nashville 1985, p. 284.
4 The 3rd-century poet, Timon, calls Heraclitus 'riddler' in frag. 43 (ed. H. Diels, *Poetarum Philosophorum Fragmenta*, Berlin 1901, p. 195), quoted in Diogenes Laertius 9.6.

5 Hippolytus, *Refutatio* 9.10.6; Heraclitus frag. B 62 DK.
6 Pap. Didot II 3–4, ed. F. H. Sandbach in his Oxford text of Menander, Oxford 1976, p. 330. For the interpretation, see the commentary on Menander by A. W. Gomme and F. H. Sandbach, Oxford 1973, pp. 728–729.
7 Philo, *Leg. All.* 1.108.
8 This doctrine is also suggested by frag. B 53 DK: 'War is the father of all and king of all, and some he has appointed gods, some he has appointed men.'
9 Commentators have largely ignored the syntactical parallels adduced here, which seem to be fairly decisive at least with regard to the syntax of the verbs. Otherwise there are two structural problems in the fragment: does **ἐκείνων** refer to the same people each time, with the corollary that the subject of the two participles must also be the same? And what is the subject of the two participles? (i) Porphyry clearly took the two pronouns as having different references, paraphrasing Heraclitus as saying 'We live their death and they live our life' (*De Antro Nympharum* 10), and this has generally been followed by modern commentators. But Philo, loc. cit., equally clearly took the two participles as having the same subject, so that **ἐκείνων** must also have the same reference each time (in his paraphrase Heraclitus is made to say, 'We live their death and we have died their life'). No evidence has been produced to show that, in Greek usage, repeated **ἐκεῖνος** can be taken as designating two different people (cf. M. Nussbaum's comments in *Phronesis* 17 (1972) p. 163), so, Porphyry notwithstanding, it is most natural to suppose that both participles have the same subject and both pronouns refer to the same set of people. (ii) Philo also clearly takes Heraclitus as meaning that 'mortals' is the subject of both participles, which corresponds to Kahn's 'strong' reading of the text (C. H. Kahn, *The Art and Thought of Heraclitus*, Cambridge 1979, p. 218), and this seems far more plausible than the alternative view, taking 'immortals' as the subject of 'living' (espoused by M. Marcovich, for instance, *Heraclitus*, Merida 1967, p. 240, and by Nussbaum, loc. cit.).
10 Frag. B 60 DK.
11 Frag. B 61 DK.
12 On Hippolytus' strategy, cf. C. Osborne, *Rethinking Early Greek Philosophy*, London 1987, pp. 15–17.
13 *Refutatio* 9.10.10–12.
14 On Hippolytus' Christology, see A. Grillmeier, *Christ in Christian Tradition*, vol. I, 2nd edn, London 1975, pp. 113–117.
15 The text is edited and studied by R. Butterworth, *Hippolytus of Rome, Contra Noetum*, London 1977, but the editor deliberately refrains from discussing questions of authorship, contenting himself with the remark, 'It is presumed for the moment that there does not seem to be any clear reason why the accepted author, Hippolytus of Rome, could not have written CN' (p. i). Grillmeier, op. cit. p. 116, draws attention to the 'Hippolytean colouring' of a passage from the work.
16 Even if 'Son' is a title properly belonging only to the incarnate Christ,

as the *Contra Noetum* maintains, the Son is still the same divine person as the eternal Logos (*Contra Noetum* 15.6–7), so the coincidence of mortality and immortality in the Son cannot be resolved by ascribing mortality to the Son and immortality to the Father.

17 *Contra Noetum* 18.1–5.

18 Pindar, *Nem.* 6.1–4.

19 *Pyth.* 3.59–62.

20 Aristotle was self-consciously going against popular moral wisdom, when he recommends, as the ideal, a life devoted entirely to intellectual pursuits, even though it might seem to be a life more divine than human; 'contrary to what people tell us, we should not, as human beings, confine ourselves to human things or, as mortals, confine ourselves to mortal things: as far as possible, we should be immortal' (*Nicomachean Ethics* 10.7.8, 1177b31–33). For the conventional wisdom, cf. Sophocles, *Trachiniae* 473; id., frag. 531.1 Nauck; Euripides, *Bacchae* 395–396; the adage (perhaps from Epicharmus) quoted by Aristotle in *Rhet.* 2.21.6 (3194b25), printed as Epicharmus B 20 DK.

21 *Iliad* 20.232–235.

22 *Hymn to Aphrodite* 214.

23 *Theogony* 949; on doubts about the genuineness of the passage, expressed even in antiquity, see M. L. West's edition, Oxford 1966, pp. 416–417.

24 *Iliad* 18.117–119, 3.243–244.

25 *Odyssey* 11.601–603. It was suspected by some ancient critics that lines 602–3 were interpolated (cf. the comment by A. Heubeck in his edition, vol. II, Milan 1983), but this has not been followed by modern critics on the whole.

26 E.g. *Iliad* 1.3–4.

27 Apollodorus 2.7.7.

28 Lucian, *Hermotimus* 7.

29 W. S. Gilbert, *Complete Operas*, Dorset Press edn, p. 242.

30 N. J. Richardson, ed., *The Homeric Hymn to Demeter*, Oxford 1974, p. 11.

31 *Hymn to Demeter* 235–245.

32 Apollodorus 3.4.3.

33 Pindar, *Ol.* 2.25.

34 Pausanias 2.31.2.

35 *Iliad* 3.243–244.

36 *Odyssey* 11.300–304.

37 *Homeri Opera* vol. V, ed. T. W. Allen, Oxford 1912, p. 103.

38 Pindar, *Nem.* 10.76–77.

39 Ibid. 80–90.

40 Ibid. 55–56.

41 Apollodorus 3.11.2.

42 *Cypria* frag. VI, Allen, ed. cit. p. 120.

43 Lucian, *Dial. Deorum* 25.

44 Hesiod, *Works and Days* 106–173.

45 Ibid. 249–255. Lines 124–125 are identical with lines 254–255, but they are not found in all the manuscripts and are certainly to be

dismissed as an interpolation. Cf. M. L. West's edition, Oxford 1978, p. 183.

46 Jan Bremmer, *The Early Greek Concept of the Soul*, Princeton 1983, chapters I and II, connects the Homeric ψυχή with beliefs found quite widely in other Indo-European cultures, suggesting that there was a common belief in a 'soul' which represented the person after death or in a state of trance or sleep, but which had no contact with normal waking consciousness.

47 *Iliad* 1.3–4.

48 For the latter see, for example, *Iliad* 22.482.

49 *Odyssey* 9.523–524.

50 *Psychagogoi* frag. 273a, in S. Radt, ed., *Tragicorum Graecorum Fragmenta* vol. III, Göttingen 1985, p. 372. Aristophanes clearly saw the comic potential in this kind of language, and has Aeschylus, parodying Euripides, refer to a dream sent from Hades as a messenger 'having a soulless soul' (ψυχὴν ἄψυχον ἔχοντα) *Frogs* 1332–1334.

51 *Odyssey* 11.90–91, 98. For the feminine, cf. for example *Odyssey* 11.471–472.

52 *Odyssey* 11.475–476, 494–495.

53 *Iliad* 23.103–107.

54 *Odyssey* 12.22.

55 Pseudo-Plutarch, *Consol. ad Apoll.* 120D; frag. 116 in the Oxford text of Pindar, ed. C. M. Bowra, Oxford 1947.

56 *Regimen* 86.

57 Cf. frags. 114, 115, 117 and 121 in Bowra's edition.

58 E. R. Dodds, *The Greeks and the Irrational*, Berkeley 1971, p. 140.

59 Op. cit. p. 52.

60 This does not, of course, mean that Homer cannot describe death in terms of soul and body going their separate ways: cf. *Odyssey* 11.216–222. The point is that soul, for Homer, represents the whole person in Hades, not a spiritual element in human beings which is unaffected by death.

61 E.g. *Iliad* 5.696, 22.467.

62 E.g. (death) *Iliad* 13.544, 16.414; (sleep) 23.62–63, 24.445.

63 *Iliad* 672; cf. Hesiod, *Theogony* 211–212.

64 *Odyssey* 13.80.

65 *Odyssey* 11.216–222.

66 *Odyssey* 11.485–491.

67 R. Garland, *The Greek Way of Death*, London 1985, p. 60.

68 *Iliad* 19.259–260.

69 *Odyssey* 24.13–14.

70 *Odyssey* 4.561–565.

71 Anselm, *Proslogion* 1.

72 Aristophanes, *Birds* 1224.

73 Aristotle, *Rhet.* 2.23 (1399b5); Xenophanes A 12 DK.

74 Kahn, op. cit. p. 328 note 293.

75 Callimachus, *Hymns* 1.8–9.

76 Apollodorus 3.13.6.

77 Herodotus 2.123.2–3.

78 Cf. W. Burkert, *Lore and Science in Ancient Pythagoreanism*, Cambridge Mass. 1972, p. 126.
79 Heraclitus B 40 DK.
80 Plato, *Meno* 81a.
81 *Dichtung und Philosophie des frühen Griechentums*, Munich 1976, p. 340.
82 Anacreon 15, in D. L. Page, ed., *Poetae Melici Graeci*, Oxford 1962.
83 Herodotus 4.94.
84 Garland, op. cit. p. 6.
85 Plato, *Gorgias* 492–493. Euripides, fragment 638 Nauck.
86 *Leg. Alleg.* 1.108.
87 L. G. Westerink, ed., *The Greek Commentaries on Plato's Phaedo* vol. II, Amsterdam 1977, p. 52.
88 R. Harder, *Über Ciceros Somnium Scipionis*, Halle 1929, p. 6.
89 Theognis 425–428, in M. L. West, ed., *Iambi et Elegi Graeci* vol. I, Oxford 1971.
90 Aristotle, frag. 44, in V. Rose, ed., *Aristotelis Fragmenta*, Stuttgart 1967.
91 Catullus 5.1.
92 Seneca, *De Brevitate Vitae* 2.2.
93 Xenophon, *Mem.* 3.3.11.
94 Euripides, *Alcestis* 802, though admittedly the word used here is βίος, which is less directly contrasted with death than ζωή is.
95 Aristophanes, *Frogs* 1082.
96 Ibid. 1476–1478.
97 Ibid. 177. The translation is suggested by W. B. Stanford in his commentary, London 1968, p. 87.

2

Plato's *Phaedo* is often, naturally enough, taken to be an elaborate proof of the immortality of the human soul or ψυχή. As such, it probably does not work. But it may still be worth taking another look at the dialogue, not in the hope of vindicating any demonstration of immortality, but rather in the hope of seeing more precisely what is at stake and what Plato's real interest may be.

The first mention of immortality in the dialogue is remarkably casual. It comes just after the conclusion of Socrates' first argument, which attempts to show that the living come into being from the dead and therefore (in Socrates' words) 'the souls of the dead exist' (τὰς τῶν τεθνεώτων ψυχὰς εἶναι) (72d). Cebes then comments that Socrates' contention that learning is really recollection, if true, would also show that 'the soul existed somewhere before coming into being in this human form; so in this way too the soul seems to be something immortal' (72e). It is significant that it is Cebes, the disciple of the Pythagorean Philolaus (61d), who introduces the word 'immortal' into the discussion, as immortality in the sense outlined by Herodotus was certainly a Pythagorean tenet. It is Cebes again, later on, who insists that it is not enough to prove that the soul pre-exists this present life, nor to show that the soul can outlast the body; it might, after all, endure birth and death repeatedly, but then finally wear out and perish. What is needed is a proof that the soul is absolutely immortal and imperishable (88ab). It is in response to this plea that Socrates produces his massive final argument, which is designed to show that the soul is, strictly, unsusceptible of death, immortal and imperishable, and which concludes triumphantly, 'So, Cebes, soul is immortal and imperishable and our souls will indeed exist in Hades' (106e).

Cebes' allusion to the doctrine of recollection is presumably meant to remind us of the earlier argument in the *Meno*. There (81a) Socrates invokes the doctrine of immortality, which he ascribes to priests and 'divine poets' like Pindar, to support his belief that learning is recollection. According to this doctrine the soul of man is immortal, dying and coming to birth again alternately, but never perishing. The awkwardness of saying that an immortal soul 'dies' is evidently felt, and Socrates softens it a bit by using the word τελευτᾶν (literally 'come to an end') and adding that this is 'what they call dying' (ἀποθνήσκειν), but for all that τελευτᾶν is a perfectly normal Greek word for 'dying'. In the course of its successive phases, the soul has seen 'what is here and what is in Hades and everything, so there is nothing it has not learned' (81c). Socrates proves his point by his famous geometrical experiment with the uneducated slave boy. No one has taught him geometry and at the beginning of the experiment he did not have the knowledge he patently did have at the end, so he must have had a sort of unconscious knowledge all along, which he cannot have acquired in this life. He must therefore have acquired it at some other time, and this must have been some time 'when he was not human' (ἄνθρωπος) (85–86). Socrates then infers that this unconscious knowledge, waiting to be activated by questioning, must have been there both when he was human and when he was not, so his soul must always ('the whole time', τὸν ἀεὶ χρόνον) have been in a state of having learned, since all the time he is either human or not human. Therefore the soul must be immortal (86ab).

This is a wretchedly bad argument. Immortality is inferred from the presence of truth in the soul the whole time, so immortality must be taken to mean existing the whole time; that truth is in the soul the whole time is inferred from its presence there both when one is human and when one is not, backed by the principle that one is either human or not human the whole time. But there are, of course, several ways of not being human, one of which is simply not to exist at all. The most that can be proved by Socrates' argument is that the soul must have pre-existed one's present life, and in the *Phaedo* this is pointed out by Simmias (77b), the other disciple of Philolaus who is involved in the conversation (61d).

Bad though the argument is, it raises some interesting points. First of all, it is striking that ante-natal existence is not regarded as human. It is before becoming human that one has learned things. So there is no question, strictly, of human immortality. And the soul, like the traditional Greek ψυχή, evidently goes underground when it is present in a human life, so that its knowledge is unconscious unless it is laboriously reactivated. It essentially represents a mode of existence alternative to that of ordinary conscious human life. And finally, precisely because it is soul that is immortal, it is essentially soul that undergoes the whole sequence of births and deaths, even if a half-hearted attempt is made to mitigate the paradox by using the word τελευτᾶν and hinting that ἀποθνήσκειν is rather a misnomer.

In the *Phaedo* Plato proceeds more cautiously. We are well into the dialogue before immortality is even mentioned, and there is good reason for this. The beginning of the conversation between Socrates and his friends, far from being about immortality, is essentially about death and being dead. Socrates makes it quite clear that, at least in some cases, the adage is correct: it is better to be dead than to be alive. And he justifies this assertion by affirming his hope that 'there is something in store for the dead'; a philosopher, at least, can be very hopeful that 'he will receive the greatest benefits there, when he has died' (62–63). Indeed philosophy is a rehearsal for 'dying and being dead' (64a). Seneca is probably right to say that this is a dialogue about death.[1]

From the outset the real topic of conversation is not immortality, but what it is like being dead, and it is to this topic that we return at the end, with the great myth of the hereafter (107–115). It is only in order to justify the hope that it is a good thing to be dead, at least for a philosopher, that the question is raised whether the soul continues to exist after death, and it is only the insistence of Cebes that turns the discussion of this into a discussion of immortality.

Socrates defends his contention that philosophy is a rehearsal for death on the basis of a definition of death (64c): dying means 'the separation (ἀπαλλαγή) of the soul from the body' and having died (or being dead – the perfect infinitive τεθνάναι can be translated either way) means that the body has come to be (γεγονέναι) on its own apart from the soul and the soul is (εἶναι) on its own apart from the body.

Socrates had been accused of offering a tendentious definition, which biases the discussion in favour of the soul's existence on its own after death,[2] but this is unfair.[3] His definition is in principle quite neutral, though it is, no doubt deliberately, worded in an ambiguous way. In the context of the dialogue as a whole it is tempting to translate it much less neutrally, but the immediate context should restrain us. ἀπαλλαγή often means 'release' and in 67d the corresponding verb in a similar context almost certainly does mean 'release', and the noun is replaced in 68a by two nouns which bring out the two possible ways of taking ἀπαλλαγή: 'release and separation' (λύσις καὶ χωρισμός). But in the definition itself the noun is neutralised, surely, by saying that the body is ἀπαλλαγέν from the soul, as well as vice versa, and there is no suggestion that death is a 'release' for the body. So the rendering 'separation' must be right here, however pregnant the ambiguity may be. Similarly we may wonder whether τεθνάναι is meant to refer to the state of being dead, as it certainly must do in 64a. But it is surely absurd to suppose that the body goes on existing on its own the whole time that people are dead,[4] so it is more natural here to take the perfect infinitive simply to mean 'having died': dying is a process, having died means that the process is completed, without preempting the discussion of what happens to the separated elements. Finally, ought we to take εἶναι as simply equivalent to γεγονέναι, in which case no particular claim is implicit in saying that, after the process of dying is complete, body and soul are both separate, neither necessarily continuing to exist in any significant sense? Or should we translate εἶναι 'exist', in which case Socrates is perhaps smuggling into his definition the claim that he wants to make about the continuing existence of the soul after death? Once again, I think we have to say that the definition itself should be interpreted neutrally, but with an awareness of its potential for being developed in a tendentious way.

Taken neutrally Socrates' definition is quite uncontroversial. It would fit Homeric usage without difficulty, and even more easily the more modern view found, for instance, in the epitaph on the Athenians who died in 432 in the battle of Potidaea, which states that 'the *aether* received their souls, but earth their bodies.'[5] As Garland remarks, this in no way suggests any personal immortality of the soul.[6] Its meaning is brought out in several passages in Euripides. In the *Supplices*, performed only a few years after Potidaea,[7] Theseus argues that the Argives who were killed in their attack on Thebes should be released for burial: 'And each thing should go back to the place from which it came into the light, the spirit/breath (πνεῦμα) to the *aether*, the body to the earth.'[8] Soul is here clearly identified with breath. If any notion of immortality is involved it is quite impersonal, as we learn from a fragment of the *Chrysippus*, which presents Earth and Aether as the parents of men and gods. 'And what is born from Earth goes back to earth, and what is born of Aether goes back to the pole of heaven. Nothing of what comes to be dies, but, one being separated from another, it shows a different appearance.'[9] Death is denied then, not because there is any personal survival, but only inasmuch as the separated ingredients in a human being continue to exist by being reabsorbed into their source. Finally Theonoe, in the *Helen*, announces that 'the mind of those who have died does not live, but it has an immortal intelligence (γνώμη), falling into immortal *aether*,'[10] where personal life is expressly denied to the mind which falls into immortal *aether*, so that the surviving intelligence is clearly not personal.

The neutral nature of Socrates' definition is shown further by the fact that Chrysippus the Stoic could use it as an argument for the materiality of the soul,[11] and Lucretius the Epicurean could use it in connection with his triumphant celebration of the fact that death is nothing to us, because when we are dead we no longer exist in any personal way.[12]

The ambiguous language used by Socrates no doubt makes it

easier for him to exploit his definition for his own purposes, but Plato does not in fact allow himself to cheat. The dialogue's official agent provocateur, Cebes, raises the question whether the soul does not simply disperse like breath or smoke when it is separated from the body (70a). In response Socrates, as in the *Meno*, appeals to an 'ancient doctrine' according to which souls pass from here to Hades and back again. But here, unlike the *Meno*, there is no mention of the soul being immortal. All that is claimed is that souls *exist* in between lives (70c). And it is noticeable that this time Socrates apparently feels no embarrassment about saying that the soul dies and comes to birth again. The effect of his first argument, that birth and death are cyclical, is to show that 'the soul exists when it has died (ἐπειδὰν ἀποθάνῃ)' (77d).

Plato has surely been quite deliberate in suppressing immortality. The last thing he needs is a soul that is exempt from death, if he is to maintain that it is better to be dead than alive. And, on Socrates' definition of death, it is nonsensical to say that the soul is incapable of dying. As the Neoplatonist commentator, Damascius, points out, it is precisely soul that is the subject of death.[13]

Indeed the basic thrust of Socrates' exposition is to make dying into an achievement word. The philosophical soul, which has trained itself in death by dissociating itself as far as possible from the body, succeeds in being completely separated from the body at death and 'truly' goes to Hades (80d), to spend its time thereafter with the gods (81b), whereas the soul which has not been properly trained remains 'body-shaped' even in death, and, being full of body, it does not go purely to Hades (83d) or succeed in becoming separate on its own (81c), that is, it does not succeed in fulfilling the definition of death. It is afraid of Hades and hangs around tombs (81cd).

In interpreting the *Phaedo* it is useful to be aware both how close we still are to the Homeric ψυχή and where we have departed from it. In principle ψυχή is still a mode of existence alternative to ordinary, waking consciousness. As such it occupies the interstices of human life. One of the most startling of Plato's philosophical innovations was to attempt to use ψυχή in this sense to provide a way out of the Socratic aporia. Like Socrates, Plato wanted to accept the rightness of our common instinct to say that 'there really is such a thing' as justice, piety and so on. But Socratic dialectic could never succeed in identifying them. So how do we know them? Plato's answer is a dramatic one, even if in the long run it did not prove as fruitful as he had hoped: we know things like justice and piety because we saw them before we ever began to live as human beings, when we existed as soul.[14] And this must be soul in the sense we have found in Pindar, soul which is awake when we are asleep and alive when we are dead, which operates continually only when we are dead. From the point of view of soul then, of course death is better than life.

Soul, in this sense, is not human in its own right, nor, in the first part of the *Phaedo*, is it ever said to be alive in its own right. And, as in Homer, it has an ambiguous relationship to human identity, though this ambiguity now shows signs of becoming troublesome. Soul existed 'before *we* came into being' (76e), the souls that are now ours acquired knowledge before we began to exist as human beings (76c). Yet Socrates also refers to his impending death in terms of his own departure (60c), and he says that, once he is dead, *he* will have gone away, leaving only his body for his friends to bury (115d); and one of the things he looks forward to after death is meeting *people* (ἄνθρωποι) who are better than those on earth (63b). This is reminiscent of the way in which Homer can say either that the dead person is in Hades or that the person is left lying on the battlefield, but in Homer this does not really matter, since both the corpse and the ψυχή *are* the dead person, considered from different points of view. In Plato, on the other hand, inasmuch as he is influenced by the esoteric tradition of immortality, soul cannot be said to be the person. Even in the first argument in the *Phaedo*, before 'immortality' is actually mentioned, Socrates appeals to an 'ancient doctrine' which postulates an endless cycle of births and deaths, incarnations and disincarnations (70c), which makes it very difficult to see what claim any individual has on any particular soul, except for the duration of his bodily life. If what Socrates essentially wants to claim is that it will be better for *him* to be dead (one of the advantages being the possibility of meeting other *people* who are dead), it is surely most unhelpful to appeal to a notion of soul which denies that the person who is alive shares a common identity with that which continues to exist after that person is dead.

The situation in Plato is more complicated than it was in Homer, not only because of the influence of esoteric doctrines but also because ψυχή now refers to the seat of consciousness in the living, waking human being, as in the poem of Anacreon quoted in Chapter 1. This is why the soul has to struggle to be free.

It is often suggested that the *Phaedo* is unlike Plato's other works in ascribing to a conflict between body and soul the tensions which elsewhere are seen as evidence of a conflict within the soul,[15] but this is at best only partly true. Even in the *Phaedo* the essential struggle goes on within the soul. If the soul is in a state of captivity in the body, it is nevertheless the soul itself which connives at this captivity and becomes vagrant and troubled (82e, 79c). It is the soul which feels the pleasures and pains which distort its perception of reality (83c).

The conflict is essentially between two different notions of soul, which are now both attached to the same soul. There is soul as the bearer of everyday life, and there is soul which works properly only when it is on its own, which, in other contexts, is by definition operative only when bodily consciousness ceases. It is soul in this latter sense which is invoked by Plato to account for human knowledge, and in the *Phaedo* it is made quite clear that, as far as it possibly can, it should go about its business on its own:

> Reality must be viewed by the soul; and it seems that we shall get the wisdom we desire and claim to be lovers of when we die, not while we are alive. If it is not possible to know anything purely while we are with the body, then there are two possibilities: either it will never be open to us to obtain knowledge, or it will be open to us when we have died. (66e)

The soul which can do the job which Plato wants done, namely acquire knowledge, is the old-fashioned soul, which comes into its own when we are dead and has no part to play in waking life, except as a kind of subconscious. If we are to live by it here and now, it can only be by living, as far as we can, as if we were dead. But unfortunately this kind of soul gets mixed up, during human life, with the other kind of soul, which is seduced by all manner of human concerns and interests. If soul identifies itself as being the latter kind of soul, then it will never really succeed in dying, but will hanker after bodily life. The locating of both kinds of soul in the same entity results in soul having to choose between two kinds of definition of itself, so that soul in itself becomes an ambiguous and inconstant thing, needing to be disciplined by philosophy if it is to realise its higher potential.

This inconstancy in the soul is another reason for not wanting to call it immortal. Cebes, as we have seen, is the first to introduce the notion of 'immortality' into the discussion, and Socrates does not at first take it up with reference to the soul, but with reference to the realities which are the objects of knowledge. He distinguishes between two kinds of beings (79a), the visible and the invisible. Only the latter are constant and unchanging, and it is to them that soul, being invisible, is akin, though Socrates carefully refrains from saying that soul itself is constant and unchanging. So when the soul uses the body in its exploration of reality it is dragged by the body towards things which are never constant, but when it operates on its own it 'goes to what is pure, always real, immortal and constant' and it becomes constant itself through its contact with what is constant, and this is what that wisdom means which is the goal of the philosopher (79cd).

The body is akin to what is human, mortal, polymorphous, capable of dissolution, never constant, but the soul is akin to what is divine, immortal, uniform, incapable of dissolution (80b). Yet even some parts of the body, like the bones and sinews, do not decay and are 'in a manner of speaking immortal' (80b), so it is all the more unlikely that the soul should be dissolved: it is either entirely indissoluble or something very close to being so (80b).

Yet precisely because the soul itself may not be pure at the time of death, but may still be entangled with the body, it would be inappropriate to ascribe to the soul the fully-fledged constancy and immortality which belong to the eternal realities which are the objects of knowledge. It is surely quite deliberately that Plato refrains from making Socrates draw the obvious inference from the invisibility of the soul that it too is immortal, and confines him to claiming that the soul has kinship with what is immortal. As in the fragment from Euripides' *Chrysippus*, quoted earlier on, what does not die is, strictly, the ultimate, unchanging elements which underly the complex realities we find in this world.

It seems, then, that Plato has become more sensitive to the terminological and conceptual difficulties involved in the esoteric doctrine of the immortality of the soul, and is trying to get as far as he can with the more traditional Greek notion of ψυχή as the bearer of existence, rather than life, and most typically the existence of the dead.

But Cebes will not let go, so Socrates is eventually forced to tackle the immortality of the soul directly. Plato emphasises that this initiates a new phase in the discussion, by making Socrates check with Cebes that he is proposing a new definition of death as the destruction of the soul (ψυχῆς ὄλεθρος) (91d). Verbally this new definition could claim the authority of Homer: in *Iliad* 22.325 the phrase ψυχῆς ὄλεθρος occurs, clearly meaning death. There is no question here of the destruction of the soul as the bearer of post mortem existence; in this context ψυχή means life, but precisely life as something that can be lost, as in 9.401–405, where Achilles, in the course of his rejection of Agamemnon's peace overtures, says that not all the reported wealth of Troy is worth his ψυχή: goods can always be acquired or captured, but once the soul has departed it cannot be captured and brought back again. In 22.161 the prize at stake in the race of Hector and Achilles round Troy is said to be Hector's ψυχή, his life. There is nothing odd in the later development of this kind of language, which gives us phrases like that used of Helen in Aeschylus' *Agamemnon*, where she is said to have 'destroyed many souls at Troy', meaning 'many lives' (πολλὰς ψυχὰς ὀλέσασα),[16] or in the lament of the dead Polydorus at the beginning of Euripides' *Hecuba:* 'Troy and the soul of Hector have been destroyed.'[17]

Whatever verbal ancestry we may find for Cebes' definition, however, its meaning in the *Phaedo* is hardly traditional. It certainly raises very precisely the essential question which Plato has to tackle, if he is to maintain his position that it is better to be dead than alive: his whole exposition rests on the belief that the soul exists after death. That the soul is not destroyed must therefore be demonstrated. But if we call the putative destruction of the soul 'death', we get the bizarre consequence that neither the human body nor the human composite can properly be said to die. And this is noticed by Plato. He presents Cebes as worrying that, when the soul leaves its last body, it perishes itself 'and precisely this is death, the destruction of the soul, since the body never stops perishing' (91d), which seems to imply that the perishing of the body is such a continual affair that there is no significantly decisive event in its history except the perishing of the soul. And it is presumably in deference to the new definition of death that, when Socrates wishes to refer to death in a more ordinary sense in 95d, as the termination of a human life, he designates it 'what is called death' (ἐν τῷ καλουμένῳ θανάτῳ).

It is not immediately clear why Plato introduces a new definition of death at this point. He could, surely, have discussed the indestructibility of the soul without it. Presumably he wants to retain the hallowed notion of immortality, even though he has become aware of the problems it causes, and cannot give it any sense in terms of the more traditional, commonsense definition of the death which Socrates proposed at the outset. Maybe he also hopes to safeguard what has gone before in the dialogue by signalling a new definition of death at this point. Since one of his main concerns is to offer a kind of *ars moriendi*, the last thing he needs is a doctrine which would debar the soul from dying altogether, so he has to make it clear that the death which is denied by the claim that the soul is immortal is not death in the ordinary sense, but death in the quite precise sense of the extinction of the soul.

As long as we bear in mind that we are now talking about 'death' in two different senses, we need not be too puzzled to discover that the reason why it is important to be sure that the soul is immortal is that only so can we justify the philosopher's confidence that, when he has died, he will profit from his philosophical labours (95c). Plato's interest continues to be focused essentially on the question what it is like to be dead (in the ordinary sense); he is now prepared to say that the question is nonsensical if, after death, the soul is dead too, which is not quite consistent with his earlier way of talking.

The argument with which Socrates tries to dispel Cebes' anxieties is notoriously perplexing, and we should not try to make it clearer to ourselves than it was for Plato, whose theory of forms was still fairly rudimentary, as was the ontology he built on it. Earlier in the dialogue Socrates had announced his policy of studying reality by means of language (λόγοι) (99e), and it is clear that, although the doctrine of forms is certainly meant to be making ontological claims, a form is essentially to be regarded as the secure and primary proprietor of some word (a noun or adjective), which is then shared by whatever else there may be which participates in the form (cf. 102b, 103e). The argument can therefore be seen as, for practical purposes, a linguistic one.

The first gambit in the argument is to show that the irreconcilable contrariety that there is between opposite forms extends in some cases to things other than the opposite forms themselves (102–104). Hotness can never be coldness (there cannot be any such thing as cold heat), even though, in general, hot things can turn into cold things; hot tea turns into cold tea without much difficulty, but when it does so the form of hotness which was in the tea disappears. The hot tea does not become cold hot tea. But in some cases a form which has an opposite is a necessary concomitant of something which is not itself one of a pair of opposites. Thus fire is always hot; cold fire is as impossible as cold heat. Conversely hot snow is as impossible as hot coldness. And the number three can no more be even than oddness itself can be evenness. It does not seem to matter that three can be described as 'the form of three' (104d), whereas by 'fire' and 'snow' Socrates probably does not mean us to understand the forms of these things.[18]

Forms in themselves are immortal and secure in their self-possession, but immanent forms, such as 'the big in us' (102d), may find themselves threatened by the approach of their opposites. Since it is impossible for 'the big in us' to become small, if we, who were big, become small, then the 'big' that was in us must somehow have disappeared – either it has gone away or it has perished, and Socrates does not seem to care which (102d).

It is the same with things which, without being themselves opposite to anything, are always accompanied by some quality which does have an opposite. Rather than become cold, fire must either clear off or perish, as must snow when threatened by heat, and the number three when threatened by evenness.

Now these bearers of opposites, as we may call them, can themselves be invoked to provide an explanation of certain phenomena. Whereas, before, Socrates had confined himself to entirely safe explanations of the type, 'What makes something big is bigness', he is now prepared to be more adventurous and say that, not only does heat make a body hot, so does fire. Not only does sickness make a body sick, so does fever. Not only does oddness make a number odd, so does oneness (105c).

This list of examples is even more of a ragbag than the one we were already working with. No doubt fever connotes sickness as much as fire connotes heat, but not in the same way. Fire imparts heat and is itself hot, whereas fever imparts sickness without itself being sick.

Unabashed by the heterogeneity of his examples, Socrates now uses his last point in reverse. If the presence of fire or fever makes the body hot or sick, what is it whose presence makes the body alive? Cebes obligingly provides the answer, 'Soul'. And he agrees with Socrates that this is always the case: wherever soul 'gets hold of' something (κατάσχῃ), it comes bringing life with it (105d) – notice that κατάσχῃ was used in 104d of the *form* of three getting hold of something. Since life is something that has an opposite, namely death, Socrates infers that soul is in the same category as fire, snow and the number three, not to mention fever: it is an opposite-bearer, and as such totally excludes the opposite of its own tame opposite. Soul is therefore incompatible with death, as snow is incompatible with heat, and can therefore be called 'deathless' (ἀθάνατος, immortal), just as snow can be called 'heatless' (105de).

Opposite-bearers, when faced with the contrary opposite, must either get out of the way or perish. Soul too therefore must either take itself off or perish, if death approaches. All that remains, then, is to show that it does the former, not the latter, when death supervenes.

In the case of most of our opposite-bearers there is nothing to stop them perishing, because the privative epithets proper to them do not entail imperishability. But if unevenness did entail imperishability, then threeness would be indestructible, and if heatlessness entailed imperishability, then snow would be indestructible, and would depart safe and sound at the onset of heat. And surely immortality does entail indestructibility (105e–106d).

Cebes, unfortunately, accepts without demur this facile move from immortality to imperishability, apparently because he assumes that 'immortal' connotes 'everlasting', and Socrates settles the matter to his own satisfaction and that of his friends with yet another ragbag: no one would want to say that anything immortal perishes, such as 'god or the form of life or anything else which is immortal' (106d). Since nobody demurs, Socrates concludes triumphantly that the soul is immortal and imperishable, so that 'when death assaults a man, his mortal part dies, it seems, but the immortal part goes away safe and sound' (106e). So 'our souls will really exist in Hades' (107a), which is what Socrates has been trying to prove all along.

Socrates' apodeictic justification of the move from immortality to imperishability was evidently felt to be unsatisfactory by later Platonists. From at least the time of Albinus[19] onwards we find an increasing concern to provide more substantial proofs of the imperishability of the soul as a probandum in its own right.[20] But this is only part of the more general problem: what kind of immortality is being claimed for what kind of soul?

In the course of the dialogue we have been offered two definitions of death, which would yield corresponding definitions of deathlessness, immortality. Socrates' definition rules out immortality for the soul, since it is soul that is the essential subject of the separation of the soul from the body. That is one reason why a new definition of death had to be proposed once Plato wanted to turn his attention to immortality. Cebes' definition would make immortality equivalent to the non-perishability of the soul, and this is formally what Socrates tries to prove. But if it had been taken seriously it would have rendered otiose the move from immortality to imperishability, since the two terms would coincide. However the final stage of Socrates' proof evidently takes imperishability as something still needing to be demonstrated, even if in the outcome the demonstration offered is perfunctory in the extreme and rests almost entirely on the assumption that, if soul is immortal, it must belong in the same sort of class as god and the form of life. This harks back, in a way, to Socrates' earlier usage: it is forms that are fully immortal, in the sense that they are utterly constant and indefectible. The gods, at least in the *Phaedrus* (249c), are divine because of their relationship to the world of real value, the forms, and earlier on in the *Phaedo* it is on the same basis that the soul is said to acquire a sort of constancy, though at that stage Socrates scrupulously avoided mentioning any immortality of the soul. But if soul is now to be transported by right, rather than by philosophical achievement, to this level of constancy, what becomes of the whole drama of the soul, what becomes of the *ars moriendi* Socrates has been expounding so far, with its warning that real death is a goal devoutly to be sought, though its achievement is far from being a foregone conclusion?

But then it is not immortality in the sense of the imperishability of the soul that is involved in the actual proof of the soul's immortality. The proof rests on the fact that soul brings life to the body, and death is the opposite of life. This suggests that death here must mean the death of the body, in which case the soul is immortal in a quite trivial sense and we are no nearer to dealing with Cebes' difficulties. The conclusion of the proof in 106e, however, implies that death means primarily the death of the composite human being, even though it is only what is mortal that actually dies. If it is death in this sense that the soul is incapable of, then Socrates' proof contradicts all that he has been saying earlier on, and still gets us no nearer to responding to Cebes.

In itself a proof that the soul is not liable to the death of the body or the death of the body-soul compound is far from justifying the inference that the soul is therefore indestructible. As Strato points out in his famous attack on Plato's proofs, soul might be deathless in the same sense as a stone is deathless. All that means is that we do not call its perishing 'death'.[21] Alternatively we may concede that the soul is not vulnerable to the death that is opposed to the life that soul imparts to the body or to the human composite, but why should there not be some other kind of death which is opposite to the life that soul itself possesses? Nothing has been said to prove that soul would not be vulnerable to that sort of death.[22]

As it stands in Plato, the burden of the proof of imperishability rests on the presumption that the whole class of immortals is like god or the forms of life. But if Socrates' proof of immortality works at all, it makes the immortals a much less exclusive club. As Strato points out, it would make every living being immortal, since a dead living being is as impossible as a dead soul.[23] It would make all souls immortal, including those of irrational animals and plants, since such souls impart life just as much as a human soul does.[24]

This is not the place to go into Strato's objections in detail, but it seems to me that he does show convincingly that it is far from clear that Plato has proved that the human soul is immortal in any interesting sense or that, if it is immortal, it is necessarily imperishable.

And in any case, what sort of soul are we talking about? Granted the various ragbags that Socrates throws at us, are we to take it that soul is like snow (a thing possessing a quality), like the number three (a form possessing and imparting a quality) or like fever (a condition, perhaps at a pinch a thing, imparting but not possessing a quality)?

There are certainly some indications that soul is to be thought of as a kind of form, and these were duly noted by the Neoplatonist commentators.[25] If this is what Plato meant, then of course the immortality of the soul will be like that of the form of life, but soul in this sense will be a far cry from the soul whose adventures Socrates was describing earlier, and its immortality will not secure anything like continuing personal existence.

It seems unlikely that we are meant to see the soul as being like a fever. If the connection between soul and life is simply that the soul imparts life, as a fever imparts sickness, then all that would follow would be the impossibility of soul failing to provide life, or perhaps the impossibility of its imparting death, whereas Plato expressely deduces the impossibility of there being dead soul (106b). so presumably soul is to be regarded as having life as well as imparting it. And of course this generates its own muddle. If the soul is alive in its own right (something Plato had scrupulously avoided saying in the earlier part of the dialogue), what is the relationship between its life and the life of the composite human being? It is surely significant that after the proof of immortality Socrates refers to life in the ordinary sense as 'what we call life' (107c), just as earlier on in this section he was forced to talk about 'what is called death'. And in his myth of the hereafter he refers to some of the dead going to the true earth, where there are many animals and human beings (111a), and philosophers go to an even better place and live there (ζῶσι) without bodies for ever (114c).

Soul, then, is presumably like snow in being a thing possessing a quality, in spite of its affinity to the forms. And this, I think, is all that Plato gets out of his laborious discussion of immortality. It justifies him in talking about the souls of the dead being alive. And this inevitably tends to reduce life in the ordinary sense to 'so-called life'. We seem to be heading back to Euripides' suggestion that maybe death is life and life is death. Which is all great fun, no doubt, but I wonder whether it is not rather a red herring for Plato. Surely the most engaging and, in a way, the most compelling part of the *Phaedo* is its picture of the drama of the soul, trying even in life to learn how to die, so that at the end it can triumphantly succeed in dying, in becoming separate from the body. This psycho-drama is not illuminated by any ascription to the soul of any life other than the tangled life of the human composite or of any identity other than that of the person who lived for a time in the body.

Plato's original instinct was, I think, a sound one. He would have done better to stick to the traditional Greek readiness to believe that the soul goes on existing after death, and that in that way the person goes on existing after death, and then to explore what it is like being dead, with all that he surmised about dead people's access to a world of invisible and more solid reality. But all this can be done better if we avoid the notion that the soul is itself alive, and especially the notion that it is immortal and immortal by right. Once we start calling the soul 'immortal', in the context of this kind of discussion, we risk denying precisely the continuity between the living and the dead which launched the whole issue in the first place and we shall find it hard to avoid depriving the soul of its adventures and robbing death too cheaply of its sting.

NOTES

1 Seneca, *De Providentia* 3.12.
2 D. Gallop, in his commentary in the Clarendon Plato Series, Oxford 1975, pp. 86–87.
3 R. Hackforth, in spite of Gallop's strictures, is correct in saying that the definition 'represents the normal contemporary view' and 'does not prejudge the question of the soul's survival' (*Plato's Phaedo*, Cambridge 1955, p. 44).
4 Gallop notes, as one of the difficulties in Plato's definition, that it unnecessarily requires the continuing separate evidence of the body (op. cit. p. 87), a point also raised by D. Bostock, *Plato's Phaedo*, Oxford 1986, p. 21. But Gallop's note on the possible translations of the perfect infinitive, τεθνάναι, is unduly narrow (p. 226): it can refer to the completion of the process of dying, without having to refer to a resultant 'state of being dead', if this means anything more than the sheer fact of being dead.
5 M. N. Tod, *Selection of Greek Historical Inscriptions*, vol. I, Oxford 1933, p. 127, no. 59 line 6.
6 Op. cit. p. 75.
7 It is dated to the period 424–420 by J. Diggle, in his Oxford Text of Euripides, vol. II, Oxford 1981, p. 2.
8 Euripides, *Supplices* 532–534.
9 Fragment 839 Nauck.
10 *Helen* 1014–1016.
11 J. von Arnim, *Stoicorum Veterum Fragmenta* vol. II, Stuttgart 1968, no. 790.
12 Lucretius 3.838–839.
13 Ed. cit. p. 50.
14 This is expounded most dramatically in *Phaedrus* 245c–250c. I have been persuaded by a succession of unpublished papers by Dr Julius Tomin that the ancient view, that the *Phaedrus* is the earliest of Plato's dialogues, may well be correct. In this case the *Phaedrus* can be seen as a spectacular manifesto, at the outset of Plato's philosophical career, followed by dialogues in which Plato undertakes the hard work of trying to develop and substantiate the theories announced in general and dogmatic terms in the *Phaedrus*.
15 Cf. Dodds, *Greeks and the Irrational* pp. 213–214; Hackforth, op. cit. p. 49; Gallop, op. cit. p. 89; W. K. C. Guthrie, *History of Greek Philosophy* vol. IV, Cambridge 1975, pp. 346–347; Bostock, op. cit. pp. 131–132.
16 Aeschylus, *Agamemnon* 1455–1457.
17 Euripides, *Hecuba* 21–22.
18 Cf. Gallop, op. cit. pp. 197–199; Bostock, op. cit. pp. 186–189.
19 *Didaskalikos* 25.2.
20 Cf. Damascius' commentary on the *Phaedo*, ed. cit. pp. 236–238, 332–334.
21 Strato's arguments are reported by Damascius, ed. cit., I §438.
22 Ibid. §441.
23 Ibid. §431.

24 Ibid. §434–435.
25 Cf. Damascius, ed. cit. II §76.

3

In the *Phaedo* Plato explores and gives new content to the conventional Greek notion that being dead is better than being alive, and in the process he makes dying into a positive achievement, whose successful accomplishment is paradoxically far from guaranteed. There is, of course, a price to be paid. If it is only the life of the soul that has real value, and if this psychic life can only be obtained at the cost of human death, life (or so-called life) in this world cannot help but lose all or most of its value. And if the soul, strictly, learns nothing from its sojourn in this world that it did not already know, and know better than it ever could while living in this world, then this world has absolutely no value at all. The *Phaedo*, not surprisingly, contains far and away the most negative assessment of this world ever found in Plato. All the same, granted the initial 'mistake' of being born in the first place, death, as was recognised by popular Greek pessimism, becomes a viable objective to give shape to life, and Plato succeeds in making it a far more positive objective than it ever was for mere pessimism. But if death constitutes the goal of mundane life, what happens once that goal is reached? The psychodrama, so vividly depicted in the earlier part of Socrates' exposition, comes to an end in death, and it is far from clear what the philosophical soul, whose post mortem existence Socrates is concerned to establish, is actually to do once it has successfully completed the process of dying. If soul goes on living after death, what is the purpose of this new life?

In the myth which concludes the conversation in the *Phaedo* the philosophers are said to live in dwelling-places even fairer than the pure abode allotted on the 'true earth' to those who have shown exceptional holiness on this earth, but Socrates coyly refuses to tell us anything about these dwelling-places, on the grounds that they are difficult to describe and he has insufficient time (114c). It is of course unfair to expect any philosopher or theologian to give us a satisfying account of everlasting beatitude. Even Hick acknowledges that 'it may well be possible to speculate more profitably about pareschatology than about eschatology,'[1] and the Sacred Congregation for the Doctrine of the Faith, as we have seen, reminds us of our essential ignorance on such matters.[2] All the same it would be nice to know how the dead philosophers of the *Phaedo* are meant to be occupied. In the *Apology*, perhaps not very seriously, Socrates indicates that he proposes, if it turns out that the doctrine of immortality is true, to carry on after death exactly what he has been doing so far, making a nuisance of himself quizzing supposedly wise people about their wisdom and, no doubt, showing up the dead as being no more wise than the living (41bc). The *Phaedo*, however, like the *Phaedrus*, holds out the possibility of enjoying posthumously just that clear vision of reality which the philosopher cannot attain in the body (66e, 246–249). What makes death attractive to the philosopher is precisely the access it gives to the vision of 'the real', which he desires so passionately. The philosopher is a 'chaser' of the real (66ac), and the erotic overtones of this 'chase'[3] are explicitated when Socrates goes on to say, 'We claim to be in love with wisdom (ἐρασταὶ φρονήσεως)' (66d). Death makes possible the consummation of this love. But what happens then? Can a pleasure, whose essential nature is to be the fulfilment of an appetite, last for ever? Othello certainly wanted to die at the height of his amorous contentment, but that was because he feared that the future could never bring him anything so good again.[4] Death would free him from the threat of 'unknown fate', freezing his situation, as it were, in its most satisfactory condition. But the dead philosophers of the *Phaedo* have got to go on living for ever, having attained the fulfilment of their quest.

Plato himself seems to have entertained some doubts about the sufficiency of the vision of the real. In the *Symposium*, where the erotic connotations of the philosophical quest are far more pronounced, the rapturous vision of the individual beloved is meant to lead on, step by step, to the even more excellent vision of the Beautiful Itself (211d).[5] But this is not the final goal. Immortality, he suggests, is normally sought by way of procreation, so what is desired by love is not just the beautiful, but 'begetting in the beautiful' (206de). The nearest we can hope to come to real immortality is to beget true virtues in The Beautiful Itself (212a).

In the *Symposium* it is not entirely clear whether the begetting of true virtues means acquiring true virtues for oneself or whether it means fostering them in others.[6] In the *Republic* it is quite plain that philosophers are supposed to descend again from their contemplation of reality to enlighten and take responsibility for others, though they may have to be forced to comply (519–520). But by now Plato is much less pessimistic, it seems, about the possibility of attaining the vision of reality while still living in the body; and, judging from the Myth of Er, which concludes the *Republic*, he is now no longer envisaging the possibility of a complete and final escape from the cycle of rebirth even for philosophers.[7]

So far as I know, Plato nowhere discusses explicitly the question whether there is or is not a final goal at which the soul can in principle be said to arrive definitively, so it is not possible to say whether he had become fully conscious of the problems posed by the suggestion in the *Phaedo* that the dead philosopher can expect to live a bodiless life for ever in some privileged location. The problem certainly did surface, some centuries later, in christianity. At any rate by the sixth century AD, in Origenist circles, people were speculating on the likelihood of souls getting bored with the contemplation of God. The anti-Origenist anathemas pronounced in 543 condemn, among others, the proposition that 'the souls of men pre-existed, as being formerly minds and holy powers, but they became sated (κόρον λαβούσας) with contemplating God and turned to something worse.'[8] Although this precise interpretation of the original fall is not found in so many words earlier on,[9] it looks as if Gregory of Nyssa had a similar worry and that his famous doctrine of *epektasis* is partly intended as a remedy for it: in the *Life of Moses* he is very insistent that the inexhaustibility of God justifies an interpretation of seeing God as meaning never reaching the point where one's desire is sated (μηδέποτε τῆς ἐπιθυμίας κόρον εὑρεῖν).[10] Since there is no limit to the goodness and beauty of God, there is no point in our approach to God at which satiety is reached.

The same problem has of course been raised in modern times, and Swinburne gives essentially the same answer as Gregory of Nyssa:

> Only a task which made continued progress valuable for its own sake, but which would take an infinite time to finish would be worth doing for ever . . . The growing development of a friendship with God who . . . has ever new aspects of himself to reveal, and the bringing of others into an ever-developing relationship with God, would provide a life worth living for ever. . . [God,] being (by definition) omnipotent and omniscient, will ever be able to hold our interest by showing us new facets of reality, and above all his own nature.[11]

Whether this kind of picture of heaven really resolves the problem of boredom depends, I suppose, largely on temperament. I am not sure that I would have the patience endlessly to pursue an ever-receding goal or to sit through a literally interminable divine strip-tease cum lecture. In any case, it certainly lacks the element of finality characteristic of the classic account of beatitude offered by Boethius: 'The whole concern of mortals, put to work in the labour of many different kinds of pursuit, proceeds in a variety of ways, but strives to reach a single goal, beatitude. And that is the good thing which leaves nothing more that you could desire, once you attain it.'[12] St Thomas uses this principle of the complete satisfaction of desire in his account of why it is impossible to lose beatitude, once it is obtained: one would only turn away from the vision of God if it were not completely satisfying, and this is impossible.[13] He also uses it in support of his contention that we shall actually know the *essence* of the First Cause (God), because nothing less than this would satisfy our intellectual curiosity, so if we did not reach this knowledge of God's essence, we should still be in a state of desire, and therefore not in bliss.[14]

There is an amusing showdown between an epektasis-type and a Boethian type of beatitude in C. S. Lewis' *Great Divorce*. Among the denizens of hell, who have taken the opportunity of one of their periodic days off, is a bishop, who is accosted by a friend of his in the in-between place where their bus takes them. Rather untraditionally, Lewis supposes that the visitors do not have to go back to hell if they do not want to, and the bishop's friend is trying to persuade the bishop to come to heaven instead. The bishop demands some assurances first, including a guarantee that he will find 'an atmosphere of free inquiry' there. His friend can offer no such thing: 'I will bring you to the land not of questions but of answers, and you shall see the face of God.'

'Ah,' replies the bishop, 'but we must all interpret those beautiful words in our own way! For me there is no such thing as a final answer. The free wind of inquiry must *always* continue to blow through the mind, must it not? "Prove all things" . . . to travel hopefully is better than to arrive.'

To this the friend retorts, 'If that were true, and known to be true, how could anyone travel hopefully? There would be nothing to hope for.'

The bishop counters this with, 'But you must feel yourself that there is something stifling abut the idea of finality? Stagnation, my dear boy, what is more soul-destroying than stagnation?'

The friend suggests that the bishop feels like this because he has never experienced truth except 'with the abstract intellect'. In heaven, by contrast, truth can be tasted like honey and it embraces us like a bridegroom. Further, he argues, 'Once you were a child. Once you knew what inquiry was for. There was a time when you asked questions because you wanted answers, and were glad when you had found them.' The bishop, however, has long put away childish things, and in any case he cannot visit heaven just now, because he has an important paper to read to the infernal Theological Society.[15]

There is a valid point being made here. If questioning gives up looking for answers, it gives up being real questioning, and travelling without any kind of goal would be neither hopeful nor particularly enjoyable. But at the same time the difficulty of making finality attractive is evident. If the bishop's problem is that hitherto he has only experienced truth with the abstract intellect, we may wonder how pleasing an alternative a diet of endless honey and embraces would be.

The worthwhileness of post mortem existence is a problem which will concern us again later on. For the moment though, our business is with death.

The *Phaedo* makes death an achievement, the supreme achievement of this life, but, as we have seen, it does so by making immortality an alternative to life, rather than, as in more traditional Greek parlance, an alternative to death; and it runs the risk of consigning those who succeed in dying to a rather aimless life thereafter. But the risk of boredom is not the only hazard facing believers in immortality.

The case against immortality is put with considerable imaginative power in the third volume of Ursula Le Guin's Earthsea trilogy, *The Farthest Shore*. The world created in these books rests on the power of words and names; it is a world of magicians, who seek out the true names of things and bestow true names on people. And it is being drained of life, in the third volume, by a corrupt wizard called Cob who has broken the boundary between life and death to secure endless life for himself. The archmage Ged, seeking to restore wholeness to the world, has to affirm mortality as the very principle of finiteness, particularity and, therefore, of real existence. The earnest, confused young prince, Arren, supposed that Ged, if anyone, must know the way to 'life without death,' which they have met various people seeking. But Ged replies:

> I know what they think they seek. But I know that they will die . . . That I will die. That you will die . . . And I prize that knowledge. It is a great gift. It is the gift of selfhood . . . That selfhood, our torment and glory, our humanity, does not endure. It changes and it goes, a wave on the sea. Would you have the sea grow still and the tides cease to save one wave, to save yourself?[16]

Later on, in a place which prompts Arren to comment, 'This land is as dead as the land of death itself,' Ged retorts sharply:

> Do not say that! . . . Look at this land; look about you. This is your kingdom, the kingdom of life. This is your immortality.

> Look at the hills, the mortal hills. They do not endure for ever. The hills with the living grass on them, and the streams of water running . . . In all the world, in all the worlds, in all the immensity of time, there is no other like each of those streams, rising cold out of the earth where no eye sees it, running through the sunlight and the darkness to the sea. Deep are the springs of being, deeper than life, than death . . . [17]

To secure immortality for himself the wretched Cob has had to give up his own name, the particularity which made him real and human. As the archmage says to him in their final encounter:

> You exist, without name, without form. You cannot see the light of day; you cannot see the dark. You sold the green earth and the sun and the stars to save yourself. But you have no self. All that which you sold, that is yourself. You have given everything for nothing.[18]

In the land of the dead everyone bears his own name, because there he is nothing 'but a shadow and a name.'[19] Death sets the seal on a particular, unique identity. To refuse death is to refuse identity, to refuse to live as a specific, limited being within the ceaseless flow of time. The refusal of death is in fact a refusal of life, of everything.

There is a very basic point, which we could almost call an aesthetic point, here, as well as a modestly metaphysical belief about the nature of reality. As Aristotle sensibly points out, a story must form a proper whole, and as such have a beginning, a middle and an end,[20] and much the same can be said about life itself if it is to be seen as an intelligible whole. If people in many ages and many cultures have turned instinctively to stories as a way of trying to make sense of their own lives, it is surely because we need to see our own lives as a kind of story. And a life that simply stretches on and on indefinitely could never constitute a real story. That is one reason for the Greek adage about not calling anyone happy until he is dead: before pronouncing a verdict on anyone's happiness we need to see how the story ends.[21] This is why Seneca, in similar vein, suggests that when people are at the height of their good fortune we should pray for them to die, 'because amid all the inconstancy and turmoil of things, nothing is certain except what is past.'[22]

One of the reasons why the *Iliad* is such a powerful poem is that it insists ruthlessly on mortality. I hope it is no longer necessary to argue for the literary integrity of the *Iliad*; its unity of action, which impressed Aristotle,[23] and its general coherence are surely inconceivable unless the text as we have it is essentially the product of a single poetic mind. And it seems highly probably that its insistence on mortality represents a deliberate and original choice on the part of its author.[24] In the *Iliad* there is a sharp line drawn between mortals and immortals; as Apollo warns Diomedes, 'They are never alike, the race of immortal gods and the race of men who walk the earth' (5.441–442). Not a single mortal in the story is allowed to escape his mortality, whereas in the non-Homeric epics immortality is lavishly bestowed on people. Even Achilles, whose death broods so effectively over the last books of the *Iliad*, is mysteriously translated after death to the 'White Island' according to the *Aethiopis*, presumably to enjoy some kind of posthumous existence there, though it is not clear how much of the later story of his post mortem good fortune goes back to the epic.[25] One version, said to have appeared first in the sixth-century lyric poet Ibycus, actually has him marry Medea in the Elysian fields,[26] a rather doubtful benefit, one might fancy.

The declared subject of the *Iliad* is the wrath of Achilles (1.1), and we speedily learn that what prompted his wrath was Agamemnon's appropriation of the girl Briseis, who had been given to Achilles as part of his war-spoils. But it is not the loss of the girl as such that matters most, it is the loss of his honour, his γέρας, embodied in the prize of which Agamemnon deprives him. γέρας is a crucial notion in the *Iliad*. The gods have their γέρας in the form of sacrifices (4.49, 24.70); old men have theirs in their role as counsellors (4.323, 9.422). Warriors have theirs in the form of booty. When Achilles is threatened with the loss of his γέρας, he says he would rather go home than remain at Troy without honour (ἄτιμος) (1.169–171). Later on, in the long speech in which he rejects Agamemnon's overtures for peace, he develops the theme. Agamemnon's conduct makes it pointless to fight for him, since cowards and warriors receive the same honour, and everyone dies, whether he has done nothing or toiled greatly (9.318–320). Achilles brought back immense treasure from his battles, and handed it all over to Agamemnon, who had apparently stayed behind at the ships, and Agamemnon kept most of it for himself, doling out only a little to the other leaders. And now even what had been allocated to Achilles has been taken away (9.330–336). Achilles' mother has told him that a choice of fates lies ahead of him: he can stay at Troy and fight, in which case he will not return home, but will win undying fame, or he can return home, where a long life awaits him but no fame (9.410–416). In the circumstances all the fabled wealth of Troy does not seem to be worth his life (ψυχή), so he might as well go home to his old father (9.393–409).

It is clear that Achilles is not repudiating the heroic ideal here; he is complaining that Agamemnon is making it an irrelevant ideal.

Everyone has to die, and if no difference is made in the honour given to warriors and cowards, what is the point of being a warrior?

The connection between being a warrior and mortality is explicitated by Sarpedon in 12.322–328:

> If by running away from this war we were going to be always ageless and immortal, I myself would not be fighting in the front ranks nor would I be sending you into battle which brings honour to men. But as it is, a myriad fates of death stand over us, come what may, and no mortal can escape them. Let us go and either give glory to someone or someone will give glory to us.

Precisely because there is no escape from death, it is worth seeking glory in battle, with all its risk of death.

Later on, in connection with this same Sarpedon, who is specially beloved of Zeus, we hear of another kind of γέρας, the γέρας of those who have died. In book XVI Sarpedon is being pursued by Patroclus, and Zeus laments his fated death, adding that he is in two minds whether or not to snatch him out of the battle and land him safely in Lycia. Hera is not amused: 'What a thing to say!' she remarks. 'Are you wanting to rescue from ill-sounding death a man who is mortal and fated long since?' What she proposes instead is that Sarpedon should be left to die at the hands of Patroclus, but then Death and Sleep should be sent to take his body to Lycia to be buried by his family, for this is the γέρας of the dead (16.431–457). And this is indeed what happens. In the austere world of the *Iliad* Zeus too, like the poet, knows that the temptation to rescue mortals from their fated mortality is an unreal one. When Zeus is tempted again to rescue Hector, and is once again ticked off by Hera, he explains that he was not being serious (22.174–184).

The γέρας of the dead is mentioned again in 23.9, where Achilles says, 'Let us mourn Patroclus, for that is the γέρας of those who have died.' And, most spectacularly, it reappears, even though the word is not used, right at the end of the poem, with the funeral of Hector.

It is incredible that people have doubted whether book XXIV really belongs to the *Iliad*, and one may hope that Macleod's meticulous argument will set such doubts to rest once and for all.[27] The wrath of Achilles, after the death of Patroclus, is redirected, but not resolved. It is only in the extraordinary scene in book XXIV, where Achilles accepts Priam's supplication and achieves a kind of sympathy with him, agreeing – contrary to his earlier vehement assurances (23.21, 182–183) – to return Hector's body for burial, that the episode of Achilles' wrath comes to a satisfying conclusion.

And it is entirely right, as well as being dramatic and unexpected, that the poem should end with Hector's funeral. Most of the *Iliad* concerns a temporary period of victory for the Trojans, owing to Achilles' withdrawal from the war, and the funeral of Hector is explicitly a portent of the eventual triumph of the Greeks and the destruction of Troy, which we all know to be the outcome of the war. But only this precise ending could at the same time do justice to the very sympathetic way in which Hector has been portrayed in the poem. He too has his γέρας. And it is also fitting that Achilles, whose anger over the loss of his γέρας launched the whole story of the *Iliad*, ends up making a gesture of goodwill towards the father of his enemy which, as we learn from Zeus himself, will win him a new glory, on top of the return of his original γέρας (24.110). The scene between Achilles and Priam does not describe any real reconciliation of the warring parties, this is made quite clear, but it does show how a bond of sympathy can be forged in spite of continuing enmity. Both Achilles and Priam learn from each other to see their own grief as part of the common lot of humanity as a whole (24.524–526). In the last books of the poem we are never allowed to forget Achilles' own impending death, so the parallel that is drawn between Priam's lot and that of Achilles' old father, Peleus, is a genuine one, and beyond that there is a curious but effective human solidarity between Achilles, in his pain over the death of his friend, and Priam grieving over the death of his son, which avenged the death of Patroclus (24.509–512). And Achilles' grief has already been shown as an occasion for his associates to weep with him, but for their own various griefs (19.302). The gods have allocated it to wretched mortals to live in pain – it is the gods who live without care (24.525–526). This common destiny from which no human life escapes is the lesson taught by Achilles, and it echoes the comment made earlier by Apollo that 'the fates have made the human spirit long-suffering' (24.49).

The *Iliad* gives us a genuinely tragic picture of the human condition; there is no facile evasion. In this context there can be no question of death being an achievement, nor is it in itself anything but tragic. Nevertheless there is a kind of fulfilment in the proper paying of the γέρας of the dead, which rounds off each human story, and facing up to death with endurance and heroism to the end does give a certain splendour to our poor mortal life. Pindar was being true to his Homeric inspiration when he wrote:

> Short is the time in which what is pleasant in mortal life will grow; and even so it falls to the ground, shaken by an adverse decree. Beings of a day, what is anyone, what is no one? Man

> is a dream of a shadow. But when a god-given radiance comes,
> a bright light shines on men and a gentle life.[28]

This 'radiance', however, presupposes an interpretative context, and this is provided by poetry. As Pindar again says:

> When a man comes to the house of Hades, having done brave deeds, without song, he has breathed in vain and won little pleasure by his toil. But graciousness is poured over you by the sweet-worded lyre and the pleasing pipe, and the Muses, the daughters of Zeus, nurture widely your fame.[29]

What makes all the pain of life worthwhile is that it should become the matter of poetry. In the *Odyssey*, just before Odysseus reveals his identity to Alcinous, Alcinous says that the gods brought about the fate of the Greeks and of Troy, and doomed men to destruction, 'so that they would be a song for future ages' (ἵνα ᾖσι καὶ ἐσσομένοισιν ἀοιδή) (8.578–580), and this is the hope expressed by Helen in the *Iliad*. She is lamenting to Hector the destruction she and Paris have been responsible for; but it is Zeus who has laid this evil fate on them, 'so that afterwards we will be matter of song for people to come' (ὡς καὶ ὀπίσσω ἀνθρώποισι πελώμεθ' ἀοίδιμοι ἐσσομένοισι)(6.357–358).

It is no doubt the tragic tales from an earlier past that Achilles was singing, when Agamemnon's embassy found him 'singing the fames of men' (9.189), just as for later generations he himself was matter for song. As Griffin says, 'The hero dies, not so much for his own glory, not even so much for his friends, as for the glory of song, which explains to a spell-bound audience the greatness and fragility of the life of man.'[30] Or, as Vermeule says, 'the finished lives' of people long ago 'had a normative power to illuminate the incomplete experience of their descendants.'[31]

Taplin makes a similar point about classical tragedy:

> Tragedy is only an illusion in so far as any claim to make sense of all the evils of our life is an illusion (and perhaps tragedy does not claim this). The 'tragedies' of real life, unlike those on the stage, are often shapeless, sordid, capricious, meaningless. But supposing this to be true (as I do), what then? It is not *human* to be content with this useless, even if ultimate truth. We *must* try to understand, to cope, to respond. It is in this attempt that tragedy – that most great art – has its place. For it gives the hurtful twists of life a shape and meaning which are *persuasive*, which can be lived with . . . By enthralling its audiences tragedy unites emotion and meaning so as to give

them an experience which, by creating a perspective on the misfortunes of human life, helps them to understand and cope with those misfortunes.[32]

Precisely by presenting human pain in a coherent literary form, epic or tragedy offers at least the appearance of making some kind of sense of it all. But this would be quite impossible – good old Aristotle again! – without a beginning, a middle and, above all, an end. This is why mortality is, at least, artistically necessary. A life that simply went on and on and on indefinitely could never reach a denouement.

This is at least one reason why the Homeric gods have given so many readers a sense of their 'unseriousness', their 'sublime frivolity' (*erhabener Unernst*), in Reinhardt's famous phrase.[33] Because they cannot grow old or die, nothing can ultimately make any real difference to them. Homer's gods have certainly not yet been credited with the fully-fledged invulnerability which Aristophanes satirises in the *Frogs*, in the scene where the slave Xanthias offers Dionysus to be tortured. Dionysus protests, on the grounds that he is an immortal, to which Xanthias replies, 'All the more should he be beaten, because if he is a god, he will not feel it' (633–634). Homer's gods can be hurt and distressed; but they cannot really suffer any long-term harm, at least not at the hands of men; and even Zeus' threats to punish the other gods seem somewhat unreal. On Homer's Olympus, however angry the gods may be with one another, and however resentful of Zeus' control, the days of genuine power-struggles and appalling penalties inflicted on the losers are relegated to an unspecified past.

It would be quite wrong to see the Homeric gods simply as literary decoration. Not only are they an indispensable part of the story, they are presented as often awe-inspiring and nearly always formidable powers. Even Aphrodite, who behaves like a silly ninny when she misguidedly tries to engage in battle, is a redoubtable figure in her own field of competence, which is sexual attraction. And their carefree existence, dramatically represented in the story by their ability to turn their attention away from the war in which they are sometimes passionately involved, is surely meant to be a token of their superiority and transcendence. But precisely because Homer has made his gods so anthropomorphic, the contrast between immortal and mortal attitudes becomes inescapable; and there is no doubt that immortal attitudes, if adopted by mortals, would often not be considered desirable.

The first book of the *Iliad* juxtaposes gods and men in an interesting way. It launches the story by showing how Agamemnon deprived Achilles of his γέρας. But Agamemnon's insult to Achilles was caused indirectly by his earlier insult to Apollo. As part of his war spoil Agamemnon was in possession of the daughter of a priest of Apollo, and when the priest came as a suppliant to beg for the return of his daughter he was rudely dismissed by Agamemnon, who thereby incurred the anger of the god. Apollo simply sweeps down and massacres the Greeks by sending them a plague. There is nothing left but for Agamemnon to capitulate. The outcome was never in doubt, and the story is over in less than a book, whereas the story of the wrath of Achilles fills twenty-four books. Men simply cannot compete with gods, so there cannot be any real story about a conflict between gods and men. The ease with which gods achieve their purpose is one of their salient characteristics,[34] and is no doubt an honourable attribute of gods, but if transferred to human beings it would simply trivialise them. As Griffin points out, Homer has scrupulously avoided (or eliminated) invincible warriors in his tale.[35]

Also in book I we have the famous quarrel between Agamemnon and Achilles, which constitutes the beginning of the plot of the whole epic. The same book shows us the gods quarrelling too. Thetis persuades Zeus to back up Achilles, her son, by giving victory to the Trojans for a time, and Hera, always suspicious of her husband, starts to row with him for intriguing behind her back. Zeus replies with threats, and assures her that if he sets hands on her not all the gods in Olympus will be able to rescue her. This upsets all the gods, until Hephaestus intervenes: 'This will be a bad business, not to be endured, if you two quarrel like this because of mortals and start a brawl among the gods. There will be no pleasure in our good dinner' (1.573–576). Then he makes the gods laugh by bustling round with his gammy leg, serving them all nectar. So they enjoy their dinner after all, and then they all go happily to bed. Affairs which are, quite literally, deadly serious for mortals are less important for the gods than enjoying their dinner. The row between the two Greek leaders causes the death of countless men; the row between Zeus and Hera, although it too is about something which will cause countless deaths, fizzles out in heaven without even spoiling a meal. And in any case Hera stood no more chance of succeeding against Zeus than Agamemnon did of succeeding against Apollo. For all the sound and fury, nothing serious comes or can come from celestial wrangles, at least not for the gods. The consequences for men may be dire.

Later the involvement of the gods becomes more intense, but even then dinner is not forgotten. In book XV, after Zeus has rather maliciously made Hera responsible for getting Apollo and Poseidon called back from the fighting, in which they were engaged contrary to Zeus' command, Hera is furious, and complains to Themis about how overweening Zeus is. But she still bids Themis to get dinner going in the halls of the gods, promising to give all the news then. 'And,' she goes on, 'I don't think everyone will be pleased, whether gods or men – if indeed there is anyone still enjoying his dinner' (15.95–99). Hera, as first lady of Olympus, cannot quite forget her responsibilities as hostess, and in the heat of her anger can still use the spoiling of the gods' dinner as a kind of criterion of her consort's behaviour.

There are other, more important, reminders too that the gods are not wholly serious about the war, not least Apollo's rather disdainful refusal to fight Poseidon, even when the gods have been sent into battle by Zeus himself: 'Earth-shaker, you would not reckon me to be in my right mind, if I fight you for the sake of wretched mortals . . .' (21.462–464), and indeed it is far from clear that Poseidon's challenge was serious, 'Phoebus, why do we stand apart? It is unseemly, when others have given a lead. It will be shameful to go to Olympus without fighting . . .' (21.436–438). Poseidon himself had earlier refused to fight, suggesting to Hera that they should rather sit and watch and leave the men to fight (20.133–137). Later on Hera calls back Hephaestus from the fight, saying that 'it is not seemly for an immortal god to fight like this because of mortals' (21.379–380).

The whole bizarre episode of the gods going to war seems to have little serious purpose. Zeus announces at the outset that he is going to sit on Olympus and enjoy the spectacle (20.22–23), and enjoy it he does: he laughs happily at the sight of the gods fighting (21.389–390). Theoretically the gods have been let loose to help either side to their hearts' content, because otherwise there is a risk that Achilles will succeed in taking Troy before its appointed time (20.24–30), but in fact the serious interventions of the gods are much more secret and sinister, as when Patroclus is stripped of his armour by Apollo (16.787–804) and Hector is lured to his death by Athena (22.214–299). The gods can achieve their purpose easily, without entering into the brawl themselves.

Zeus' enjoyment of the fight contrasts with the poet's comment on the human struggle, 'It would be a brazen-hearted man who could then have enjoyed seeing their toil without grieving' (13.343–344). But if it is primarily the sight of the gods fighting that amuses Zeus, it is not a very serious fight that he is watching. When it comes to human beings, he can sometimes be distressed at what is happening to them, and particularly at their impending death. In so far as there is tragedy among the gods, it is caused by their involvement with mortals.

Zeus is upset at the sight of Achilles' immortal horses lamenting the death of Patroclus, and says: 'Wretched ones, why did we give you to king Peleus, a mortal, when you are unageing and immortal? Was it that you should have pain among unfortunate men? For there is nothing more pitiable than man of all that breathes and moves upon earth' (17.443–447). And Achilles sympathises with his mother and says: 'Would that you were dwelling again with the immortal sea-nymphs and that Peleus had married a mortal wife. Now there will be abundant grief in your mind for your dead son, since you are not going to welcome him returning home' (18.86–90).

But at least among the Olympians one gets the impression that such grief does not bite very deeply. Though Zeus is particularly fond of Troy, he is not prepared to quarrel with Hera over it, and will let her destroy it, and in return she lets him destroy three cities which are particularly dear to her (4.31–54).

This kind of ruthlessness is possible to the gods precisely because they are outside the company of suffering mortals. They lack the constraints which give dignity and moral significance to human beings. Not being genuinely exposed to any long-term consequences of their actions, they can do whatever they like. Thus Achilles complains about Apollo intervening to drive him back from the walls of Troy: 'You have deprived me of great fame and saved them easily, because you had no retribution to fear afterwards. I would certainly have paid you back, if I had the power' (22.18–20). And, even if the other gods do face the threat of sanctions if they arouse the anger of Zeus, Zeus himself is answerable to no one. This is pointed out by Thetis when she is pleading with Zeus to honour Achilles: 'There is nothing for you to fear,' she says (1.515), clearly implying that he is therefore free to do anything he wants to.[36] As Griffin comments, 'It is the presence of mortality which imposes on men the compulsion to have virtues; the gods, exempt from that pressure, are, quite consistently, less "virtuous" than men.'[37]

It is interesting, in this connection, to look at book III of the *Iliad*. Paris at first appears in a highly improbable outfit, wearing a leopard-skin and sporting a bow and a sword and brandishing two spears – hardly the apparel or equipment for a serious warrior! None the less he challenges the Greeks to come and fight. But when Menelaus makes for him, he prudently withdraws into the ranks. Hector sees him and reviles him for being nothing but a glamorous playboy. Paris accepts the rebuke and changes at once into the hero that he is generally shown to be in the *Iliad*. He suggests that the war should be settled once and for all by a single combat between himself and some Greek champion, and this time he arms seriously and engages in serious battle with Menelaus. But as soon as he is liable to be hurt, Aphrodite effortlessly plucks him out of the way and packs him off to go to bed with Helen. Helen, meanwhile, had been feeling guilty and nostalgic, in spite of Priam's attempt to comfort her with the thought that it is not she who is to blame, it is the gods. When Aphrodite summons her to go to Paris, who is, she says, glisteningly beautiful, as if he were going to a dance, not returning from a battle, Helen refuses with disgust, but Aphrodite takes not the slightest notice of her moral scruples and cows her into obedience. Homer seems to go out of his way to present both Helen and Paris sympathetically. Paris, as he explains to Hector, has been given gifts by Aphrodite, and divine gifts cannot be spurned, even if they are not the gifts one would have chosen; left to himself, he is as much a hero as anyone else. But Aphrodite absolutely refuses to take him seriously as a warrior, just as she rides roughshod over Helen's nuanced sensibilities. When human beings try to attack gods, they do not last long, as Dione comfortingly assures Aphrodite herself, after she has rashly ventured into battle and been hurt by Diomedes (5.407); Aphrodite is easily healed of her pain, and the whole episode quickly resolves itself in celestial merriment (5.419–431). But when gods choose to exert their power over human beings, the human beings have no redress and no easy comfort. They have to endure their pain to the end, knowing that there is no other end in sight but death. Their very helplessness gives them a dignity that the gods lack.

The need to face pain and death provides a motivation for heroism on the part of human beings. Gods have no such motive for anything they do. On the whole the *Iliad* is reticent about the motivation of the gods. But it is now generally accepted that the author presupposes the story of the judgement of Paris, and in its light we can see why Hera and Athene are so unremittingly hostile to Troy and so bitter against Aphrodite, and conceivably why Aphrodite is so keen to flaunt her rather barbed support for Paris. In each case there is nothing more serious at stake than personal vanity. And in the interests of that vanity whole armies and towns must be destroyed, and individuals put in the most impossible positions. It is Athene who incites Diomedes to attack Aphrodite (5.131–132), even though both she and he know full well that it is the utmost foolishness for men to attack gods. Precisely because their life is endless, the life of the gods is shapeless and aimless. It is given a kind of shape from time to time by their involvement in the story of human affairs, but in itself it is dominated by petty feuds and family bickering, none of which, in Homer's relatively well-run Olympus, can ever really attain the status of genuine drama. Our last sight of the assembled gods in *Iliad* 24.97–119 shows them sitting together, apparently having a drink, and their nine-day quarrel over what should be done about Hector's body is amicably resolved by Zeus, and Thetis is warmly received by Hera. These are indeed the 'happy everlasting gods' (24.99). There are no problems that cannot be resolved over a cup of wine or a cheerful dinner.

NOTES

1 John Hick, *Death and Eternal Life*, London 1985, p. 22.
2 *Acta Apostolicae Sedis* 71 (1979) p. 942.
3 Cf. K. J. Dover, *Greek Homosexuality*, London 1978, p. 87: 'Hunting is not an uncommon metaphor of homosexual pursuit.'
4 Shakespeare, *Othello* Act 2 scene 1.
5 Plato never seems to see any philosophical potential in heterosexual love, and he does not normally envisage any consummation for homosexual love beyond a kind of 'voyeurism', which makes it easy for him to suggest that it should be sublimated into a vision of Beauty Itself. Even in *Phaedrus* 256cd, where he is unusually tolerant of indulgence in sexual activity between male lovers, he clearly regards it as an unfortunate lapse.
6 Cf. Guthrie, op. cit. vol. IV pp. 389–390.
7 In *Republic* 619de it seems that the best that can be hoped for by philosophical souls is to prosper here and hereafter and to have an easy return to this world in due course.
8 Denzinger-Schönmetzer no. 403.
9 Cf. A. Guillaumont, *Les 'Kephalaia Gnostica' d'Évagre le Pontique*, Paris 1962, pp. 142–143.
10 *Life of Moses* II 239.
11 R. Swinburne, *Faith and Reason*, Oxford 1981, pp. 135, 131.
12 Boethius, *Consol. Phil.* III prose 2.
13 *Summa Theologiae* I.II q.5 a.4.
14 Ibid. q.3 a.8
15 C. S. Lewis, *The Great Divorce*, Fontana edn 1972, pp. 40–43.
16 Ursula Le Guin, *The Farthest Shore*, London 1973, p. 131.
17 Ibid. p. 174.
18 Ibid. p. 189.
19 Ibid. p. 188.
20 Aristotle, *Poetics* 1450b21–27.
21 Cf. Herodotus 1.7 (Solon's advice to Croesus).
22 Seneca, *Consol. ad Marciam* 22.1.
23 Aristotle, *Poetics* 1451a28–30.
24 J. Griffin, 'The Epic Cycle and the Uniqueness of Homer', *Journal of Hellenic Studies* 97 (1977) pp. 39–53, especially pp. 41–43.
25 *Homeri Opera* vol. V, ed. Allen, p. 106.
26 Ibycus 10, in Page, *Poetae Melici Graeci*.
27 C. W. Macleod, in his edition of book XXIV, Cambridge 1982, pp. 8–35.
28 Pindar, *Pyth.* 8.92–97.
29 *Ol.* 10.91–96.
30 J. Griffin, *Homer on Life and Death*, Oxford 1980, p. 102. It will be

apparent to those who know this splendid book how much I am indebted to it in this chapter.

31 E. Vermeule, *Aspects of Death in Early Greek Art and Poetry*, Berkeley 1979, p. 23.

32 O. Taplin, *Greek Tragedy in Action*, London 1978, pp. 170–171.

33 K. Reinhardt, *Das Parisurteil*, Frankfurt 1938, p. 25.

34 Cf. West, *Hesiod, Works and Days* p. 139.

35 Op. cit. pp. 32–33.

36 Cf. G. S. Kirk, *The Iliad: A Commentary* vol. I, Cambridge 1985, p. 107.

37 Op. cit. pp. 92–93.

4

The *Iliad* depicts and, in a way, interprets the tragic dignity of human beings by refusing to fudge the boundaries set to human life by mortality and by the invincibility of the gods and particularly the will of Zeus. Precisely within these constraints, the universality of human suffering can generate both heroism and unexpected bonds of sympathy, and we, who share the mortality of the heroes of old, can benefit from their heroism and the completedness of their lives by telling ourselves tales and singing songs about them.

Later epic rather changes the picture, partly because it seems to have been felt necessary to mitigate the impression of divine irresponsibility which the *Iliad* tends to convey. Thus, whereas the *Iliad*, for all its insistence that the whole story is the story of the will of Zeus being fulfilled, never attempts to find any ultimate motivation for the will of Zeus, the later *Cypria* does ascribe an intelligible motivation to Zeus' will: Earth has been complaining that she is overburdened by the excessive numbers of human beings living on her, so Zeus devises a succession of wars, including the Trojan war, as a means of population-control.[1] This certainly makes Zeus' behaviour more intelligible, but it hardly makes satisfying sense for us of all the human pain involved in these wars. We may compare Nagel's comment:

> If we learned that we were being raised to provide food for other creatures fond of human flesh, who planned to turn us into cutlets before we got too stringy . . . that would still not give our lives meaning . . . Although we might acknowledge that this culinary role would make our lives meaningful to them, it is not clear how it would make them meaningful to us.[2]

Our situation, on this hypothesis, could perhaps be made meaningful to us if we add to it a further consideration, suggested by George Macdonald's fairy story, *The Golden Key*, where the mysterious 'lady' explains that 'In Fairyland the ambition of the animals is to be eaten by the people; for that is their highest end in that condition.

But they are not therefore destroyed. Out of that pot comes something more than the dead fish, you will see.' Sure enough, out of the pot comes 'a lovely little creature in human shape, with large white wings.'[3]

If we were being raised as food in this kind of fairyland, then being eaten would make sense of our lives, precisely because it was our own ambition, a purpose we could make our own, and it would make sense of our lives even if it did not result in our turning into lovely little winged creatures. But it is difficult to see what comfort there is to be gleaned for the actual victims of and participants in war from knowing that it is all serving the useful purpose of reducing the population, however urgent the problem of excess population may once again have become in our minds. Being cooked and being shot cannot of themselves make sense of our lives, because they are things that simply happen to us. They cannot feature in our personal story except as part – maybe an all-important part – of the context within which we live out our mortality. What will make sense of our story as a human story will have to have a lot more to do with how we face up to the inevitable fate which confronts us. If we wanted to be eaten, then being eaten would constitute the happy ending which would satisfy our need to see our lives as having an intelligible shape. If we did not want to be eaten, but were being raised as food, then we would have to impose an intelligible shape on an otherwise meaningless tragedy, and we would have to do this by wresting such positive values as heroism and song from inevitable tragedy.

It is the inevitability of fate and, ultimately, death which creates the tragic space within which we must look for the sense of life.

The *Odyssey* is a fascinating poem in this regard. It too is concerned with theodicy. Almost at the beginning of the poem (1.32–34) Zeus complains to the assembled immortals, 'How mortals blame the gods! They say that it is from us that ills come, but even on their own, because of their sins, they have griefs beyond their appointed lot' (οἱ δὲ καὶ αὐτοὶ σφῇσιν ἀτασθαλίῃσιν ὑπὲρ μόρον ἄλγε᾽ ἔχουσιν). In the *Iliad* it is not clear that anything can happen ὑπὲρ μόρον, beyond people's appointed lot. If something contrary to fate looks like happening, prompt action is taken by the gods to prevent it.[4] When, in *Iliad* 16.780, the Greeks are being unduly victorious, ὑπὲρ αἶσαν, Apollo soon puts a stop to it. In the *Odyssey* men are given much more scope to choose their own fate, as it were. As Lloyd-Jones brings out, people who come to a sticky end have generally brought it on themselves by doing something they were explicitly warned not to do.[5]

The world of the *Odyssey* is ruled by divine interventions much less than that of the *Iliad*; but, at the same time, it is characterised by vastly more magic and far more of its inhabitants seem to be living in or near fairyland. Odysseus himself is given the chance to remain in fairyland: Calypso invites him to stay with her forever as an immortal. But he politely declines: even though Penelope is mortal and not nearly as beautiful as Calypso, nevertheless he wants to go home to her and brave whatever hardships may be involved on the way,[6] a decision which endeared him to the Stoics.[7] The whole of his extraordinary journey can be seen as a laborious escape from the world of enchantment and faery to return to a real, mortal wife in a real home, where indeed a real battle awaits him. But what makes the happy ending fully cogent is not his reunion with Penelope, even if that is where the story formally ends; it is the prophecy of Tiresias that he will die, apparently at home, in a prosperous old age, amid the prosperity of his people.[8] Call no man happy until he is dead. Without this glimpse into the future, we would not really know how the story of Odysseus ended.

No one in the *Odyssey* is hounded by any god-sent madness (ἄτη) into doing anything disastrously wrong, as Agamemnon claims he was in the *Iliad* (19.86–89). No one is in the position of Aeschylus' Agamemnon, faced with a choice where all the options are wrong.[9] No one has to 'put on the yoke of necessity.'[10] The morality of the *Odyssey* is therefore simpler and maybe blander. But in its own way this highlights Odysseus' deliberate espousal of mortality: his virtue consists in his acceptance of necessity, in a world much less obviously constrained by factors not subject to human choice. He could have escaped from necessity and remained in fairyland.

The *Odyssey* has a happy ending and looks forward to a happy death for Odysseus; but all the same, it has given us an unforgettable picture of the finality and desolateness of death, thanks to Odysseus' trip to Hades and especially his meeting with Achilles there. His refusal of the easy option offered by Calypso is genuinely heroic, and if he had not refused it, there would have been no story of Odysseus to tell.

What happens when the boundary of mortality is breached is explored, with gentle irony, in Euripides' *Alcestis*, which is all about attempts to evade death. It is also, incidentally, the only extant Greek play in which anyone dies on stage without violence, and, through Alcestis, we are given a glimpse of the sheer appallingness of death, and, at least for Alcestis, it is unrelieved by any hope of a significant post mortem existence. As far as she is concerned, once she is dead, she is nothing (381, 387, 390).

The story really starts with Apollo's son Asclepius, who carried his medical expertise too far and started restoring the dead to life, an impropriety for which Zeus destroyed him with a thunderbolt.

Pindar had used the example of Asclepius – whom he accuses of having been led astray by cupidity – to point the moral that mortals should seek only what is fitting for them from the gods, knowing what is to hand, what their appointed lot is.[11] The wisdom of the ancients teaches us that the immortals give men two ills for every blessing; fools cannot endure this decorously (κόσμῳ), but good men can, 'turning the fair side outwards' (so that this is what shows).[12]

In the *Alcestis* no one explicitly criticises Asclepius; indeed the chorus expresses a wish that he were still around (121–126). But Euripides hints quite firmly at all the trouble he has caused. His death annoyed Apollo, who got his own back by killing the Cyclopes who manufactured thunderbolts for Zeus, and as a result he was banished to serve a mortal for a year. His master, Admetus, was kind to him, so in return he got the Fates drunk and persuaded them to let Admetus off his appointed death, provided that he could find someone else to die in his place. No one, not even his parents, was willing, except for his wife Alcestis, and at the beginning of the play her time is now up and she is due to die (3–21).

Apollo puts us in the picture at the beginning of the play and then clears off, claiming that it would be a defilement for him to be present at the actual death (22–23), just as Artemis abandons the dying Hippolytus on the same pretext.[13] And, contrary to what Dale says in his commentary,[14] that is pretty well the end of his involvement in the matter. He makes a rather half-hearted attempt to persuade Death to leave Alcestis alone, but when that fails he contents himself with a thinly veiled prophecy of what will in fact happen at the end of the play, namely that Heracles will wrest Alcestis from Death's grip by brute force (48–71). There is no suggestion that he has himself done anything or that he will do anything to procure this intervention of Heracles. Essentially he just leaves the human beings to cope as best they may with the muddle he has landed them in, a stance not untypical of Apollo in the plays of Euripides.

And what a muddle it is! The loss of such a perfect wife as Alcestis makes life for Admetus not worth living, as everyone points out, including Admetus.[15] When Alcestis is dying, he pleads with her to take him with her, to which she rather tartly replies that one death is enough (382–383). Since she is dying, he says he looks forward to joining her in death, and in the meantime he is going to live a life that is little better than death (343–368). After her death he declares that he envies the dead (866), and that his dead wife is better off than he is (933–936). The horror of outliving one's loved ones is so vivid to him that he can actually curse his father with the wish that he may live 'longer than Zeus' (713). All in all, the life won for him by his wife's death is such as to make her sacrifice quite pointless, as Dale remarks.[16]

The chorus tries to comfort him with the platitudinous but, in other contexts, quite effective comment that everyone has to die (419) and there's no escaping from Necessity, including the necessary fact that the dead are dead (962–994). Heracles too remarks that everyone has to die, and 'being mortals we must think like mortals' (782, 799), which, for him, means essentially that we should eat, drink and be merry. But the whole situation of the play undermines these commonplaces. Asclepius, after all, did bring people back from death, and Admetus himself is the living proof that there is a way to thwart death. And both Admetus and the Chorus express a wish that they could go and get Alcestis back from Hades, even if they confess their inability to do so (357–362, 455–459). Their whole position is one of not really accepting the finality of death.

Worse still, the morality of the situation is hopelessly entangled, as the scene with Admetus' father, Pheres, makes clear. There is no doubt that we are meant to be critical of Pheres; even Alcestis thought that it was more appropriate for elderly parents to die in place of their son than for a young wife and mother to die (290–297). And we are probably meant to sympathise with Admetus' remark that old people claim to be fed up with life, yet when the crunch comes, they do not really want to die (669–672). Pheres is, perhaps, an old hedonist. But then he is quite right to point out that there is no νόμος, no law or custom, requiring parents to die instead of their children (682–684), and it is perfectly fair for him to remind Admetus that, if he (Admetus) loves life, so does his father, so does everyone (691, 703–704). And it is certainly correct to assert that each one of us is meant to live one life, the one appointed for us, not two lives (712). On Admetus' principles, he could live for ever, if he could find enough obliging wives (699–701). For all practical purposes he has murdered Alcestis, and if her family knows its salt, he will pay the price for it (730–733).

The row between father and son is distasteful and is meant to be felt as such; the reaction of the Chorus, trying to shush both parties, assures us of that (673, 707). And the row is left unresolved. How could it be resolved? Human morality is essentially mortal morality, and it cannot deal with death-swopping, which is, of course, quite unlike such situations as dying in battle for one's country or risking one's own life in battle or in an epidemic in order to save someone else's. Where everyone's life is at risk already, there may be cogent reasons for increasing the risk to one's own life to diminish the risk to someone else's life. But why should Admetus' parents have to die before their time, so that he could live beyond his appointed time? It is all very well to point out, as Admetus does, that if he had died they would have had no other child to look after them in their old age (662–664). That is a familiar tragic situation. It does not constitute a moral obligation on them to die in his place, even if, granted the initial hypothesis of death-swopping, they might have been sensible to volunteer.

The only person in the play who can be seen as having made a wholly rational choice is Alcestis. She values her life, but would rather die while she is still enjoying it than go on living without her husband and all the joy associated with him (284–289). But then Alcestis is also the only character to have a straightforward view of the finality and emptiness of death. She does not complain, as Pheres does, that death is 'long' (692–693), which implies that it is a kind of pseudo-life, nor does she, like Admetus, dream of family reunions in Hades (363–368); nor is she anticipating, as the Chorus does, any posthumous fame and cult (453–454). For her, the dead are nothing (381). Her robust acceptance of mortality has given her, it seems, a rather saner view of life than most of the other characters in the play have.

And then Heracles, a comic character, as usual, comes along to provide the happy ending. Alcestis, on her return from the dead, is obliged to keep silence for a few days (1144–1146), so we do not know what she made of it. Everyone else is delighted. But yet we are hardly satisfied. Heracles famously embodies the principle that might is right,[17] and his violent interruption of the logic of death makes nonsense, even if happy nonsense, of the real tragedy we have been witnessing, a tragedy already given its particular flavour by an earlier tampering with death, and it does nothing whatsoever to resolve the moral dilemmas caused by Apollo's meddling.

The mood is quite different, but yet, perhaps, Euripides' message is not so totally different from that of Oscar Wilde, in the prose poem in which he imagines Christ finding Lazarus weeping. When he asks why he is weeping, Lazarus replies, 'But I was dead once and you raised me from the dead. What else should I do but weep?'[18] For once Oscar Wilde and St Bernard seem to be in agreement. St Bernard interprets Christ's weeping at the tomb of Lazarus as being caused, not by Lazarus' death but by the fact that he is going to be called back to life.[19]

There are several other plays in which Euripides uses a divine intervention to provide what is surely meant to be perceived as a false resolution of a plot tending naturally towards death. Aristotle's objection to *deus ex machina* denouements was that the story itself should generate its own conclusion,[20] and Euripides must have been as aware of this as Aristotle was. In the *Orestes*, for instance, Apollo's highly dramatic last-minute appearance, even if it enables everyone to live happily ever after, simply derails the plot as it has been developing so far. No one is in any doubt that Apollo gave Orestes bad advice, which put him in a morally impossible position, because it failed to do justice to the ambiguities involved in avenging his father by murdering his mother. And he then signally failed to do anything to help Orestes. Our sympathies are meant to go with Orestes and his sister and his friend, and the condemnation of Orestes and Electra to commit suicide, and Pylades' resolve to die with them, is a real tragedy. Menelaus, on the other hand, is presented as shifty, and when he lets Orestes down at his trial, he loses whatever sympathy we might have felt for him. Helen has been presented in a uniformly bad light throughout the play, and Hermione is too nondescript to arouse much interest. We are probably meant to feel that Orestes was right in supposing that he would win universal acclaim by killing Helen (1149–1152), and few tears are going to be shed for Menelaus in his bereavement, and even the projected murder of Hermione is not too shocking for us. So everything is set for a magnificent tragic conclusion, with the palace all ready to go up in flames, Helen dead and nearly everyone else about to die, and Menelaus helpless to do anything about it. And this tragedy is simply aborted, not resolved or fulfilled, by Apollo's belated arrival, which had been heralded only by the utterly mysterious disappearance of Helen just when she was about to be killed (1494–1495).

The complete disregard of Apollo for human sensibilities is shown particularly by his cool announcement that Helen is to be a god and, in fact, a patron deity of sailors (1635–1637). This last detail seems to be Euripides' own invention[21] and we are meant to be shocked by it. After all, this is Helen the ship-destroyer, as Aeschylus called her, Ἑλένη ἑλέναυς,[22] the lady no one in the play has had a good word for. Then Apollo says blandly that Menelaus had better take another wife (1638) – after all that the Greeks had gone through to get Helen back for him! And Orestes is to marry Hermione and rule in Argos, and Pylades can marry Electra (1653–1659), this being about the only point on which Apollo's bossy disposal of everyone coincides with their own plans and desires.

As Denniston suggests, Apollo's role in the whole saga of Orestes is a disgraceful one, and his 'vindication' at the end of the *Orestes* is only apparent. ' "I give you," the poet unmistakably hints, "the traditional conclusion of the story: but it is one the human conscience cannot accept." '[23] And his artificially induced happy ending is the crowning insult, trivialising the agony of its beneficiaries, fudging rather than facing the perplexities and the fatality by which Orestes and his friends are hemmed in.

It is the same with Thetis' appearance at the end of the *Andromache*. The interpretation of this play is a matter of considerable controversy, but there can be little doubt that it moves in its own odd way to the real tragedy of the death of Neoptolemus, and the main tragic character at the end of the play is certainly Peleus. Prompted only by a quite casual reference to her, Thetis suddenly appears, out of respect, as she says, for her former marriage to Peleus, and she bids him not to grieve too much – after all, she too, a goddess, lost her son Achilles, whom she had borne to Peleus. She then turns brusquely to business. What she has come to say is that Neoptolemus is to be buried at Delphi, Andromache is to be married off to Helenus, and Peleus himself is to become an immortal god and live with her for ever, and he will also see Achilles living in the White Island. So he must stop being upset over the dead, because it is the divine decree that all men must die. Peleus duly says that, at her behest, he is no longer miserable (1231–1276).

One is tempted to recall here Vellacott's comment that 'Euripides was concerned to say that to be godlike was a less laudable aim than to be human.'[24] The human seriousness of the situation is simply dismissed by Thetis, and there is something slightly displeasing about Peleus' readiness to accept her disdainful depreciation of human death. And her reference to her own bereavement is rendered unconvincing by her disclosure that Achilles is actually not really dead anyway, so even her frigid sympathy does not ring true. It is no doubt very nice to make old Peleus immortal and let him have his divine bride back, but it makes all the suffering he and everyone else has been going through rather pointless. The divine way of dealing with the situation disregards and so cheapens the human tragedy on which it supervenes, but to which it is not really relevant.

In a different way, we are left with the same feeling at the end of the *Hippolytus*. Artemis cannot really enter into the human tragedy for which she is, at least in part, responsible. Like Apollo in the *Alcestis*, her divine status forbids her to witness human death (1437–1438). In Taplin's words:

> It is the ease, the detachment, of Artemis' departure . . . which the scene conveys in performance; and this sharpens the contrast with the brief final scene, full as it is of human love and regret . . . (Artemis') farewell pales before that of the mere mortals. These are the Homeric gods, blessed, immortal and thus untragic: a foil to the misery, and yet nobility, of the mortal condition.[25]

I have dwelt at some length on these various literary texts, because they emphasise, within the Greek tradition, a point which the philosophers are reluctant to recognise, namely that human life, hemmed in as it is by uncontrollable forces and by death, is tragic. Suffering is not of course the sole reality of life, but it is a factor of sufficient prominence to justify the claim that no interpretation of life which fails to do justice to it can really ring true. This is why, as Chesterton has Father Brown explain, 'The Religion of Cheerfulness . . . is a cruel religion . . . Why couldn't they let him weep a little, like his fathers before him?'[26] Magical or miraculous interventions may bring about an unanticipated happy ending, but they fail to round off a human story convincingly because they leave unexplained, uninterpreted, the pain that has gone before. If Helen can become immortal simply because she is Zeus' daughter, the human tale of which she is a part becomes a mockery; the *Iliad*, in which there is no divinity for Helen, no exemption from death for any of the gods' children, is a more truly human and humane story. If Peleus can slough off his grief just like that and become an immortal, it is hard not to feel that he has become less than a man, not more. And interfering with the boundary of mortality which delimits a human life not only risks a false negation of tragedy, it even makes a genuine happy ending impossible, because it makes any ending impossible. The fairytale conclusion, 'And they all lived happily ever after,' only works because we treat it as having a kind of finality which belongs properly to death; it implies that nothing more really happens. The picture is complete and therefore in a way frozen. And it is only mortals whose stories can be complete in this way. It is somehow difficult to imagine a story about immortals concluding that they all lived happily ever after.

One thing which did not live happily ever after is Greek tragedy. From the fourth century BC onwards, even though we know that tragedies continued to be written and performed, apparently almost nothing in them was considered worth preserving.[27] And it is tempting to connect this total eclipse of tragedy with the shift of mood apparent in Hellenistic philosophy. Almost every school of philosophy in this period saw ethics as its chief concern and, however varied their tactics and terminology, they all agree in identifying the purpose of ethics as being to make people invulnerable or less vulnerable to the slings and arrows of outrageous fortune. They inculcate, therefore, an essentially untragic stance.

Epicurus prided himself on being an original thinker[28] and he enjoyed being rude about everyone else.[29] Among others, Theognis incurred his detestation for giving vent to the conventional Greek notion that it is best not to be born, and, failing that, one should die as quickly as possible; and almost as bad, in Epicurus' view, is the commonplace that the young should be encouraged to live well and the old to die well.[30] With a surprising echo of the *Phaedo*, Epicurus declares that practising to live well and practising to die well are the same thing.[31] His words to Menoeceus are worth quoting at some length:

> Accustom yourself to think that death is nothing to us, since all good and evil lie in sensation, and death means deprivation of sensation. So a right awareness of the fact that death is nothing to us makes the mortality of life enjoyable, not adding unlimited time, but taking away the desire for immortality. There is nothing frightening about being alive for anyone who has genuinely grasped that there is nothing frightening about not being alive. So it is useless to claim that one fears death, not because it will be grievous when it comes, but because it is grievous now while it is impending. It is fatuous to be grieved by the expectation of something that will not be troublesome when it comes. So the most terrifying of all ills, death, is nothing to us, because while we exist, death is not present, and when death is present, we do not exist. Therefore it is nothing either to the living or to the dead, because in the one case it is not there, and in the other case they are no longer there . . . The wise man does not refuse life, nor is he afraid of not living; life does not offend him, nor does he think it any ill not to be alive. Just as he does not simply choose the greater quantity of food, but the most pleasant, so he culls, not the longest time, but the most pleasant.[32]

Epicurus' doctrine that 'death is nothing to us', so memorably expressed by Lucretius,[33] rests on his physics and his account of the nature of the soul. But what concerns us now is his contention that a yearning for immortality, already used by Aristotle as the very type of a desire for what is impossible,[34] spoils our enjoyment of our mortality.

Granted that we are mortal, learning how to live well means learning how to enjoy mortality, and this means appreciating 'the limits of life' (τὰ πέρατα τοῦ βίου). Anyone who is clear about these limits, Epicurus claims, 'knows how easy it is to obtain what removes the pain caused by need and makes the whole of life complete, so that there is no need for anything that has to be struggled for.'[35]

The 'limits of life' that need to be appreciated are temporal, quantitative and qualitative:

> The flesh takes the limits of pleasure to be unlimited and supposes that unlimited time supplies it.[36] But the mind, calculating the end and limit of the flesh and dispelling fears about eternity, produces the complete life, and we no longer need

> unlimited time. It does not flee pleasure and, when circumstances bring about its departure from life, it does not perish as if it were falling short of the best life.[37]

The point seems to be that sheer bodily sensation, as such, has no built-in awareness that bodily pleasure is limited in time or in any other way. But the mind, at least in Epicurus' view, can recognise that there is a limit to pleasure and that this limit is of a kind to make temporal prolongation an irrelevant consideration. 'The limit to the greatness of pleasure is the removal of everything painful.' 'Pleasure will not increase in the flesh, when once the pain caused by need is removed; it is only varied.' 'Unlimited time has the same amount of pleasure as limited time, if one measures its limits rationally.'[38]

Epicurus' account of pleasure is an austere one, and, if he is right to claim that pleasure can only be varied not increased, once we are in the position of having no unsatisfied bodily need, then he is right to say that unlimited time cannot contain any more pleasure than limited time. Once we have achieved this state, with a reasonable expectation that it will continue,[39] we have achieved a 'complete life'. But this does mean having a correct understanding. 'It is not the belly that is insatiable, as most people say, it is a false opinion about the unlimited capacity of the belly.'[40] If we are misled by false ideas based on an uncritical acceptance of sheer sensuality, we may think we need unlimited time for at least two reasons: we may dream of some impossible fulness of pleasure and need more time to go on looking for it; or we may simply think that pleasure can be enhanced by being prolonged indefinitely. In either way we shall be distracted from enjoying our mortality.

There is, perhaps, no strict logical connection between the temporal limit to pleasure and the quantitative and qualitative links by which Epicurus sets such store, but there is more than a merely verbal link. If he wants to eliminate dreams of immortality because they are associated with an unsettling fear that mortality might be depriving us of pleasure and of the fulness of life, it is for a very similar reason that he has to head us off from other ways of exaggerating the scope of the pleasures that are necessary to us. If his ideal of the pleasant life is to be a realistic one – and its practicality was an important aspect of it for Epicurus, who tried to embody it in his community of friends – then as few hostages as possible must be surrendered to potentially disturbing excitements. And, as Epicurus was well aware, this means cutting out a great many kinds of pleasure:

> If we say that pleasure is the beginning and end of the happy

> life . . . we do not for that reason choose every pleasure; sometimes we pass over many pleasures, when the result would be more trouble than pleasure. And we consider some pains preferable to pleasures, when after we have endured the pains for a long time a greater pleasure will result . . . When we say that pleasure is our goal, we do not mean the pleasures of the dissolute and those which consist in self-indulgence.[41]

Not only will the good Epicurean shun the pleasures of the dissolute, he will avoid politics and falling in love.[42] He will pursue intellectual interests only in so far as they are needed to deliver him from disturbing misconceptions;[43] otherwise he will again be wasting his life and forgetting his mortality.[44]

We should not exaggerate the asceticism of Epicures' ideal. 'For my part,' he says, 'I do not know how to conceive of the good in abstraction from the pleasures of taste and of sex and of listening and the pleasant sensations caused by seeing a beautiful form.'[45] But, in spite of the comparison that is often made between Epicurus and Horace's *carpe diem*,[46] his goal is a settled condition of pleasure, which has to make a certain claim on the future. Enjoying our mortality does not simply mean enjoying each day as it comes. It may be true, as Epicurus claims, that 'the person who has least need of tomorrow approaches tomorrow most pleasantly,'[47] but we obviously cannot enjoy today unless we are reasonably confident that tomorrow, if there is a tomorrow, will not be too unpleasant. And in the nature of the case, there is no guarantee that we shall not be taken ill tomorrow, and Epicurus does not say, as at least the later Stoics did, that if it gets too bad we can always kill ourselves. He does assert that acute pain does not last long, and pain that does last is always outweighed by pleasure,[48] but the ultimate remedy for serious bodily pain is the recollection of past delights, as we learn from the letter which Epicurus wrote on his deathbed, when he was in considerable pain.[49] That is why he says, 'It is not the young man who should be called blessed, but the old man who has lived well . . . The old man has docked in old age as in a harbour, with good things that before he hardly dared to hope for safely stowed away in his gratitude.'[50] When the body is in pain, the responsibility for maintaining the pleasantness of life passes to mental pleasures, namely 'looking forward to hoped-for pleasures and the memory of those previously enjoyed.'[51] Philosophy, Epicurus claims, enables one who is getting old to become young again in his gratitude for the past, and it also enables the young to be old too in not fearing the future.[52] The optimism of the young, it seems, rests at least in part on the experience of the old, happy even in sickness because of their happy memories. Thus the future cannot simply be dismissed: 'We should be mindful that the future is not ours, nor is it entirely not ours; so we should not entirely await it, as if it were sure to come, nor should we despair of it, as if it were certainly not going to come.'[53]

One can see why considerations like these are important in Epicurus' system; without them he would not be able to maintain that happiness is within easy reach of everyone. But they do rather undermine his contention that we have no reason to complain of the prospect of death. What of the young man who dies before he has accumulated a stock of happy memories? Is his life 'complete'? How does he cope with serious sickness? Has Epicurus really banished the tragedy of someone cut off in his prime?

If the patch defended by the Epicureans against Fortune[54] was a small one, the Stoics retreated to an even smaller and more impregnable citadel, where the wise man would be 'undefeated by fortune, unenslaved and invulnerable'.[55] 'The wise man,' declares Seneca, 'does nothing against his will; he escapes necessity because he wills what it is going to enforce.'[56] Distinguishing sharply between what is and what is not subject to our control, the Stoic sage makes himself impervious to the vagaries of fortune by treating all that is not subject to our control – including even life and death – as 'indifferent'.[57] Even if it is often sensible to *prefer* one indifferent thing to another – the Stoic will, in ordinary circumstances, prefer health to sickness[58] – the sage will not make himself subject to any of them by desiring or fearing them. His inner freedom and stability is thus secured, proof against disturbance by anything that may or may not befall him. He 'offers himself to fate',[59] which he identifies with God's will, which he will have to obey anyway, willingly or unwillingly. 'What madness it is,' writes Seneca:

> to be dragged rather than to follow; just as it is foolishness and ignorance of one's condition to complain that you are lacking something or that something hard has befallen you, so it is to admire or be indignant over things which happen to good and bad alike – disease, I mean, deaths, infirmities and all the other things which cut across human life. Whatever must be endured, because of the way the world is constructed, must be accepted magnanimously. This is the vow we are subjected to: to bear the consequences of mortality and not to be disturbed by things which it is not in our power to avoid. We were born in a kingdom: to obey God is freedom.[60]

Contrary to the popular modern image of Stoicism, Seneca is recommending something more than glum resignation to the inevitable:

> The person who knows what to enjoy reaches the heights, the person who has not put his happiness in the power of anything outside himself. Anyone who is moved by any hope is anxious and unsure of himself, even if what he hopes for is to hand and easily sought, even if his hopes never deceive him. Above all, Lucilius, learn how to enjoy.[61]

True joy, as Seneca warns us, is a *res severa*, and it shows, not least, in people's attitude to death: the 'bland' joys of the populace do not readily go with 'making light of death' (*mortem contemnere*).[62]

Death and mortality are not a major topic, as such, in Stoicism, but death is certainly one of the most obvious things which are not subject to our control (except in the sense that we can, in the Stoic view, always escape from an intolerable life by committing suicide), so it is not surprising that both Seneca and Epictetus would have us bear death constantly in mind.[63] Death highlights true values. Seneca complains that people 'fear everything like mortals and desire everything like immortals,'[64] whereas the philosopher fears neither loss nor death, and does not commit himself to desiring anything that is vulnerable to fortune. Because of their failure to learn the lesson of mortality, people ruin their lives and suffer agonies from their desire for something in the future and their disaffection for what is present. The sage, by contrast, uses every moment profitably, and treats every day as if it were his last, and so neither yearns for tomorrow nor fears it.[65] Our attitude to the things of fortune should be that 'we receive things which are going to perish as people who are going to perish' (*accipimus peritura perituri*).[66]

The realisation of mortality also brings home to us the absurdity of putting off philosophy. It is our false desires which make us complain about the shortness of life and plan on adopting a more philosophical life later on, living 'as if we were going to live for ever'.[67]

It is interesting that this line of thought is apparently quite unaffected by the genuine Stoic belief that at least some souls will actually survive death and last until the final conflagration which will terminate this world-order;[68] Seneca alludes to this belief at the end of the *Consolatio ad Marciam*, in spite of the fact that he has earlier used the Epicurean topos that death is nothing to us because we shall be as unaffected by being dead as we were by being unborn.[69] Wisdom can no more be deferred to post mortem existence than it can be put off till old age. Living rationally means living rationally now, within the confines of mortality and in full acceptance of the unreliability of external benefits, which is dramatised for us by our mortality.

There is something undoubtedly impressive about the Stoic

refusal to be upset by the ups and downs of life, but it is not wholly unfair to think fleetingly in their connection of the wretched Pangloss in Voltaire's *Candide*, with his dogged insistence, against all the evidence, that all is for the best in the best of all possible worlds, and indeed of the king in *The Little Prince*, who secures unfailing obedience to his commands by commanding only what is going to happen anyway.[70]

It probably is unfair, but I cannot resist the temptation, to connect the three different attitudes to mortality with which we have been occupied in these two chapters with something that Charles Williams says about one of his characters in *Descent into Hell*:

> He was not a child, neither the child that had lost its toy and cried for it, nor the child that had lost its toy and would not let itself care, nor the child that had lost its toy and tried to recover it by pretending it never did care.[71]

For the tragedians and for Homer life is tragic and calls for tears, but there is no remedy except heroic endurance to the end. For the Epicureans life is sweet, but its passing does not matter. For the Stoics life is indifferent and it is foolish to be attached to it.

NOTES

1 Fragment 1 in *Homeri Opera* vol. V, ed. Allen.
2 T. Nagel, *Mortal Questions*, Cambridge 1979, p. 16.
3 G. Macdonald, *Complete Fairy Tales*, New York 1977, pp. 218–219.
4 Cf. *Iliad* 2.155, 20.30, 20.336, 21.357; also *Odyssey* 5.436.
5 H. Lloyd-Jones, *The Justice of Zeus*, Berkeley 1971, p. 29.
6 *Odyssey* 5.206–224.
7 Cf. Seneca, *Ep*. 88.5.
8 *Odyssey* 11.134–137.
9 Aeschylus, *Agamemnon* 211.
10 Ibid. 218.
11 Pindar, *Pyth*. 3.54–60.
12 Ibid. 80–83.
13 Euripides, *Hippolytus* 1437–1438. Similarly Juno abandons Turnus in the battle which is to lead to his death in Vergil, *Aeneid* 12.151.
14 A. M. Dale, *Euripides, Alcestis*, Oxford 1961, p. xxii: 'In and out among them the beneficence of Apollo, working through Heracles, has been preparing a way towards the light.' The text gives no warrant for ascribing Heracles' intervention to Apollo's initiative.
15 The servant points it out in 197–198, the Chorus in 242–243, and Admetus in 278–279.
16 Op. cit. p. 82.
17 Cf. Pindar, frag. 152 in Bowra's edition.

18 Oscar Wilde, *The Doer of Good*, in *Complete Shorter Fiction*, Oxford 1979, p. 255.
19 I have not been able to find this in Bernard, but it is ascribed to him in Hugh of St Cher's comment on John 11:35.
20 Aristotle, *Poetics* 1454a37-b2.
21 Cf. W. Willink's commentary, Oxford 1986, p. 352.
22 Aeschylus, *Agamemnon* 689.
23 J. D. Denniston, *Euripides, Electra*, Oxford 1939, p. xxii.
24 P. Vellacott, *Ironic Drama*, Cambridge 1975, p. 12.
25 Taplin, op. cit. p. 52.
26 G. K. Chesterton, *The Innocence of Father Brown*, Penguin edn 1950, p. 246.
27 Cf. B. M. W. Knox in P. E. Easterling and B. M. W. Knox, eds, *Cambridge History of Classical Literature* vol. I, Cambridge 1985, p. 345.
28 Diogenes Laertius 10.13; cf. the commentary by A. Laks in J. Bollack and A. Laks, eds, *Études sur l'Épicurisme antique*, Lille 1976, pp. 68–69.
29 Cf. Diogenes Laertius 10.7–8.
30 Epicurus, *Letter to Menoeceus* 126.
31 Ibid.
32 Ibid. 124–126.
33 Lucretius 3.830.
34 Aristotle, *Eth. Nic.* 1111b22–23.
35 *Kyriai Doxai* 21.
36 For this interpretation, cf. C. Diano, *Scritti Eipcurei*, Florence 1974, p. 21.
37 *Kyriai Doxai* 20.
38 Ibid. 3, 18, 19.
39 H. Usener, *Epicurea*, Stuttgart 1966, pp. 121–122, frag. 68.
40 *Vatican Sayings* 59.
41 *Letter to Menoeceus* 129, 131.
42 Diogenes Laertius 10.118–119.
43 *Kyriai Doxai* 11–13; frag. 221 Usener. Cf. A. A. Long and D. N. Sedley, *The Hellenistic Philosophers*, Cambridge 1987, 25 B.1 and 25 C.
44 I take this to be the point of *Vatican Sayings* 10, ascribed to Metrodorus by Clement of Alexandria, *Strom.* 5.138.2. D. Clay, in Bollack and Laks, *Études* p. 225, tries to claim it for Epicurus himself.
45 Frag. 67 Usener.
46 Horace, *Odes* 1.11.8.
47 Frag. 490 Usener.
48 *Kyriai Doxai* 4.
49 Diogenes Laertius 10.22 (Long and Sedley 24.D).
50 *Vatican Sayings* 17.
51 Long and Sedley 21 T; 439 Usener.
52 *Letter to Menoeceus* 122.
53 Ibid. 127.
54 Cf. *Vatican Sayings* 47.
55 *Stoicorum Veterum Fragmenta* I no. 449.
56 Seneca, *Ep.* 54.7.
57 *Stoicorum Veterum Fragmenta* I no. 190.

58 Cf. Diogenes Laertius 7.102–107.
59 Seneca, *De Providentia* 5.8.
60 Seneca, *De Vita Beata* 15.6–7.
61 Seneca, *Ep.* 23.2–3.
62 Ibid. 4.
63 Cf. Seneca, *Ep.* 12.6; Epictetus, *Enchiridion* 21.
64 *De Brevitate Vitae* 3.4.
65 Ibid. 7.8–9.
66 *De Providentia* 5.7.
67 *De Brevitate Vitae* 3.4.
68 Cf. J. M. Rist, *Stoic Philosophy*, Cambridge 1969, pp. 93–94.
69 The Epicurean argument is used in 19.5, survival until the final conflagration is alluded to in 24.5–26.6. For the Epicurean argument, cf. Lucretius 3.830–842; on Lucretius' possible sources, see B. P. Wallach, *Lucretius and the Diatribe against the Fear of Death*, Leiden 1976, pp. 15–20.
70 A. de Saint-Exupéry, *Le Petit Prince*, London 1958, pp. 36–41.
71 Charles Williams, *Descent into Hell*, London 1949, p. 50.

5

We have so far been looking chiefly at various ancient attitudes to death and mortality, unaffected by christianity. And it seems to me that there are essentially three positions that emerge as defensible. It is possible to see death as the tragedy which highlights the generally tragic nature of human existence, in face of which the most we can do is tell stories that give a kind of aesthetic shape to what would otherwise be meaningless pain and frustration; and the seriousness of this option is underlined by the unsatisfactoriness of stories which seek to evade the tragedy by importing magical, but essentially irrelevant, happy endings. Or we may follow the line of the *Phaedo*, which Plato himself increasingly abandoned, but which resurfaced in Middle Platonism and in what Dillon calls the 'Platonic underworld,'[1] and say that life, in the ordinary sense, is such a bad business that death is the best thing that can happen to us, provided that we internalise it sufficiently to make it a decisive break with this whole world-order. Or we may attempt to minimise our exposure to the slings and arrows, and particularly death, by trying to secure some small space within which we can be happy, either by espousing the austere hedonism of Epicurus or by aiming at the moral superiority of the Stoics.

These are probably still the three options that arise in our modern western culture, at least wherever, for one reason or another, the intellectual challenge of christianity is inoperative. Few people can really quarrel with the designation of this world as a 'vale of tears',[2] whether they infer from it that life is meaningless and we might as well eat, drink and be merry, for tomorrow we die, or whether they console themselves by telling stories of heroism. This is the tragic option, whether or not the tragedy is deliberately faced. The ethos of the *Phaedo* and the Platonic underworld can be recognised, in a debased form, in the current popularity of stories about people who have died or nearly died and come back to assure us that death is only a passage to a cosier and brighter life, usually, it seems, without any of the moral stringency involved in the *Phaedo*. The same can be said about such modern myths as *Jonathan Livingstone Seagull*. Finally, unless I am much mistaken, there is a pronounced similarity to Stoicism in the 'Being-towards-Death' preached by Heidegger in *Being and Time*,[3] and Epicurus could recognise as his heirs the various modern movements calling for a simplification of life, this call often being embodied in more or less 'drop out' communities.

Christianity introduces a new factor into the discussion, but, before we begin to consider its contribution in detail, let us review briefly the human concerns that have emerged so far from our probings. It will be important to see how far such concerns are recognised, or can be recognised, by christian theology.

First we have seen that a human life needs a genuine end, a denouement growing out of the actual development of the story, if it is to make sense.

Secondly the boundaries of human life must not be fudged in such a way as to detract from the reality of our situation in this world and to license unbridled daydreaming.

Thirdly the genuine tragedy involved in human life and death must not be brushed aside cheaply by phoney and adventitious happy endings, which do not make sense retrospectively of the pain that has gone before.

Fourthly we may wonder whether there is not some way of facing death honestly which neither commits us to the disdain shown for this life in the *Phaedo* nor confines us to the rather cramped choice between Epicurus' garden, Stoic highmindedness and Heideggerian authenticity.

Christianity, with its belief in the resurrection of the dead, is obviously committed historically to maintaining that death is not simply the end of the human story, and it has generally found it convenient to make use also of the doctrine of the immortality of the soul, though, as we shall see, this latter doctrine is far less securely enshrined in christian theology than conventional modern orthodoxy might lead us to imagine. At the same time, however, there are doctrinally important signs that christianity has been reluctant to deprive death too briskly of its finality.

The recognition of death as an essential limit is evident in the medieval adage that 'the time for repenting extends to the last moment of life.'[4] The underlying principle is stated with admirable clarity as early as the so-called Second Letter of Clement, composed probably in the first half of the second century:

> While we are on earth, let us repent. We are clay in the hand of the craftsman. If a potter is making a pot and it goes wrong or comes apart in his hands, he refashions it; but when he reaches the point of putting it in the hot oven, there is no more

> he can do for it . . . Similarly we can no longer confess or repent, once we have gone out of the world.[5]

And this is apparently what St Paul means in 2 Corinthians 5:11, an obscure verse, which I hesitantly translate, 'We must all appear before the tribunal of Christ so that each one may recover the things done through the body, in accordance with what he has done, whether good or bad.'

What is judged by God is what we have done in this life, and we are judged on the basis of where we end up, not on the over-all balance of our virtues and vices. As Ezekiel 3:17–21 makes clear, it is possible for both the righteous and sinners to change direction, and if they do, their former righteousness or sinfulness ceases to count. This is the point of the peculiarly vicious vengeance favoured by Hamlet:

> Up, sword; and know thou a more horrid hent:
> When he is drunk, asleep or in his rage,
> Or in the incestuous pleasure of his bed,
> At gaming, sweating, or about some act
> That has no relish of salvation in't,
> Then trip him, that his heels may kick at heaven,
> And that his soul may be as damn'd and black
> As hell, whereto it goes.[6]

It is also the point of all those medieval stories in which someone dies in a state of sin but is then restored to life, usually at the intercession of Mary, so that he can mend his ways, or at least make a good confession, and then die again properly.[7] Even if the miraculous intervention somewhat blurs the finality of death, it does so in order to re-affirm it: the business of this life has to be finished within the limits of this life. Precisely because there is no posthumous remedy for a bad death, the only further mercy that the devout imagination can conceive of is a chance to die again.

The definitiveness of death is underscored by the belief that souls are judged as soon as people die, a belief we shall be looking at in more detail later on. On the face of it, this immediate judgment (the 'particular judgment', as it is called) renders the last judgment otiose, and it is interesting to see how St Thomas Aquinas deals with this problem.[8] He begins by noting that 'no complete judgment can be passed on anything mutable until its course is finished.' A human life comes to an end in death, but there are several ways in which the future may still modify one's judgment of it: the dead live on in men's memory and in their children and in the effects of their deeds; we may want to consider what happens to the corpse and to the things the dead person was interested in. All of these, Thomas boldly declares, fall within the scope of God's judgment, and it is only on the last day that a final verdict can be pronounced on them.

This is so unconvincing that Thomas must surely have been tempted to say that there is some sort of personal development after death, which necessitates a second judgment at the end of time. But no, Thomas is adamant: after death, our situation (*status*) is immutable, as far as the soul is concerned, so there really is nothing left for a second judgment of the soul to deal with. All that is judged at the last judgment is certain incidental effects of one's life, which cannot affect anyone's essential reward, though Thomas allows that they may affect 'some kind of reward'. He is presumably thinking of such bonuses as haloes, traditionally expected to be bestowed on successful preachers,[9] whose posthumous influence might well continue to win converts after their death, so that it would be improper to assess their entitlement to eschatological bonuses until the end of time. But as far as the story of the soul itself is concerned, that has come to an end at death. Thomas is not prepared to budge an inch from the standard position he had argued for in the *Contra Gentiles*: the will of all the dead, whether they are in hell, in purgatory or in heaven, whether before or after their resurrection, is immutable.[10]

Origen was regarded, fairly or unfairly, as having undermined the decisiveness of death and judgment, by teaching that the soul can pass through an unlimited number of lives of various kinds in various worlds, ranging from the angelic to the demonic, apparently with no definitive arrival either in bliss or in damnation.[11] At the Council of Florence the Greeks were worried that the Latin doctrine of purgatory could easily lead to a kind of Origenism, with its belief in a temporary post mortem punishment.[12] Bessarion noted, all the same, that the Latins were not in fact indulging in Origenism, inasmuch as they believed that the will of the souls in purgatory was already immutable,[13] and he was certainly right about this. In the standard medieval textbook of theology Peter Lombard, on the authority of Augustine, makes it quite clear that our prayers and other services undertaken on behalf of the dead can only benefit those who had already merited such help during their life on earth. They can acquire no new merits. 'No one, once he finishes this life, will be able to have anything after this life except what he merited during his life.'[14]

One of Luther's propositions condemned by Leo X in 1520 was that the souls in purgatory are not sure of their salvation, or not all of them, and that it is not proved by reason or by scripture that they are incapable of meriting or increasing in charity.[15] Luther shortly afterwards decided he did not believe in purgatory anyway, but in the meantime he had provided the pope with an opportunity to reaffirm the traditional Catholic belief that death means a definitive conclusion to this life, rendering the position of the dead no longer susceptible of either risk or further personal development.

Classic Protestantism was, on the whole, more concerned to affirm the decisiveness of the last judgment than it was to insist on the decisiveness of death. Its abandonment of the doctrine of purgatory did not therefore necessarily entail a complete exclusion of the idea of posthumous progress.[16] But it was in later liberal Protestantism and in the eccentric speculation of people like Swedenborg that the notion of an energetic and constantly developing afterlife really gained momentum, culminating in the extraordinary beliefs of the Latter Day Saints.[17] It is against this background that we may situate the attempt made by some nineteenth-century Anglican theologians to interpret the twenty-second of the Thirty-Nine Articles as condemning only the *Romish* doctrine of purgatory, so that an alternative notion of purgatory could be proposed in which the dead would be seen as maturing gradually towards complete sanctification by their own endeavours and by the use of their own free will.[18]

Undoubtedly the loss of the doctrine of purgatory posed a problem for Protestantism, as the uncompromising logic of John Wesley makes clear. He believed it to be universally accepted that we must all be fully cleansed from sin before we can enter into glory and so, since most people patently do not attain complete holiness during their lives, he argued that they must be perfectly sanctified instantaneously at 'the instant of death, the moment before the soul leaves the body.' Only so could he benignly continue to insist that 'everyone must be entirely sanctified in the article of death.'[19]

Catholics seem generally to have been unwilling to deviate from the basic conviction that the story stops at death, apart from whatever purification remains to be carried out in purgatory. Notions of post mortem progress made little headway among them and were formally condemned at least once, by an episcopal synod held in 1857 at Périgueux.[20]

Cullmann was being fair to one element anyway in his Protestant inheritance when, in a famous and tendentious book, he pointed out that the New Testament focuses our post mortem hopes on resurrection, not on the immortality of the soul.[21] And indeed 'immortality' is a word rarely used in the Bible. 'Immortal' (ἀθάνατος) is found twice in the Septuagint: Wisdom 1:15 declares that righteousness is immortal, and Ecclesiasticus 17:30 declares that human beings are not immortal. The corresponding noun occurs a few times in the book of Wisdom, and there we are told that the righteous have a hope which is 'full of immortality' (3:4) and that knowing God's might is the 'root of immortality' (15:3).

In the New Testament there is the affirmation already cited, that God alone possesses immortality (1 Tim. 6:16). The only other passage to use the word ἀθανασία (and the adjective is never used) is 1 Corinthians 15:53–54. St Paul is talking about the resurrection of the dead which, he says, is 'sown in corruption and raised in incorruption' (15:42):

> Behold, I tell you a mystery. We shall not all fall asleep, but we shall all be changed, in a moment, in the twinkling of an eye, at the last trump. For the trumpet will sound and the dead will be raised incorruptible and we shall be changed. For this corruptible thing must be clothed in incorruption and this mortal thing must be clothed in immortality. And when this corruptible thing is clothed in incorruption and this mortal thing in immortality, then will come about the word which is written, 'Death is swallowed up in victory. Where, death, is your victory, where, death, is your sting?' (15:51–55)

There is no hint here that there is anything in us which is innately immortal. It is as a result of a change that that which is now mortal becomes immortal. Our lot is evidently isomorphic with that of Christ who, 'having been raised from the dead, dies no more' (Rom. 6:9). And if mortality is 'clothed in' immortality, this suggests that immortality (which belongs by right only to God) is imparted as a gift to those who have put on Christ. And there is no question of immortality negating death altogether; what is claimed is that those who have died and been resurrected are no longer liable to any further death thereafter.

However, as even Cullmann concedes, the dead are not simply annihilated and then resurrected ex nihilo. As in Homer, they continue to exist, even if they cannot be said to be alive. They can be said to be 'asleep' and even to have some special relationship with Christ. The good thief is promised that he will be with Christ in Paradise 'today' (Luke 23:43), and Paul longs to 'be dissolved and be with Christ' (Phil. 1:23).[22]

On the face of it, very much more than this is implied by Matthew 22:31–32 and parallel texts, where Jesus deals with the Sadducees' trick question about the resurrection: 'About the resurrection of the dead, have you not read what is said to you by God? "I am the God of Abraham and the God of Isaac and the God of Jacob"? God is not the God of the dead, but of the living.' This suggests that Abraham and co. must be alive now; and, if this is to work as an argument for the resurrection, it looks as if it ought to mean that they are already resurrected, which seems to land us in the belief repudiated as heretical in 2 Timothy 2:18, that the resurrection has already occurred.

It is instructive to see how patristic and medieval commentators deal with this text. Chrysostom interprets Christ's words as meaning, 'He is not the God of the non-existent, who have disappeared once and for all with no prospect of rising again.' Just as Adam died on the day that he ate the forbidden fruit, in the sense that he was condemned to die, even though in fact he went on living, so Abraham and co., 'even if they were dead, were alive in the promise of resurrection.' So there is no contradiction between this text and Romans 14:9, which says that Christ 'died and lived so as to become Lord of the dead and of the living.' The 'dead' referred to by St Paul are also going to live again.[23]

St Jerome, in his commentary on Matthew, explains why Christ does not cite better proof texts: the Sadducees, he says, only accepted the authority of the Pentateuch. And 'I am the God of Abraham etc.' is meant to prove 'that souls continue (*permanere*) after death, because it could not be the case that God is the God of people who do not exist at all', and this implies the consequent resurrection of the body, since bodies are involved with the soul in all the good and bad we do in life.[24]

Both these texts are included by St Thomas in the *Catena Aurea*, and in his lectures on Matthew Thomas follows Jerome's interpretation closely.[25]

It is interesting to notice the terminological instinct, to which I have drawn attention, still at work in the patristic texts. In spite of Christ's words, the commentators at first talk about the continuing existence of the soul and avoid saying that it is alive. By the time of Thomas though, this instinct seems to have weakened. At least if the *reportatio* is to be trusted, Thomas was prepared to interpret Christ as meaning that the dead are alive in the spirit or with regard to their souls (*secundum animam*).

The basic belief, in the New Testament, is that the dead are neither totally extinct nor alive. In the vision of judgment in Apoc. 20.13–14 we read that 'the sea gave up the dead (νεκρούς) that were in it, and death and Hades gave up the dead that were in them, and they were all judged according to their works. And death and Hades were thrown into the lake of fire.' *Hades*, as already in the Septuagint, translates the Hebrew *Sheol*, and it refers, in a rather mythological way, to the place of death, conceived of as being somewhere in the depths of the earth (which is why the sea gives up its dead separately). It is not until after the resurrection and the judgment that the dead pass to any place of torment or bliss; and after the judgment there is no further need for a place of sheer death (which is why death and Hades are themselves thrown into the lake of fire, which is the 'second death').

The credal statement that Christ 'descended into hell' (*ad inferna* in the earliest known Latin versions)[26] underscores the fact that Christ really died: like all the other dead, he went to Hades. But it did not take the christian imagination long to develop this simple point into a lively drama of Christ storming Hades and delivering the dead saints of the Old Testament. Rightly or wrongly (and probably rightly) an allusion to this despoiling of hell was soon found in Matthew 27:52–53 ('The tombs were opened and many bodies of the saints who were asleep arose and, coming out of their tombs, after his resurrection, went into the holy city and appeared to many'), and in 1 Peter 3:18–19 ('. . . having been put to death in the flesh and made alive in the Spirit, in which he also went and preached to the spirits in captivity').

The idea that Christ preached to the dead suggests that they were both in need of and capable of some kind of posthumous conversion, and this idea was soon found to be unacceptable, so the emphasis shifted to the picture of Christ triumphantly defeating the powers of hell and death and rescuing those who had already believed in him.[27]

The harrowing of hell is an exciting story, but it raises some questions which a more systematic theology has to try and answer. In his discussion of Christ's descent into hell, St Thomas insists that there can be no question of a real change of direction for any of the dead: the damned remain damned, and the souls in purgatory stay there, unless they were in any case ready to be released; it was only the saints who were delivered from captivity, where their only pain was the delay in their admission to glory.[28] In the *Summa* Thomas accepts that the saints thus liberated were now received into the glory of heaven,[29] but he does not tackle the question which he had to raise in his lectures on Matthew: were the people whose 'resurrection' is mentioned in Matthew 27:52–53 restored, like Lazarus, to a mortal life which would necessitate their dying again? In that case, in Thomas' view, Christ was doing them a disservice, not a favour.[30] But he apparently did not see fit ever to incorporate this collective anticipation of the resurrection into any more general account of the resurrection of the dead, which was probably prudent of him.

The basic point that emerges from all of this is that the dead really are dead, even if in some sense they continue to exist and can even have certain things happen to them. Any idea of the dead actively developing or improving their situation is firmly excluded.

In the Apostolic Fathers there is little sign of any interest in the immortality of the soul.[31] Except in Ignatius of Antioch, the focus is essentially on the general resurrection and the last judgment.

Slightly later Justin Martyr, rather surprisingly, actually attacks the doctrine of the immortality of the soul.[32] In the *Dialogue with Trypho* he presents himself as having been converted from a Platonist belief in immortality and metempsychosis by an old man he met one day. The argument against the immortality of the soul is, first, that if it is immortal it must also be ingenerate, which is impossible if the whole world had a beginning in time, which Justin concedes. This is at best an ad hominem argument.[33] On the other hand, the old man goes on to say that he is not claiming that all souls die, which would be a godsend for sinners (notice the echo of *Phaedo* 107c). His position, which he seems to regard as the standard christian position,[34] is that the souls of the righteous go to some 'better place' to await the day of judgment, while unrighteous souls go to a 'worse place'. So the souls which are worthy of God 'die no more' (a phrase reminiscent of Rom. 6:9, presumably implying that these souls, like Christ, having died once, will die no more). The souls of the unrighteous are punished for as long as God wants to punish them.

The old man then proposes another argument: either the soul is life or it is alive. If it is life, then it must be something else which it makes alive, not itself. But nobody would deny that the soul is alive, therefore it is not life itself, it is only a sharer in life. So 'the soul shares in life, when God wants it to live.' Therefore in the same way it will cease to share in life when God does not want it to live any more. Unlike God, it does not possess life as its own property.[35] Human beings do not exist permanently (διὰ παντός). Body and soul are not permanently united, and, when it is time for the soul to be no more, the life-giving spirit departs from it and the soul is no more, but returns to the place from which it was taken.

How this is to be squared with the statement in 1 *Apol.* 12.1, that 'everyone goes to eternal punishment or salvation according to his deeds,' is not clear. Barnard suggests that Justin's ideas varied according to different circumstances,[36] which may be true. In any case, his fundamental point is clear: the soul does not possess life by right and so, a fortiori, does not possess immortality by right. And his position can be made coherent on the assumption that there is a temporary punishment after death for the wicked, then they lapse out of real existence for a while and are subsequently resurrected at the judgment, after which they are sent into eternal punishment. The souls of the righteous, on the other hand, do not, strictly, die, except in the sense that they undergo the death of the human being; after that, they die no more.

On the whole, christian thinkers were more hospitable to the idea of immortality than Justin was, but even as late as the fourteenth century, in the course of the famous dispute about the beatific vision provoked by John XXII, it could still be argued that souls do not attain immortality until the resurrection.[37]

It was not until 1513 that the immortality of the soul was formally declared to be required Catholic doctrine, at the fifth Lateran Council.[38] And the nature of this conciliar declaration is such as to leave considerable room for doubt about its genuine doctrinal force. The dispute which prompted the conciliar intervention was a philosophical one. What was at stake was not christian doctrine, but the correct interpretation of Aristotle. A significant number of philosophers, of differing intellectual persuasions, were maintaining that Aristotelian doctrine, properly understood, left no room for belief in the immortality of the individual soul. No one was denying individual immortality as an article of faith. The worry that the conciliar Bull is addressing is essentially about the relationship between philosophy and christian doctrine. It is in this context that Leo X, with the support of the council, declares that the individual human soul is immortal, and that it is wrong to maintain otherwise, even as a matter of philosophy. He then goes on to oblige philosophers to do all they can to provide philosophical support for the immortality of the soul.[39]

The actual point of doctrine which is felt to be at risk from philosophical doubts about the credentials of immortality, as Leo's Bull makes clear, is the reality of the resurrection and eternal bliss or punishment. A denial of the immortality of the soul is seen as entailing a denial of these essential doctrines, without which – and the Bull echoes St Paul's words in 1 Corinthians 15:19 – we would be 'the most wretched of men'. It is simply presumed that orthodox christian eschatology cannot survive without belief in immortality, but the language of immortality is in fact supplied by the philosophers the Bull is attacking. Their denial, in the name of Aristotle, that there can be any kind of continuing individual existence after death is couched in terms of a denial of personal immortality. The essential content of the Bull is surely the affirmation that any philosophical position which makes the posthumous existence of the individual impossible is incompatible with christian belief. The problematic of the time simply does not raise the question whether it is, strictly, necessary to use the language of 'immortality of the soul' to secure the point needed by christian orthodoxy.

The purpose of the Bull, in any case, is not so much to reaffirm christian belief (which no one was expressly disputing), but to impose on philosophers a responsibility to support, and not to attack, the doctrine of the immortality of the soul. One of the two people at the Council who objected to this part of the Bull was the eminent Thomist, Thomas de Vio Cajetan, Master of the Dominican Order.[40] In this he was evidently following the example of St Albert and St Thomas, who similarly denied the propriety of trying to settle philosophical issues simply by dogmatic decrees.[41] And, in spite of the Bull of 1513, Cajetan became more and more willing to express his doubts about the possibility of offering any decisive philosophical arguments for the immortality of the soul.[42]

It is hardly going too far to say that 'the Council's decision' on this point 'is of no consequence and had no practical significance.'[43] Its chief interest for our present purpose is that it shows how far it was assumed, by the sixteenth century, that the immortality of the soul was an essential, if not the essential, element in christian eschatology.

The increasing use by christians of this notion that the soul is immortal by right, combined with the conviction that the soul can in principle go straight to its reward at death without waiting for the resurrection, could easily lead to a decidedly bland view of death, such as we find in the Anglican Homilies:

> A true Christian . . . conceiveth great and many causes, undoubtedly grounded upon the infallible and everlasting truth of the word of God, which move him, not only to put away the fear of bodily death, but also, for the manifold benefits and singular commodities which ensue unto every faithful person by reason of the same, to wish, desire and long heartily for it. For death shall be to him no death at all, but a very deliverance from death . . . [44]

A more modern writer, Mgr José Escrivá, the founder of Opus Dei, is so moved by the delights of death that he, presumably unintentionally, echoes Euripides:

> Haven't you heard the mournful tone with which the worldly complain that 'each day that passes is a step nearer death'? It is. And I tell you: rejoice, apostolic soul, for each day that passes brings you closer to Life.
>
> For others, death is a stumbling block, a source of terror. For us, death – Life – is an encouragement and a stimulus.[45]

It is true, no doubt, that Paul longed to be dissolved and to be with Christ, regarding the continuation of his life as a nuisance to be endured for the sake of others. As far as he was concerned, 'To die is gain' (Phil. 1:21–24). But on the whole, as Cullmann emphasises, the New Testament presents death as being 'the last enemy' (1 Cor. 15:26).[46] Christ himself offered 'prayers and supplications to the one who could save him from death, with great cries and tears' (Heb. 5:7), and he is presented as responding to the death of Lazarus with such grief that it attracted comment, and he was also 'indignant' (ἐμβριμώμενος), suggesting that he saw death as an outrage (John 11:35–38). In the Middle Ages St Thomas is still insisting that death is 'naturally abhorrent to human nature',[47] and he argues that death is a bad thing, even if, as in the case of the martyrs, it is also meritorious: saints can always make good use of bad things.[48]

St Thomas acknowledges that our bodily nature, in itself, is liable to death. But, if Adam had not sinned, he would not have died or been liable to death, thanks to a special power bestowed on him by God. Death is thus, strictly, not natural to us, it is a punishment inflicted on us because of Adam's sin.[49]

It is no doubt difficult for most christians today to accept that there ever was a humanity that was in principle not destined to die. But at least we can note the concern, both of the biblical writers and of theologians like St Thomas, to give a theological significance to the feeling that there is something outrageous about human beings dying.

If Adam and Eve had not sinned, according to the traditional story, they would not have died. But this does not mean that they would simply have gone on living indefinitely in their garden with their friendly animals and their ever-increasing progeny. According to Augustine, the original happiness of Eden would have lasted:

> until, through that blessing which says, 'Grow and multiply', the number of the predestined was achieved, and another, greater happiness was given, the same as was given to the blessed angels, in which there would now be absolutely no fear that anyone would sin or that anyone would die. Then the life of the saints, with no preceding experience of toil, of grief, of death, would be like that which there will be after our experience of all these things, when the resurrection of the dead restores our bodies to incorruptibility.[50]

Augustine was convinced, surely rightly, that complete happiness requires not merely a guarantee that it will not come to an end, but that the blessed *know* that their continuance in bliss is guaranteed,[51] so Adam, before the fall, however happy he was, lacked the fulness of beatitude, because there was always the risk that he would fall, as indeed he did. If he had refrained from sinning he would have received the further gift of complete bliss without having to die,[52] but this would have involved a change in his situation as radical, in its own way, as death. This is what gives point to the insistence that he would have 'attained blessed immortality without passing through death':[53] after the fall, it is only by dying that we can come to that indefectibility which makes happiness complete. So even without sin, Adam needed to be 'changed' in ways that are now associated with death and resurrection. His body was to become a 'spiritual body'[54] and he was to become incapable of sinning.[55]

Even apart from sin then, and its consequence in death, there has to be a decisive shift from a mutable situation to a definitive one. And, according to St Thomas, this is true of angels as well as of unfallen humanity. Thomas takes for granted the Augustinian account of what would have happened to Adam if he had not fallen,[56] and what he says about the angels is, mutatis mutandis, of a piece with it. The angels cannot have been created in bliss, because that would have made it impossible for any of them to fall.[57] Since angels, unlike us, go straight to the point, their first act of choice merited either definitive bliss or irremediable damnation.[58] Once their choice was made, the blessed angels could not sin thereafter[59] nor could the fallen angels repent.[60] Nor can the blessed angels make any further progress because, as St Thomas says with reference to the kind of fulfilment which is achieved by merit rather than by one's own resources, 'It belongs to what is at its final goal, not to move, but to have been changed' (*ei quod est in ultimo termino non convenit moveri, sed mutatum esse*).[61]

There is a similar element of finality in the condition of both angels and men. As Damascene noted, 'The fall is for angels what death is for men; they cannot repent after their fall any more than men can repent after death.'[62] And there is the same finality in what the scholastics call the 'confirmation' of the good angels and of the saints.

Granted this insistence on finality, can we not say that death, which is a punishment for the sin of Adam, is a kind of fallen version of the finality which is essential if either angels or men are to arrive at a real and complete beatitude?

Every story has to have an ending, we have said, and the endings must really grow out of the story. In the case of unfallen beings, their confirmation provides the ending, and the Augustinian insistence that beatitude is merited (even if all merit rests entirely on divine grace) secures just this coherence between the story and its ending. In the case of devils too the outcome of damnation provides a fitting, if sad, conclusion to the story of their irremediable choice of evil. But death, although it ends a story in one sense, is an unsatisfactory ending. All too often it does not round off a life which can be seen as complete, it just cuts it off brutally. And it is but the last in a whole succession of apparently meaningless frustrations.

Human beings are not irremediably evil, so the eternal thwartedness which makes a proper conclusion to the tale of the fallen angels, can never be seen without further ado as the right way to end a human story, at least from within the perspective of the still continuing story. Human lives are characterised over and over again by unfulfilled promise. If death is but the last and most insuperable obstacle to fulfilment, it is indeed a fallen finality.

Finality of some kind there must be, so may we not wonder whether death itself, as a fallen finality, cannot in some sense be redeemed? If there is to be a happy ending, it must grow out of the story whose ending it is, and it must respect, even as it fulfils, the tragic nature of the story.[63] That is, it must respect death and its fallenness. And this, it seems to me, is exactly what we find celebrated in some of the earliest surviving liturgical texts of the western church, in phrases which have been adopted, with only minor changes, into the modern Roman rite, where they have, alas, fallen victim to the theological and linguistic insensitivity of the vernacularisers.

That death is redeemed is asserted in so many words in a preface first found in a seventh-century sacramentary: *Nostrorum omnium mors cruce Christi redempta est* ('the death of all of us is redeemed by the cross of Christ').[64] In the modern rite this has been turned into the even more epigrammatic declaration, 'Our death is redeemed by his death'[65] – a far more daring claim than the one proposed in the vernacular version, 'His death is our ransom from death.'

The continuity between the story and its ending is affirmed in another preface, first found in a sacramentary dating from the sixth or seventh century: 'We know that it belongs to your immeasurable glory to succour mortals with your Godhead, but also to provide for us, from mortality itself, a remedy, and to derive the salvation of all the lost from the very source of their perishing.'[66] In the modern vernacular, this has shrunk to the trivial statement, 'You came to our rescue as God, but you wanted us to be saved by one like us.'[67]

Finally the abiding reality of the tragedy of death is magnificently expressed in a preface first attested in several eighth-century rites: 'He never stops offering himself for us . . . because he never dies, being sacrificed, but always lives slain' (*numquam moritur immolatus, sed semper vivit occisus*).[68] The extraordinary juxtaposition of *vivit* and *occisus* is naturally rendered harmless in the vernacular: 'The Lamb, once slain, who lives for ever.'[69]

If the risen Christ bears the marks of his passion, as both Luke and John say he does (Luke 24:39; John 20:20,27), this gives a kind of permanency to the paradoxical yoking together of death and immortality which is involved in the death of the Son of God. In the striking words of an ancient Spanish liturgy, 'He is proclaimed immortal in death.'[70] The fact of his having died is built into his risen life. Death may be swallowed up into victory (1 Cor. 15:54), it may even be said to have been destroyed (2 Tim. 1:10), in the sense that it has no more power over Christ or any of those who are risen in him. This does not mean that death is simply forgotten, a thing of the past that is now left behind.

We seem to be faced here with a paradox even more startling than the one pronounced by Heraclitus, which we were considering in Chapter 1. What is being alleged is no mere alternation between being mortal and being immortal, no mere combination of death in one sense with life in another sense. Nor is the paradox muted by any appeal to what I have called the 'hybrid' view of human nature. The claim is not that the soul of Christ continues to live, nor that he just goes on living in his Godhead: it is in his full humanity, body and soul, that he 'lives slain'.

Nevertheless the christian paradox is susceptible of a much more serious analysis than that of Heraclitus. Heraclitus' firework, examined dispassionately, turns out to have more rhetorical than philosophical punch. If living human beings are dead immortals, the 'death' inherent in their human life only means the cessation of a particular kind of life, not the cessation of all life. If their new-found mortality makes them liable to death in a more rigorous sense, then they were clearly never really immortal in the first place, any more than we would predicate immortality, except in a very diluted sense, of someone of whom we might say, 'He could live for ever, so long as he does not contract some fatal disease or get shot.'

Heraclitus presupposes the common Greek idea that there is no essential difference of genus between gods and men, and takes it up in a rather heterodox fashion. If the gods are immortal, on this view, that can only mean that they are not liable to human death unless they change their status and become human. The case is similar to that of the millionnaire who is not liable to die a pauper's death, unless he loses his fortune and becomes a pauper – which he could always do. No significant immunity is involved in either situation.

The christian paradox rests on the opposite presumption, that there is a radical and essential difference between God and creatures. The difference is so radical that there is no inherent impossibility in the idea of a being who is both God and man, and who is, therefore, both immortal and mortal. Incompatibility implies some kind of common ground. It is impossible to be both a snail and a rhinoceros, because snails and rhinoceroses belong to a common genus, they are both animals. A pillar box cannot simultaneously be red and green all over, because red and green are both colours.

Being both divine and human is, logically, more like being large, pink and smelly. Compatibility is guaranteed by difference of genus.

Hippolytus was right to suspect that Heraclitean paradoxes do little to assist in the formulation of christian orthodoxy, even if he did not quite spot where the problem lay. Heraclitus' immortals have to stop being immortal in order to become mortal, but, in christian belief, God did not stop being God in order to become man. Christ is simultaneously divine and human, mortal and immortal. Between his death on the cross and his resurrection he was simultaneously immortal as God and dead as man. This is logically no more absurd than the evident fact that a living human being is at the same time characterised by a certain amount of dead matter (hair, nails and so on).

Since death is an irreversible condition, we may say that, after the resurrection, Christ as man was both dead and alive. 'I am the living one and I became dead, and look, I am alive' (Apoc. 1.18). Resurrection is a quite different notion from survival. That a resurrected human being should be called 'immortal' is natural: he has already died, and there is no necessary reason why he should ever die again, any more than there is any likelihood of someone who has already been born being born again, except in some metaphorical sense. He is immortal precisely because dead. If, by the gift of God, he is also alive, so much the better for him. Strictly, however, the life that is capable of *containing* death is the divine life, imparted to human beings by grace, not some life inherent in the human soul. The resurrection is not simply the resumption, after an interval, of life as before, such as is recounted in the story of the resuscitation of Lazarus; it is a sharing in the divine-human life of Christ.

No one would deny that there are paradoxes here, but they are tough paradoxes, which do not dissolve into empty rhetorical ornament when examined more closely; and they can be seen to rest on firm logical ground.

If death can be redeemed, then, so that being dead becomes a facet of being alive again in Christ after the resurrection, can we not go further and surmise that all the 'deaths' which characterise life on earth, all the dead ends and frustrations, all the uncompleted goods and aborted initiatives and failed attempts may in some way be redeemed too? This was certainly the hope of Julian of Norwich, who assures us that none of what happens in time and none of the toil and suffering that we have to endure in this world will be wasted; it will *all* be turned to God's worship and our endless joy. *All* shall be well.[71] She specifies in particular that, in heaven, sin itself 'shalle be no shame, but wurshype to man.'[72]

It does seem, then, that the christian tradition contains the wherewithal to attempt an account of redemption, of the 'happy ending', which would not disappoint the desires I outlined at the beginning of this chapter. There is evidence of a concern for finality, for a decisive conclusion to the development of life. The seriousness and tragedy of this life is recognised, and provision is made for its abiding significance, in spite of the overwhelming happiness of the promised happy ending. And we do seem to be offered a way of facing death, and so of facing life, that escapes from the *Phaedo*'s belittling of this life and from the moralists' various ways of narrowing down our engagement in the multiple interests and concerns which this life makes available. Precisely because death itself is redeemed, the fear of death can be overcome, if I may put it like this, without highmindedness. In Charles Williams' novel, *Shadows of Ecstasy*, Considine's endeavour to hold death at bay indefinitely and his hope of discovering a way to defeat death by dying and then returning to life, is challenged on the one side by the civilised and gentlemanly agnostic Sir Bernard Travers, who 'couldn't imagine himself wanting to die and live, because that (it seemed to him) would be to spoil the whole point of death,'[73] and on the other side by the gently wise Isabel, who challenges Considine with the question:

> 'Mightn't the missionaries you killed have joined with something which was greater than you because it had known defeat? Have you known defeat?'
>
> 'No,' Considine said and stood up. 'I've mastered myself from the beginning and all things that I've needed are mine. Why should man know defeat?' . . .
>
> Isabel, as if from a depth of meditation, answered, 'But those that die may be lordlier than you: they are obedient to defeat. Can you live truly till you have been quite defeated?'[74]

Travers raises the question of finality, but Isabel raises the more specifically christian question: the determination not to be mastered by fate leads, as we have found with Epicurus and the Stoics, to a considerable loss of nerve about engaging in many aspects of life. Christianity, with its hope that death, accepted precisely as an evil, can be redeemed, suggests a more general way of accepting the risk of engaging with life: being defeated by fortune, however genuinely painful and tragic it may be, is perhaps only one side of a tremendous enterprise of redemption.

NOTES

1 J. Dillon, *The Middle Platonists*, London 1977, p. 384.
2 The phrase is found most famously in the antiphon, *Salve regina*.
3 'Anticipation, however, unlike inauthentic Being-towards-death, does not evade the fact that death is not to be outstripped; instead, anticipation frees itself *for* accepting this. When, by anticipation, one becomes free *for* one's own death, one is liberated from one's lostness in those possibilities which may accidentally thrust themselves upon one; and one is liberated in such a way that for the first time one can authentically understand and choose among the factical possibilities lying ahead of that possibility which is not to be outstripped.' 'Every Dasein always exists factically. It is not a free-floating self-projection; but its character is determined by thrownness as a Fact of the entity which it is; and, so determined, it has in each already been delivered over to existence . . . In the face of its thrownness Dasein flees to the relief which comes with the supposed freedom of the they-self.' 'The temptation to overlook the finitude of the primordial and authentic future and therefore the finitude of temporality, or alternatively, to hold "*a priori*" that such finitude is impossible, arises from the way in which the ordinary understanding of time is constantly thrusting itself to the fore.' 'Fear has been characterised as an inauthentic state-of-mind.' 'We have called concernful Being alongside the "world" our "dealings in and with the environment" . . . In this kind of concern Dasein's authentic existence too maintains itself, even when for such existence this concern is "a matter of indifference". The ready-to-hand things with which we concern ourselves are not the causes of our concern.' 'Only by the anticipation of death is every accidental and "provisional" possibility driven out. Only Being-free *for* death, gives Dasein its goal outright and pushes existence into its finitude. Once one has grasped the finitude of one's existence, it snatches one back from the endless multiplicity of possibilities which offer themselves as closest to one – those of comfortableness, shirking, and taking things lightly – and brings Dasein into the simplicity of its *fate*. This is how we designate Dasein's primordial historizing, which lies in authentic resoluteness and in which Dasein *hands* itself *down* to itself, free for death, in a possibility which it has inherited and yet has chosen.' (M. Heidegger, *Being and Time*, trans. J. Macquarrie and E. Robinson, Oxford 1978, pp. 308, 321, 379, 391, 403, 435). It seems to me that statements like these can without much unfairness be translated into the Stoic terminology of fate, of choosing which must in any case be, of fear as a 'passion' (πάθος, by definition an 'inauthentic' response to a situation), of the real value of that which is 'up to us' (τὰ ἐφ' ἡμῖν) and that which is not and is therefore 'indifferent'. The ethical mood of Heidegger strikes me as being remarkably close to that of Seneca.
4 Peter Lombard, IV *Sent.* d.20 c.1.1; Gratian, *Decretum, De Poen.* d.7 I (Friedberg I 1244).
5 2 Clement 8.1–3.

6 Shakespeare, *Hamlet* Act 3 scene 4. Cf. the supposedly historical example of the Milanese character, too wicked to name, reported by Jean Bodin (1520–1596): he forced his enemy to renounce his religion and then, when he had done so, killed him, with the comment, 'This is real vengeance, which snatches life from the body and will bring everlasting torment to the soul' (*De Republica* V 6, Lyons 1586 p. 608). The episode is alluded to by Thomas Browne, *Religio Medici* II 6 and *Pseudodoxia Epidemica* VII 19.3.
7 To quote but two easily accessible examples, cf. *Gesta Romanorum*, ed. S. J. H. Herrtage, Early English Text Society ES 33, pp. 404–406; Nigel of Canterbury *Miracles of the Virgin Mary*, ed. J. Ziolkowski, Toronto 1986, pp. 39–45, 48–51.
8 *Summa Theologiae* III q.59 a.5.
9 Cf. Humbert of Romans, *De Eruditione Praedicatorum* V 49–55, trans. in S. Tugwell, *Early Dominicans*, New York 1982, pp. 198–200.
10 *Contra Gentiles* IV 93–95.
11 Jerome, *Ep.* 124.3–4.
12 L. Petit and G. Hofmann, eds, *De Purgatorio Disputationes* (Concilium Florentinum A VIII ii), Rome 1969, p. 15.
13 Ibid. p. 29.
14 IV *Sent.* d.45 c.2.
15 Denzinger-Schönmetzer no. 1488.
16 Cf. C. McDannell and B. Lang, *Heaven, A History*, New Haven/London 1988, pp. 184, 204–205.
17 Ibid. chapters 7–9.
18 Cf. E. C. S. Gibson, *The Thirty-Nine Articles*, London 1906, pp. 553–554 (first published in 1896–1897).
19 A. C. Outler, ed., *John Wesley*, Oxford 1964, p. 167; J. Wesley, *A Plain Account of Christian Perfection*, London 1968, p. 112. Cf. R. Davies and G. Rupp, eds., *History of the Methodist Church in Great Britain* vol. I, London 1965, p. 105.
20 McDannell and Lang pp. 289–291, 304.
21 O. Cullmann, *Immortality of the Soul or Resurrection of the Dead?*, London 1958. This book is based on the Ingersoll Lecture on the Immortality of Man, delivered in 1955.
22 Cullmann, op. cit. pp. 49–57.
23 John Chrysostom, *Homilies on Matthew* 70.3.
24 Corpus Christianorum Series Latina vol. 77 p. 207.
25 *Catena Aurea* p. 254 in vol. XI of the Parma edition. *Super Matt.* paras. 1802–1804 in the Marietti edition.
26 Denzinger-Schönmetzer no. 16.
27 Cf. J. N. D. Kelly, *Early Christian Creeds*, London 1960, p. 381.
28 *Summa Theologiae* III q.52 articles 5–8.
29 Ibid. art. 5.
30 *Super Matt.*, ed. cit. para. 2395.
31 Cf. T. H. C. van Eijk, *La Résurrection des Morts chez les Pères Apostoliques*, Paris 1974, pp. 152–153.
32 Justin, *Dialogue with Trypho* 3–6.
33 It was a disputed question in Middle Platonism whether the world

had a beginning in time. Plutarch and Atticus argued that it had, Albinus that it had not (cf. Dillon, op. cit. pp. 207, 252–254, 286–287). Justin explicitly sides with Plutarch and Atticus. It was widely assumed by Greek philosophers that immortality entailed being ingenerate too, but Atticus, who espoused belief in the temporal beginning of the world, also denied that coming into being in time precluded being preserved for ever thereafter (ibid. p. 253), so Justin, as a Platonist, was making unnecessary concessions to his 'old man'.

34 I take it that this is the point of his appeal to the authority of revelation in *Dial.* 7.

35 This argument seems to be influenced by Plato, *Timaeus* 41.

36 L. W. Barnard, *Justin Martyr*, Cambridge 1967, p. 167.

37 Cited by Thomas Waleys. See T. Kaeppeli, *Le Procès contre Thomas Waleys OP*, Rome 1936, p. 101.

38 J. Alberigo and others, eds., *Conciliorum Oecumenicorum Decreta*, Bologna 1973, p. 605.

39 On the background to the declaration of 1513 and the controversies that continued after it, see the introduction by M. H. Laurent to I. Coquelle's edition of Cajetan's commentary on Aristotle's *De Anima*, Rome 1938; E. Gilson, 'Autour de Pomponazzi', *Archives d'Histoire Doctrinale et Littéraire du Moyen Age* 28 (1962) pp. 163–279.

40 Laurent, op. cit. pp. XXXVIII-XXXIX.

41 Cf. S. Tugwell, *Albert and Thomas*, New York 1988, pp. 14, 32–33, 227–228.

42 Cf. Laurent, op. cit. pp. XXXIV-XXXV.

43 O. de la Brosse, *Latran V et Trente*, Paris 1975, p. 91.

44 First Part of the Sermon on the Fear of Death, *Certain Sermons or Homilies appointed to be read in Churches in the time of Queen Elizabeth*, London 1908, p. 95.

45 J. M. Escrivá, *The Way*, New York 1963, p. 173, paras 737–738.

46 Cullmann, op. cit. pp. 19–27.

47 *Summa Theologiae* III q.46 a.6.

48 Ibid. II.II q.164 a.1.

49 Ibid. I q.97 a.1, II.II q.164 a.1.

50 Augustine, *De Civitate Dei* 14.10.

51 Cf. ibid. 10.30.

52 *De Corr, et Grat.* 10.28.

53 *Civ. Dei* 12.22.

54 *Gen. ad Litt.* 6.28.39.

55 *Corr. et Grat*, loc. cit.

56 Cf. *Summa Theol.* I q.100 a.2, q.102 a.4.

57 Ibid. I q.62 a.1.

58 Ibid. I q.62 a.5, q.63 a.6.

59 Ibid. I q.62 a.8.

60 Ibid. I q.64 a.2.

61 Ibid. I q.62 a.9.

62 John Damascene, *Expositio Fidei* 18, partly quoted by St Thomas in I q.64 a.2.

63 There has been some controversy over whether or not christianity is

compatible with tragedy; for a sensible comment, see J. F. Worthen, 'Christianity and the Limits of Tragedy', *New Blackfriars* 70 (1989) pp. 109–117.

64 E. Moeller, ed., *Corpus Praefationum*, Corpus Christianorum Series Latina vol. 161, Turnhout 1980–1981, no. 1528.

65 Second Easter Preface.

66 *Corpus Praefationum* no. 11 (ad cuius immensam gloriam pertinere cognoscimus, ut mortalibus tua deitate succurreres, sed et nobis provideres de ipsa mortalitate remedium, et perditos quosque unde perierant inde salvares).

67 Third Preface for Sundays per annum.

68 *Corpus Praefationum* no. 1242.

69 Third Easter Preface.

70 A. Hänggi and I. Pahl, *Prex Eucharistica*, Fribourg 1968, p. 506.

71 Julian of Norwich, Long Text chapters 32, 39, 62 (ed. E. Colledge and J. Walsh, Toronto 1978, pp. 422, 452, 610–611).

72 Ibid. chapter 38, p. 445.

73 Charles Williams, *Shadows of Ecstasy*, London 1965, p. 85.

74 Ibid. pp. 130–131.

Part II

Eternity and the End

6

'Who knows,' wondered the character in Euripides, 'whether life isn't death and death isn't life?' A similar thought seems to have occurred to some of the early christians. Thus, when Ignatius of Antioch wants to urge the Roman christians not to do anything to interfere with his martyrdom, he can say what he wants quite plainly: 'I desire to die' (Rom. 7.2), but he can also reverse the terms and say, 'Do not prevent me from living, do not want me to die' (Rom. 6.2), where clearly 'living' means 'dying' and 'dying' means 'living'. It is presumably the similar conviction, that life begins at death, that underlies the custom of referring to the anniversary of a martyr's death as his 'birthday', a usage attested at least from the martyrdom of Polycarp onwards.[1]

In Ignatius' letters we can glimpse something of the conceptual context which legitimises this kind of language. The incarnation, death and resurrection of Christ are seen as having established a new criterion of what is meant by human life. He has become 'perfect' or 'complete' man (τέλειος ἄνθρωπος) (Sm. 4.2), and we in turn become alive and human because of him. He is 'our true life' (Sm. 4.1). But this true life that he has and that he is for us is inseparable from his passion and death: his passion is our resurrection (Sm. 5.3). So 'unless we volunteer to die into his passion, his life is not in us' (Mag. 5.2). And Ignatius insists that he really suffered, died and rose again *in the flesh* (Sm. 2–3). He is the 'one physician' who is both flesh and spirit, 'God coming to be in flesh, true life in death' (Eph. 7.2). After the resurrection, the apostles were united to him 'in his flesh and in his spirit . . . (He) ate and drank with them, as a being of flesh, even though he was spiritually united to the Father' (Sm. 3.2–3). When Ignatius says he is our 'true life', he is primarily insisting on the full human reality of Christ's life, against any docetic denial of that reality, and claiming that it is that full human reality which underpins and makes sense of our life, and not least Ignatius' own suffering and impending martyrdom (Sm. 4.1–2; cf. Trall. 10). Apart from him, we have no true life, but he was truly raised from the dead and, if we believe in him, the Father will raise us too in him (Trall. 9.2).

'True life', for us, is essentially an eschatological prospect. 'It is the last times . . . Let us fear the wrath which is to come or love the grace which is present, one or the other, provided only that we are found in Christ Jesus in view of true life' (εἰς τὸ ἀληθινὸν ζῆν) (Eph. 11.1). Life is something 'set before us' as a goal (Eph. 17.1, Mag. 5.1), meaning 'incorruptibility and eternal life' (Pol. 2.3). But here and now we must learn how to live the kind of life that christianity is all about (Mag. 10.1), and this means operating firmly within the unity of the church, 'breaking the one bread, which is the medicine of immortality, the antidote to death, giving life in Jesus Christ for ever' (Eph. 20.2). Outside the 'sanctuary' (the unity of the church) no one can share in the 'bread of God' (Eph. 5.2), because the structured hierarchical unity of the church *is* 'the type and teaching of incorruptibility' (τύπος καὶ διδαχὴ ἀφθαρσίας) (Mag. 6.2) – it is, we might say, the 'print-out' or 'offprint' of immortality. 'When you are subject to the bishop, as to Jesus Christ, you seem to me not to be living by human standards (κατὰ ἄνθρωπον), but in line with Jesus Christ, who died for us, so that, believing in his death, you may escape death' (Trall. 2.1).

Ignatius is aware of various wrong beliefs that come between us and our life, if we indulge in them. In general the heretics envisaged by Ignatius seem to be docetists preaching a spiritualised form of Judaism (they apparently come from a pagan background and do not practise circumcision – Phld. 6.1), and the only consequence of their doctrine according to Ignatius is that they deprive themselves of the real life which they refuse to acknowledge in Christ, inasmuch as they deny the reality of his passion and of his resurrection in the flesh. They suppose that he only seemed to suffer, but it is they who are only a seeming (αὐτοὶ ὄντες τὸ δοκεῖν) (Trall. 10). They are not 'the Father's planting. If they were, they would appear as branches of the cross and their fruit would be incorruptible. It is through the cross that he calls you, in his passion, as being his members' (Trall. 11.1–2). True believers 'no longer keep the sabbath, but live by Sunday, on which our life arose through him and his death, which some people deny' (Mag. 9.1). But, as far as Ignatius is concerned, these Judaisers are 'tombstones . . . on which only the names of human beings are inscribed' (Phld. 6.1). The fate of those who deny the reality of the passion and the resurrection is in line with their own beliefs: they are 'without bodies and like demons' (Sm. 2). They only have the shape, without the reality, of human beings (Sm. 4.1). In denying that Christ 'bore flesh' they show themselves to be 'bearing corpses' (Sm. 5.2). As a result of their denial of the flesh of Christ, they cut themselves off from charity (ἀγάπη), both in the sense that they fail to practise charity, not caring for widows and orphans and others in need, and in the sense that they hold aloof from the eucharist, 'because they do not confess that the eucharist is the flesh of our saviour Jesus Christ, which suffered for our sins, which the Father in his kindness raised up again.' But 'it would be better for them to have charity, so that they could rise again' (Sm. 6.2–7.1).

It is probably with an eye on some kind of heretical disbelief in the flesh of Christ that Ignatius proposes his own interpretation of the gap between carnal and spiritual people: 'Spiritual people cannot do carnal things . . . even what you do in the flesh is spiritual, because you do everything in Jesus Christ' (Eph. 8.2). True belief, far from encouraging a systematic dissociation of flesh from spirit, insists on the union of the two in Christ and therefore in the practice of his disciples too.

Apart from the hint in this passage which I have just quoted, Ignatius does not normally talk in so many words about the union of flesh and spirit in us. It is the union of flesh and spirit in Christ which is all-important (Mag. 1.2). Maybe in Ignatius' view flesh, in the case of the rest of us, remains a somewhat ambiguous affair, and it is only at our own resurrection that flesh and spirit will be fully integrated, as they are now in Christ. Although normally Ignatius uses the word 'flesh' (σάρξ) in a positive sense, he does occasionally refer to the flesh in more negative terms (e.g. Mag. 6.2, Rom. 2.1, 8.3), though even there he stops far short of the Pauline strictures on the flesh. Also we should notice that the two allusions to 'matter' (ὕλη) are every bit as pejorative as anything we find in Platonist writings (Rom. 6.2, 7.2). Nevertheless it is clear that the union of flesh and spirit in Christ is meant to be reflected in a union of faith and practice, of word and reality, in the believer.

Ignatius explicitly associates the union of flesh and spirit in Christ with the union of faith and charity in the church (Mag. 1.1), and the moral and theological resonances of this association can be seen in Eph. 14.1–15.3:

> None of this eludes you, if you have faith and charity perfectly in Jesus Christ, which is the beginning and end of life. Faith is the beginning, charity the end, and the two coming together in unity are God, and all the rest that concerns human goodness follows from them. No one who professes faith sins, nor does anyone who has obtained charity hate. The tree is manifest from its fruit, and similarly those who profess to belong to Christ will be seen by way of the things they do. For now it is not a matter of profession, but of effective faith, if only one is found faithful to the end. It is better to be silent and to be than to speak and not be. Teaching is good, if the speaker is also a doer. There is one teacher who spoke and it came to be,

> and what he did in silence is worthy of the Father. Anyone who has truly received the word of Jesus can also hear his quietness, so that he may be perfect, so that he may act in what he says and be known in his silence. Nothing is hidden from the Lord; even our secrets are near to him. So let us do everything as having him dwelling in us . . .

As usual, Ignatius is pouring out his thoughts in a red-hot jumble, but it is clear enough what he is getting at. There is to be a complete harmony between what we are, what we say and what we do, and all of this is to be both modelled on and derived from the unity of word and silence in Christ, the one teacher whose words actually bring things into being (his word being evidently identified with the word which is the divine instrument of creation). Ignatius seems to have been sensitive to the Hellenistic propensity to connect God with silence; for him Christ is 'the Word coming forth from the silence' (σιγή) (Mag. 8.2).[2] But he also anticipates later Platonist speculation about the One: Christ is 'the one Jesus Christ, who came forth from the one Father and is in the One and went to the One' (Mag. 7.2). Ignatius himself draws attention to his own interest in unity (Phld. 8.1), and the 'unities' he celebrates in the churches include, not just the unity of the flesh and spirit of Christ and the unity of faith and charity, but also – and most importantly, as he says – the unity of Jesus and the Father (Mag. 1.1).[3]

Our life as human beings depends, so to speak, on our being plugged into the whole system of unities. Christ is united with the Father, the Word with the silence that guarantees its reality and efficacy; in Christ flesh and spirit are united, and we are united with him in flesh and spirit by our faith and our charity, expressed in our sacramental and moral adhesion to the church. This ensures that we ourselves become real, unlike the heretics who are only apparent human beings.

In the case of Ignatius himself, all of this is sharply focused on his impending martyrdom. It is there that he hopes to become a human being (ἄνθρωπος) (Rom. 6.2), and surely this is, at least in part, because it is there that he must definitively display the unity of what he professes to be and what he is (Rom. 3.2). It is there that word and silence will come together. If the Romans keep silent (do not intervene to stop his martyrdom) then, he says, 'I shall become a word of God, but if you love my flesh, I shall just be a noise again' (Rom. 2.1).[4] It is precisely Ignatius' death that will establish the necessary link between word and silence. Or, to change the image, it will be his disappearance from the world that will establish his reality, just as 'Jesus Christ, being in the Father, appears all the more' (Rom. 3.2–3). 'Nothing that appears is good'

(3.3): there is always something ambiguous about an appearance. It can always be just a mere appearance. Until his actual death Ignatius could always be regarded as only appearing to be a christian. His disappearance, his martyrdom, will show once and for all that he is real. By 'imitating the passion of my God' (Rom. 6.3) he will enter into the full reality of him who was silent in his death (this is surely one of the works wrought in silence which was 'worthy of the Father') (cf. Eph. 19.1) and who, by disappearing from the world (going to the Father, the One), displayed and continues to display his power to give life to us in the church.

If it is by volunteering to die in the passion of Christ that we share in the risen life of Christ, it is not surprising that Ignatius, already condemned in principle to die for Christ, should appear to echo Euripides' character in speaking as if real life only begins at death. But his problematic is radically different from that which we find in any pagan writer. There is no room in his perspective for an immortal soul needing to be freed from the body in order to enjoy the fulness of its own life. Ignatius shows no interest in the soul at all, though he does once list soul, with flesh and spirit, apparently only to produce a neat triad to balance a triad of virtues he wants to mention (Phld 11.2): 'They will be honoured by the Lord Jesus Christ, in whom they hope in flesh, soul and spirit, in faith, in charity, in harmony.' For Ignatius, immortality goes with the resurrection of Christ, and what he is most insistent on there is the reality of the flesh of the risen Christ. Where Plato, at least teasingly, could wonder whether life in the body is not really death, Ignatius seems almost to be wondering whether life in this world is sufficiently incarnate to count as life at all. If we do not share in the life of Christ, we are 'bodiless'. And if, at least in Ignatius' own case, death itself is the privileged means to life, it is surely because it is in martyrdom that the believer most fully identifies his flesh with the passion of Christ, which is our resurrection.

Even apart from martyrdom, it looks as if Ignatius would have to ascribe a decisive importance to death. If fidelity 'to the end' is all-important (Eph. 14.2; cf. Rom. 10.3), there must be an end, and it is difficult to see what end this could be except death. And if the guiding principle of the christian life is conformity to Christ and abiding in him 'in flesh and spirit' (cf. Eph. 10.3), it at least makes sense that christians should hope to enter into life by literally dying with Christ and rising with him.

So, although Ignatius' use of the words 'life' and 'death' shifts the focus of our attention away from death in its ordinary sense, towards a more definitive life and death, identified as a participation or non-participation in Christ, his doctrine does not negate the concern I have been expressing that there should be a real finality, allowing the human story to reach a proper conclusion. In spite of his suggestion that death is, at least for himself, a beginning, Ignatius talks explicitly about things having an end, a conclusion (τέλος) (Mag. 5.1). Paradoxically the conclusion of every human story is said to be life or death (ibid.), but if it turns out to be life, this is not simply life going on, it is eternal life, incorruptibility; it is an arrival, not just a further process, let alone a new point of departure.

Precisely because things have an end, and the desirable end is a life which is proposed as a reward (Pol. 2.3), the culmination of a process of discipleship, Ignatius ensures that the happy ending, should there be such, is a true denouement, and that it excludes the kind of escape into fantasy which Seneca feared to be the consequence of a failure to face up to death. Indeed Ignatius' insistence on the model of Christ's passion and death functions quite overtly as a way of disallowing any flight into irresponsible spirituality. The demands of day to day practical charity, and the obligation to respond with generosity even to the hostility and arrogance of persecutors, are both linked to the reality of Christ's passion (Sm. 6.2, Eph. 10.3), and discipleship is not allowed to degenerate into curiosity about higher things (Trall. 5.2; cf. Sm. 6).

Ignatius' message is an intensely personal one, but many of the ideas we find in his letters are recognisably akin to things we find in other early christian writings.

The use of the word 'life' to refer to something aimed at and hoped for in the future is familiar from the New Testament. Take, for example, the contrast between the broad way which leads to destruction and the cramped way which leads to life (Matt. 7:13–14), or the assurance that it is better to enter into life maimed than to be cast into the eternal fire with two hands and two feet (Matt. 18:8). And it is clear that 'life' in this future sense is identical with 'eternal life' (notice how the mention of eternal life in Matt. 19.16 is taken up in the following verse with a mere 'life'). This New Testament usage is a distinct innovation by comparison with the superficially similar passage in Deuteronomy 30:15, where Moses says to the people, 'See, I have set before you this day life and good, death and evil.' The promise of life here means only long life in the promised land, as the following verses make clear.

That Christ is the giver of life and that the life he gives is himself is a topic enjoying a certain prominence in St John (e.g. 5:40, 6:33, 11:25 and, not least, the famous verse 14:6, where Jesus declares, 'I am the way and the truth and the life').

It is quite natural in this early christian context that Hermas should tell us that 'before a man bears the name of the Son of God he is dead' (νεκρός).[5]

If Christ constitutes a new criterion of what it means to be alive, and Adam is properly stated to have received the breath of life from God so that he became a 'living soul' (*nephesh hayyah*) (Gen. 2:7), it is not difficult to infer that there is a problem about the status of the first Adam, or, in other words, a question about the humanity, not just the life, of those who are not made alive in Christ. Ignatius, we noted, hopes to become human at the time of his martyrdom. Ignatius' implicit questioning of the creation story in Genesis, or at least its application, is found in a much more explicit form in the letter of Barnabas. Barnabas is not noted for his clarity, but there seems little doubt that he is proposing a reinterpretation of the story of the creation of Adam as being prophetic and as having a future reference. He begins by identifying the land flowing with milk and honey as Christ, on the grounds that man is γῆ πάσχουσα (6.9), with an explicit reference to the fashioning of Adam out of the earth. The phrase γῆ πάσχουσα has to be translated both as 'suffering land', to do justice to Barnabas' desire to connect it with the promised land and with the passion of Christ, and also as 'earth which has had something done to it', to do justice to the reference to the creation story. Barnabas then goes on to claim that it is with an eye on us, the christians, that God says to his Son, 'Let us make man in our image and likeness, and let them rule the beasts of the earth and the birds of heaven and the fish in the sea.' Then, 'seeing our good fashioning,' the Lord said, 'Grow and multiply and fill the earth.' So Adam in the Genesis story is actually to be taken as meaning Christ and those who believe in Christ, and Barnabas develops this point with a rather circuitous proof that indeed the whole passage refers to 'us'. His argument culminates in the question who can now rule the beasts or the fish or the birds. He evidently assumes that the answer is that no one can, so he can underline the need to 'grow and multiply'. The text of Genesis will be fulfilled when we become perfect heirs of the Lord's covenant (6.12–19).

That Barnabas really did mean to resituate the creation story as pointing to the future is confirmed by his treatment of the sabbath. When the Bible says that the Lord finished the work of creation in six days and rested on the seventh, what it means, he tells us, is that the Lord will bring the world to an end in six thousand years (on the principle that for the Lord one day is equivalent to a thousand years, a principle presumably derived from Ps. 90:4 and used in a similarly general way in 2 Pet. 3:8). The Lord will rest from his labours when his Son has 'put an end to the time of the lawless one' at the last judgment (15.3–5). Barnabas' line here is the same as that taken in John 5:17, where Jesus defends himself against the charge of breaking the sabbath by claiming, 'My Father is still working,' that is, we have not yet reached the sabbath.

Barnabas also points out that scripture says that the sabbath must be hallowed 'with pure hands and a pure heart', a condition which, he maintains, no one can yet realise. It is when all has been made new by the Lord and there is no more lawlessness, when we have been justified and have received the promise, that we shall be able to keep the sabbath (15.6–7).

One of Barnabas' main concerns is that we should not imagine that we are already justified (4.10), so it suits his purpose very well to read the creation story as telling us about a process of creation in which we are still engaged. We are still being created, and before we can enter into the inheritance of Adam we must first grow up. As yet, we are only children – or, to quote Barnabas more precisely, we 'have a soul that is a child' (6.11).

Barnabas sometimes gives the impression that he wants simply to apply the story of the creation of Adam to Christ and to us, which would raise very serious questions about the nature of the human race as it existed before and apart from Christ. If the implication is taken seriously, that human beings apart from Christ are not really human beings, as envisaged by God, then we are well on the way to the sort of anthropology developed in the various Gnostic systems, and indeed it is likely that Gnostic speculation grew out of precisely the sort of questioning of Genesis that we have been looking at. It is perhaps in order to exclude such unacceptable inferences that Barnabas rather confuses his exposition by inserting allusions to recreation (6.11, 16.8) and to a 'second creation', in which God 'makes the last things like the first' (6.13).

There is a similar confusion about the relationship between the old and new covenants, and in this case it is rather more certain that Barnabas is deliberately trying to exclude an unacceptable kind of radicalism. Near the beginning of the letter, Barnabas produces a proof that God did not want sacrifices, as practised by Judaism, and then comments that he 'abolished these things, so that the new law of our Lord Jesus Christ, being without any yoke of constraint, would have an offering not made with hands' (2.4–6). The line of argument is familiar from the speech of Stephen in Acts 7 and it raises the urgent question where the old law, with its sacrificial precepts, came from. The answer of the pseudo-Clementines is well known, and has been shown to be rooted in Jewish speculation: some parts of the Old Testament are interpolated and do not come from God at all.[6] Later, in his *Letter to Flora*, the Valentinian Ptolemy develops a whole theory about the different sources of different parts of the Old Testament along similar lines. Barnabas is surely precluding this sort of development with his theory that there never really was an old law distinct from the law of Christ: the Jews misunderstood God's commandments, because 'a wicked angel instructed them' (9.4). This theory of a diabolically inspired misinterpretation of what was genuinely God's law looks very like a deliberate alternative to the theory that some parts of the putative law were actually fabricated by a wicked angel. But, strictly, this means that Barnabas should not have talked about a 'new law' superseding a previous law, if all along there was in fact only one law, rightly or wrongly interpreted.

Ignatius' concern for the unity of flesh and spirit in Christ and the corresponding integrity of word and deed, being and appearance, faith and charity, in the believer, is related to the widespread early christian belief that the coming of the kingdom is associated with 'the two becoming one, and the outer and the inner'. Whatever the original context of the apocryphal saying in which this doctrine is presented – possibly in the Gospel of the Egyptians[7] and certainly in the Gospel of Thomas[8] it is connected with speculation about an eschatological return to the original androgynous unity of Adam before the creation of Eve – it is interpreted in the so-called Second Letter of Clement as follows:

> The two are one, when we speak the truth to each other and so there is one soul without hypocrisy in two bodies. And 'the outer as the inner' means this: 'the inner' refers to the soul, 'the outer' to the body. Therefore, just as the body is evident, so the soul should be manifest in good works. (12.2–4)

This reinforces the author's message, that we must confess Christ by doing what he says (3.4), but it acquires a particular interest in view of the polemic against people who are apparently maintaining that it does not really matter what we do in the flesh. 'None of you should say that this flesh is not judged or raised.' It was in the flesh that Christ, who was first spirit, called us, and it was accordingly in the flesh that we were saved and converted, and it is in the flesh that we shall receive our reward (9.1–5). The church likewise, 'created before the sun and moon', was spiritual, but was revealed in the flesh of Christ, being the body of Christ:

> showing us that, if any of us keeps her (the church) in the flesh . . . he will receive her in the Holy Spirit. This flesh is the antitype of the spirit, so no one who corrupts the antitype will share in the original. So, brethren, this means: watch over the flesh, so that you may receive the Spirit. If we say that the church is the flesh and Christ the Spirit, then anyone who insults the flesh insults the church, and such a one will not share in the Spirit, that is, Christ. (14.1–4)

The point of this emphasis on the flesh is the same as the point that the author of 2 Clement finds in the principle of the 'outer' being 'as the inner': christians are meant to be visibly christian. As Ignatius put it, they will be seen by way of what they do. It is on the basis of what we do, visibly, in the flesh, that we shall be judged (2 Clem. 8.2–4), and, if we are faithful, it is in the full visibility of the flesh that we shall be rewarded.

A similar point is made, probably with a similar polemical edge, in Hermas: the incarnation of the Son of God establishes the principle that we must keep our flesh holy, subservient to the holy spirit which God has made to dwell in it, and if we do so, the spirit will bear witness on behalf of the flesh and it too will be justified and rewarded (Sim. 5.6–7). But even more interesting is Hermas' account of the virtue of truth, even though it is not overtly related to the question about the flesh. God has made to dwell in our flesh a spirit which is without deception (ἄψευστον). If we do not practise truth, we defile and oppress this spirit, and so cannot render it back intact to God, thereby cheating and making light of the Lord. Hermas bursts into tears when he hears this from his angelic mentor, and says he has never spoken the truth in his life. It is clear from the context that this means that he has never presented himself honestly to other people, but has allowed them to believe him to be much better than he really is. The kind of truth in question is essentially a matter of visibility, of being seen for what we are, without hypocrisy. And the need for this honesty derives from the nature of the spirit we have received from God (Mand. 3). The spirit or spirits made to dwell in our flesh are the principle of our christian existence and the means whereby God himself dwells in us,[9] and there seems to be an elemental thrust towards visibility, towards honest self-manifestation, inherent in this gift. However tiresome Heideggerian etymologies may be, however unlikely it is that Hermas was conscious of any such etymologies, it does look as if there is a real sense here that ἀλήθεια (truth) means an abandonment of the attempt to remain unobserved (λανθάνειν).

In the *Phaedo* the soul needed to escape from the body in order to perceive truth. In the early christian writings we have been looking at the concern is rather with *being true*, and this means escaping from the ambiguity of appearance (which can always degenerate into mere appearance, in which case 'nothing that appears is good'). In Christ the link between inner reality and outer appearance is established definitively, in the union between his spirit and his flesh. And his appearance is, paradoxically, enhanced, as Ignatius sees it, by his disappearance, his being in the Father after the ascension. But this is far from entailing any abandonment of his flesh. Ignatius insists on the reality of the flesh in his resurrection. Ignatius too hopes to disappear, and his disappearance in martyrdom will finally eliminate any ambiguity there might be about his appearance: then he will fully be and be seen to be a christian. The ambiguous noise he has been will be replaced by a fully-fledged word of God. And, if he dies thus, it is in the hope of rising again, in an unambiguous unity of flesh and spirit.

However, if, for the moment, flesh is ambiguous and may serve to conceal as well as to reveal, and if we follow the line of exegesis which seeks to apply to the future the story of the creation of Adam, may we not raise the further question whether genuine fleshliness is not something still to come? The heterodox Gospel of Philip takes this step. The reconstruction of the text is not quite certain, but there seems little doubt about the general sense: 'The Lord rose from the dead . . . He had flesh, but this flesh is true flesh. Our flesh on the other hand is not true, but a flesh in imitation of the true.'[10] The stripping off of our clothes at baptism symbolised our putting off of the false body, to be clothed in a genuine body: 'The living water is a body. It is necessary that we put on the living man. Therefore, when he is about to go down into the water, he unclothes himself, in order that he may put on the living man.'[11]

It is presumably already against a background of speculation like this that the author of 2 Clement insists so strongly on the resurrection of *this* flesh (9.1–5). On the face of it, it is rather tempting to suggest that St Paul's doctrine that the body is 'sown as an animal body, but raised as a spiritual body' (1 Cor. 15:44) could be developed into an understanding of real bodiliness as something belonging to the resurrection, while our present bodiliness is only a pale reflection of what bodies should be. C. S. Lewis gives rather a nice picture of the insubstantiality of our present bodies in *The Great Divorce:* the 'living' dreamer discovers that it is he who is the ghost, unable even to bend the grass beneath his feet.[12] But what has to be insisted on is that the recipient of God's reward at the resurrection is really the person who lived a bodily life in this world. That is the connection the author of 2 Clement wants to emphasise.

It is also a connection underlined by St Paul, on what I take to be the most natural reading of 2 Corinthians 5:4. In marked contrast to the Gospel of Philip, he says that we do not want to be unclothed, but to have more clothes on top of our present clothing (ἐπενδύσασθαι), so that what is mortal will be swallowed up by life. That is to say, our desire is not to slough off mortality, but to have our mortality subsumed into eternal life. St Thomas, it is true, interprets St Paul as merely pointing out that we have this desire which is, in fact, misguided;[13] but there is nothing in the text to indicate that St Paul is dissociating himself from this desire or criticising it. And he seems to be making a similar point in 1 Corinthians 15: 53–54, where he says that mortality itself will 'put on' immortality. Similarly in Romans 8:11 we are assured that it is our 'mortal bodies' that will be made alive by him who raised Christ Jesus from the dead.

The great difference between orthodoxy and heterodoxy is that the heretical Gnostics did not acknowledge, let alone value, any continuity between mortality and immortality, whereas the orthodox, however much they may have identified real life and real humanity with the new life in Christ, never seriously denied the reality and significance of this mortal life. For St Paul it is our 'mortal bodies' that are to be raised. For the author of the Gnostic Letter to Rheginos, 'The visible members which are dead shall not be saved, only the living members which exist within them would arise.'[14]

The Gnostics, if I may risk the generalisation, cannot ascribe any real significance to life in this world because, as the Gospel of Philip says, 'The world came about through a mistake.'[15] The Gospel of Truth gives a vivid and, indeed, moving account of the nightmarish quality of this world; but in the last analysis it is all simply a fog of error. Real human existence is produced by the Father quite independently of this illusory world:

> If he wishes, he (the Father) manifests whomever he wishes by giving him form and giving him a name, and he gives a name to him and brings it about that those come into existence who before they come into existence are ignorant of him who fashioned them. I do not say, then, that they are nothing at all who have not yet come into existence, but they are in him who will wish that they come into existence when he wishes . . . he who has no root (i.e. in the Father) has no fruit either, but though he thinks to himself, 'I have come into being', yet he will perish by himself. For this reason, he who did not exist at all will never come into existence.[16]

There is thus a complete dichotomy between the people who merely think they exist and those who do really exist, and the life and existence of the latter owes nothing to this unreal world of mortality. And so there is no real story to be told about the life of the 'real people' in this world, except the kind of story that budding writers used to be warned against, the sort of story that ends, 'Then I woke up. It had all been a dream.' The Gospel of Truth uses the analogy of returning to one's senses after being blind drunk.[17]

This is one major point at issue between Irenaeus and the Gnostics. Both agree that the crucial problem is to explain how and why we find ourselves in this patently unsatisfactory condition in such a very unsatisfactory world. Irenaeus shows, I think convincingly, that, for all the splendid drama of the aeons and especially the one that Armstrong calls 'naughty Sophie',[18] the Gnostic myth fails to make sense of human life, because nothing really comes of it on their view.[19] The spiritual beings that we are meant to be seem to have been quite pointlessly subjected to a regime of nightmare because of a celestial accident. Irenaeus in reply proposes a far more cogent tale, which unfolds throughout the last three books of his monumental work, *Adversus Haereses*. We are creatures of flesh because God actually wanted, amazingly, to produce creatures of frail flesh that could, nevertheless, be made eventually capable of true life, which consists, according to Irenaeus, in the vision of God.[20] The unsatisfactoriness is due to the fact that we are essentially the kind of creature that needs a long time to come to maturity, and we have not yet got very far on the way. If Adam had been made perfect at the outset (which God could quite well have achieved, had he wanted to), the result would not have been the same kind of Adam.[21] So the whole long story of this world is the story of the fashioning of man.[22] Without this kind of story there would have been an entirely different end-product. The happy ending which we await will therefore be a genuine denouement, whereas in the Gnostic system we end up simply being what we always were, spiritual beings who have nothing to do with this pseudo-world. One is reminded of the conclusion of Anna Russell's delightfully mischievous 'analysis' of Wagner's *Ring of the Nibelungs:* 'After sitting through this whole operation . . . you're exactly where you started twenty hours ago.'

If life in this world is unreal, so obviously is death. The orthodox belief that it is mortality which will put on immortality has to accommodate the obvious fact that our mortality is not immortal. Mortality ceases to be mortal, in the ordinary course of events, by dying. In a perfectly down to earth sense this must be true: once someone is dead, he is no longer liable to death. By being raised from the dead, one acquires life without regaining the old liability to death, inasmuch as one shares in the life of Christ who 'dies no more'. But the resurrection is essentially the resurrection of the dead, of that which has died. According to St Thomas, the common view in the schools was that even the people still alive at the end of the world will die, even if they are raised again immediately.[23] Death is a necessary and decisive factor in the process whereby human beings become immortal. For the Gnostics, by contrast, the resurrection is not the resurrection of what has died, so it can precede death (this is the heresy already denounced in 2 Tim. 2:18). As the Letter to Rheginos says, 'The resurrection is always the disclosure of those who have risen,' it is 'the revelation of what is.'

'Nothing, then, redeems us from this world, but the All which we are, we are saved.'[24] This, I take it, implies that salvation does not necessitate any redemption from this world, because what is saved was never really involved in this world. What apparently needed redemption was in fact ship-shape all along. So all that is in store for the elect is to receive again what they were at first.[25]

The emphasis on the resurrection of 'this flesh', which we find in orthodox writers, is the safeguard of the reality of this life, with its termination in death, however much the fulness of humanity and life may be located in the new life in Christ which we have by virtue of our baptism. Immortality may already have been given in some sense,[26] but if so it coexists with mortality: 'If Christ is in you, the body is dead because of sin, but the spirit is life because of righteousness. And if the Spirit of him who raised Jesus from the dead dwells in you, then he who raised Christ Jesus from the dead will give life to your mortal bodies too through the Spirit who dwells in you' (Rom. 8:10–11).

This is a far cry from any mere 'hybrid' anthropology. Immortality is not something which the soul possesses by right, it is something the whole person has by God's gift of his own Spirit. On the other hand the insistence on the flesh is not meant to settle questions about the material identity of the person who dies and the person who is resurrected, it is meant to underline the real continuity of personal identity between the person who lives this life in the flesh and the person who will be rewarded hereafter at the judgment.

NOTES

1 *Martyrium Polycarpi* 18.3.
2 Cf. S. Tugwell, *The Apostolic Fathers*, London 1989, chapter 6 note 9.
3 For this interpretation of the genitives in this sentence, see Tugwell, op. cit. chapter 6 note 21, and the extended commentary in the text of the chapter.
4 There is a textual problem here; cf. Tugwell, op. cit. chapter 6 note 28.
5 Hermas, Sim. 9.16.3. (93.3).
6 G. Strecker, *Das Judenchristentum in den Pseudoklementinen*, Berlin 1958, pp. 166–187.
7 Cf. Clement of Alexandria, *Strom.* 3.92–93.
8 Logion 22.
9 On Hermas' doctrine of 'spirit(s)', see Tugwell, op. cit., chapter 4.
10 R. McL. Wilson, *The Gospel of Philip*, London 1962, pp. 135–136.
11 Trans. W. W. Isenberg, in J. M. Robinson, ed., *The Nag Hammadi Library in English*, San Francisco 1977, p. 145.

12 *The Great Divorce*, ed. cit. pp. 27–28, 30.
13 *Super Ep. Pauli*, 2 Cor. paras. 157–159 in the Marietti edition.
14 *Letter to Rheginos*, trans. M. L. Peel, in Robinson, p. 52.
15 Logion 99 (in Wilson).
16 *Gospel of Truth*, trans. G. W. MacRae, in Robinson, p. 42.
17 Ibid. p. 40.
18 B. Aland, ed., *Gnosis* (Festschrift für Hans Jonas), Göttingen 1978, p. 90.
19 The crucial question is raised explicitly by Irenaeus in *Adv. Haer.* II 19.6: why was it necessary, on the Gnostic account, for spiritual beings to be incarnated in this world?
20 'The life of man is the vision of God' (*Adv. Haer.* IV 20.7).
21 *Adv. Haer.* IV 38.
22 Cf. the lapidary comment in *Adv. Haer.* V 15.2: 'The works of God are the fashioning of man' (*opera dei plasmatio est hominis*).
23 *Summa Theol.* I.II q.81 a.3 ad 1.
24 Robinson pp. 52–53.
25 Ibid. p. 53.
26 Cf. *Didache* 10.2, 1 Clement 35.2.

7

Judging from the Acts of the Apostles, the earliest christian preaching laid great stress on the resurrection. It was precisely as a 'witness to the resurrection' of Christ that someone was needed to replace Judas in the company of the apostles (Acts 1:22) and, after Pentecost, we are told that the apostles 'gave witness with great power to the resurrection of the Lord Jesus' (4:33). And the resurrection of Jesus was evidently presented as giving grounds for believing in our own hope of resurrection: what annoyed the priests and the Sadducees was the apostolic proclamation of 'the resurrection of the dead in Jesus' (4:2). It was the doctrine of 'Jesus and the resurrection' that intrigued and, on the whole, amused the Epicureans and Stoics in Athens (17:18,32).

The opponents of resurrection are clearly identified: they are people who believe that once you are dead, you are dead and that's the end of it. Cullmann's problematic seems to be quite absent from the early church. Although he is essentially right to say that the hope of the christians, as expressed in the New Testament, is focused on resurrection, not on the immortality of the soul, neither the New Testament nor the fathers appear to consider it important to insist on resurrection as distinct from the immortality or survival of the soul. Celsus objected to the christian doctrine of resurrection, not in the name of some more purely spiritual doctrine of survival, but because it seemed to him that the christians were appropriating, only in a garbled form, the authentic Platonist doctrine of reincarnation.[1] Tertullian, in his treatise on the resurrection, sees himself as defending christian belief, not against pagan beliefs about immortality, but against the popular conviction that nothing survives after death, a conviction, he reckons, that is shared by some philosophers, notably Epicureans and Stoics. The Platonists, on the other hand, do believe in the immortality of the soul and in its return to bodily life, though they have not got the doctrine of resurrection quite right.[2] Gregory of Nyssa, in his *De Anima et Resurrectione*, presents himself as being accused by Macrina of undue grief at the death of Basil: such grief, she says, quoting 1 Thessalonians 4:13, is proper only to people who 'have no hope'.[3] Gregory confesses that it is the doctrine of the church that 'the soul endures for ever' (εἰσαεὶ διαμένειν), but it is difficult to believe.[4] Gregory is far from meaning that the immortality of the soul is the essential christian belief, as distinct from resurrection; on the contrary, his view is that people are incredulous about the resurrection because they do not find it easy to believe in any kind of human continuation after death. The continuation of the soul is therefore adduced and supported by arguments, in order to add credibility to the doctrine of the resurrection.[5] Platonist arguments can obviously be useful here, but Gregory points out an essential difference between Platonism and Christianity: the Platonists believe that the soul enters into all kinds of bodies, but the christian doctrine is that the soul resumes the same body as it had before.[6] If it is not the same body that is restored to the soul, then the result will not be the same person, in which case resurrection has nothing to do with me, if someone else instead of me is restored to life.[7] The survival of the soul guarantees the identity of the resurrected person with the person who died, because the soul keeps an eye on the matter that belongs to its body, so that it can be reclaimed at the resurrection.[8]

Nemesius likewise adduces the immortality of the soul to support the doctrine of the resurrection.[9] He too relies on Platonist proofs to refute philosophers who denied the immortality of the soul, though he points out that these proofs are difficult to understand and suggests that for believers the evidence of scripture suffices.[10] What scriptural evidence he has in mind he does not say, but it is likely that he is thinking of scriptural evidence for the resurrection.

Nemesius was well informed about Greek philosophy, and yet he shows no signs of anyone objecting to the christian doctrine of the resurrection precisely because of its insistence on the body. On the contrary, he affirms that all the Greeks who believe in the immortality of the soul also believe in reincarnation.[11] The only point at issue, in his mind, is what sort of bodies human souls go into, and he contents himself with a rejection of the idea that human souls can enter into non-human bodies; in this, he says, he is following Iamblichus against some other Platonists.[12] The only philosophical objection to resurrection that he mentions comes from people who claim that the christian doctrine is a misunderstanding of the Stoic belief in cyclical history, against which Nemesius points out that the christians insist that the resurrection occurs only once, definitively.[13]

Justin, as we have seen, attacks the immortality of the soul, but in general the battle-lines are drawn elsewhere in the early church. The controversy is not between proponents of resurrection and proponents of the immortality of the soul, it is about the much more basic question whether or not we have anything to hope for after death. There was therefore no urgent need to choose between different ways of stating the hope that the christians have. St Paul talks clearly about the dead being raised at the second coming of Christ (1 Thess. 4:16), and yet he can also use language that suggests that it is being in the body which separates us from the Lord, so that as soon as we leave the body we shall be with the Lord (2 Cor. 5:6–8; Phil. 1:21–24).

If there is, as we saw in the previous chapter, a certain emphasis in some early christian writings on the resurrection of the *flesh*, this is not due to any polemic against philosophical notions of the immortality of the soul. In so far as it is polemical at all, its target seems to be heretical christians abusing the doctrine that we are made new in Christ to support their contention that the works of the 'old man' do not matter. St Paul talks indifferently, it seems, either about the 'old' and 'new' man or about the 'inner man' and the 'outer man' (Col. 3:9–10, 2 Cor. 4:16). Whichever language was used, what was at risk and needed to be given special emphasis was the continuity between inner and outer, old and new. The spirit, the principle of new life in us, must therefore not be divorced from the flesh. It is the mortal body that is to be made immortal, so it is not just discarded and superseded. The emphasis on the resurrection of the *flesh* thus serves to explicitate the continuity between the new life in Christ and the life that we live here and now in the flesh.

On the whole, then, the christians could and did regard the immortality of the soul as a notion which could be helpful to them in affirming their beliefs. But there are some signs that they were not willing to let immortality become too exclusively the property of the soul. In the New Testament immortality belongs to God in the first place, and then to resurrected human beings, beginning with Jesus Christ, and in that case the sense is that, once raised from the dead, Christ and those who are made alive with him and in him 'die no more'. It is quite natural, then, that the church should have retained the possibility of using the word 'immortality' to refer, not to something that we all possess now, by virtue of our souls, but to something we hope to possess in the future, by virtue of the resurrection. Thus one of the ancient liturgical prefaces contains a reference to our being cheered up 'by the hope of future immortality' (*spe futurae immortalitatis erigimur*).[14] The phrase *futurae immortalitatis* probably derives from the apocryphal IV Esdras 7.43, a book which was surprisingly influential in early christian thinking about the hereafter. A variant of this preface, derived from an eighteenth-century neo-Gallican liturgy, with a very similar phrase about 'future immortality', is found in the modern Roman missal.[15] In this text the 'promise of future immortality' is evidently related to the 'hope of blessed resurrection' which is also mentioned. Much of the text was rewritten for the new missal, but the reference to 'future immortality' survived unchanged, so it is evidently still considered acceptable in the eyes of the Sacred Congregation to talk of immortality as future.

Whether a full study of patristic use of the words 'immortal' and 'immortality' would disclose any significant pattern, I do not know; but it is, I think, quite interesting that Nemesius, who is concerned to argue for the immortality of the soul, first raises the topic of immortality in connection with the whole human person. The Hebrews, he says, maintain that Adam was at first neither mortal nor immortal, on the grounds that, if he was already mortal, it was superfluous to threaten him with death if he sinned, whereas, if he was already immortal, he would not have needed to sustain his life with food – which incidentally shows that the 'death' here envisaged as being negated by 'immortality' must mean bodily death. Nemesius himself prefers to say that Adam was originally mortal, but potentially immortal; by sinning, though, he fell from the perfection and immortality he could have attained, to be restored to them later by grace.[16]

Nemesius then goes on to say that man has two special privileges: unlike the angels he can obtain forgiveness for his sins, and unlike the other animals his body, which is mortal, is made immortal: after death it is raised up again and passes to immortality. 'And it attains this,' he adds, 'by means of the immortality of the soul.'[17] The immortality of the soul is introduced therefore strictly in view of the immortality of the whole person and specifically the immortality of the body.

Gregory of Nyssa seems to have a similar sense that the language of 'immortality' does not properly belong to the soul. In his sermon *De Mortuis* he is quite happy to talk about post mortem life, but he does not introduce the word 'immortal' until he mentions the 'outer man' and says that he too will be freed from corruption at the resurrection, when what is mortal is changed into something immortal.[18] In *De Anima et Resurrectione* he does discuss the soul, sometimes, in terms of immortality,[19] but he is surely being deliberately precise (and perhaps faithful to Plato as well as to christianity) in preferring generally to talk about the soul 'enduring' (διαμένειν) or 'existing after life in the flesh'.[20] 'Immortality' strides boldly on to the stage only when the resurrection is being talked about: it is then that 'that which has died is changed to the condition of an immortal nature.'[21]

We shall be hearing more from Gregory of Nyssa in due course. For the moment the point I am trying to establish is that the original message of christianity was not resurrection versus immortality, but hope versus hopelessness. The christians are supposed to have a hope which reaches beyond death and looks forward to a renewal of personal life. The survival of the soul is not seen as a rival to this hope; on the contrary, it helps to shore up belief in the resurrection. Where the pagans who believe in immortality go wrong is not that they fail to include the body in their hopes, but that they fail to appreciate that it will be the same body that lives again, not some other body.

This hope that the christians have generates its own response to death, whether our own death or the death of others. 'We do not want you to be ignorant, brethren, about those who have fallen asleep, in case you should grieve like the others who have no hope. If we believe that Jesus died and rose again, so God will also, because of Jesus, bring those who have fallen asleep together with him' (1 Thess. 4:13–14). The very terminology can be seen as significant: a sixth-century prayer for the dead remarks that God 'wanted the dissolution of souls departing from their bodies to be, not destruction, but sleep' (*non interitum sed somnum*).[22] St Bernard comments that the death of Lazarus is called 'sleep' because he was Christ's friend.[23]

Seneca tried to console Marcia for the death of her son with the thought that she had enjoyed having him while he was alive, and it is surely better to be happy for a time than never to be happy at all.[24] His general moral is that we must learn to appreciate things on the basis of their and our mortality.[25] Contrast the attitude of St Catherine of Siena: during the plague of 1374 in Siena seven of her young nieces and nephews died. She prepared the corpses and buried them one by one with her own hands, saying over each of them, 'This one I shall never lose now' (*costui non perderò io oggimai.*)[26]

Inasmuch as it is the inevitability of loss that prompts the Stoic (and, for that matter, Epicurean) retrenchment of affective engagement with the people and things we encounter in this life, it is clear that the hope of the christians can, in principle, sustain a much less nervous attitude to such affective engagement.

The difference christian hope makes to our view of our own life and death is dramatically indicated by St Paul when he exclaims, 'If it is only in this life that we have hoped in Christ, we are more wretched than everyone!' (1 Cor. 15:19). 'If the dead are not raised, let us eat and drink, for tomorrow we die' (1 Cor. 15:32). If there is no hope beyond death, then we might just as well concentrate on enjoying ourselves here and now – St Paul seems to have little use for Homeric heroism, Epicurean self-restraint or Stoic high-mindedness! It is because there is a hope extending beyond death that it makes sense to accept the nuisances of life:

> Always carrying around in our bodies the death of Jesus, so that the life of Jesus too may be manifested in our bodies. For

> we who are alive are always being handed over to death for the sake of Jesus, so that the life of Jesus may be manifested in our mortal flesh. (2 Cor. 4:10–11).

The life and death of Jesus make sense of our enduring the very real nastinesses of life, without seeking to protect ourselves from them as a prime objective. Otherwise our death would simply be the final indignity, showing up as ultimately pointless all the suffering which had gone before. Because there is hope beyond death, it makes sense for us to be exposed to death; and because it makes sense for us to be exposed to death, it also makes sense for us to be exposed to life, with all its slings and arrows.

The important thing, therefore, is to affirm hope. To explain dispassionately exactly what happens to people immediately after their death is not an essential part of the gospel, and it is not surprising if early christian writings give us a rather confused answer, if we insist on asking that question. According to St Paul we are already dead and risen with Christ, so that our life is hidden with him in God and will appear when Christ appears (Col. 3:1–4); we could certainly not be worse off, therefore, if we were actually dead, and Paul reckons we would be better off, because we would be 'with Christ'. Similarly the Apocalypse says, 'Blessed are the dead who from now on die in the Lord' (14.13). The parable of dives and Lazarus appears to suggest that immediately upon their death, the rich man goes to the place of torment, while Lazarus is taken to Abraham's bosom, and there is nothing in the story to imply that they are still awaiting a further judgment, or a more definitive punishment or reward (Luke 16:19–26). On the other hand the dramatic picture of the whole human race being assembled for judgment and allocated the punishment or reward that each individual has merited is too vivid to be disregarded (cf. Matt: 25.31–46; 2 Cor. 4:10).

Two ways of harmonising these different considerations can be recognised in the literature of the early christian centuries.

One possibility is to postulate a three-stage story: this life, an interim state, and then the judgment leading to everyone's final reward. This is the picture we found in Justin, apparently representing the normal doctrine of the period: at death people go to nice or nasty waiting-rooms, depending on their moral qualities. There they await the judgment.

It is difficult to see quite what the point is of sorting souls out like this into good and bad, only to keep them hanging around until the judgment, and later western doctrine abandoned the whole idea of waiting-rooms, which is why there is a heading in the index of Rouët de Journel's *Enchiridion Patristicum*, 'Iam ante iudicium generale animae aut beatae sunt aut torquentur.'[27] It is with growing amusement, as one looks up the texts referred to, that one discovers that practically all of them actually deny that souls are already blessed or in torment before the judgment. In fact the *Enchiridion* itself provides evidence of a significant reaction in the opposite direction. Lactantius denies that there is any judgment of souls immediately after death, and quite logically infers that all souls are kept in a common prison (*in una communique custodia*) until the judgment.[28] And it is interesting to note that he treats 'immortality' as a reward imparted at the judgment, even though he is also prepared to say that souls are immortal.

Cyril of Alexandria also argues that the judgment comes after the resurrection, which follows the second coming of Christ; until then, therefore, no one receives either reward or punishment.[29]

Aphrahat too declares that all alike fall into a state of sleep at death, such that they cannot tell good from bad, though he does suggest that the righteous sleep better than the unrighteous.[30]

This version of the three-stage theory certainly safeguards the dramatic integrity of the last judgment; but it does make it rather difficult to see why St Paul was in such a hurry to die.[31]

Hilary returns to the position of Justin, citing the parable of dives and Lazarus as proof that there is an immediate punishment of sinners as soon as they die, while the righteous go to Abraham's bosom; there both await the judgment, which will allot them either eternal bliss or eternal pain.[32]

Augustine's normal doctrine, at least in his mature works, is that souls are kept in 'hidden receptacles' until the judgment, at rest or in care depending on their deserts.[33] But he had not found it easy to accept this doctrine. In an earlier writing, *De Genesi ad Litteram*, he had raised the question why the resurrection of the body was necessary for the attainment of beautitude, if the mind could enjoy beatitude on its own. He allows that it is the case that souls cannot enjoy the beatific vision without the body, as angels can, but he is evidently perplexed as to why this should be so. Maybe, he suggests, it is because souls retain a natural desire to be reunited with their bodies, which prevents them from giving themselves up totally to the delights of heaven.[34] Earlier still, without addressing the question directly, he had rather implied that it was only the presence of the body which hindered the soul from giving itself entirely to the enjoyment of truth, so that death was precisely what it most desired.[35] In the *Retractationes* he still seems willing to leave it as a 'big question' whether souls before the resurrection can enjoy the face to face vision of God.[36]

Augustine's difficulty is a real one, as we have already noted: it is not easy to make sense of souls being kept waiting in incomplete bliss or punishment. And if there is already a discrimination between good and bad souls, it is clear that in some sense they must already be judged when they die, and Jerome is explicit about this: in his commentary on Joel he says that the 'day of the Lord' is to be taken as the day of judgment or the day of the individual's departure from the body, 'because what is to come on the day of judgment for everyone is fulfilled in the case of individuals on the day of their death.'[37] But in that case we already have the problem of what is left for the last judgment to judge.

Ambrose, in a highly Platonist work, *De Bono Mortis*, used the so-called fourth book of Esdras to fill out the picture. His line is essentially that death is a good thing, because it frees the soul from the hindrance of the body (2.5);[38] as far as possible even now we should distance ourselves from the concerns of the body and 'live in heaven' (cf. Phil. 3:20) (3.10). In this perspective the question arises particularly acutely why, at death, the souls of the righteous should not immediately pass to their reward. Ambrose makes no attempt to show that they are held back by any need or desire for the resurrection of the body, which is not surprising. Nor does he try to give any particular content to the last judgment, at least not explicitly. But he is quite clear that souls have to wait for the 'fulness of time' in appropriate 'habitations' or 'store-rooms' (*promptuaria*). As IV Esdras 5.42 says, the judgment is 'like a crown', and all alike must wait for their crown: the swiftness of those who come first and the slowness of those who come after makes no difference. And if those who come first appear to be superior to those who come after, this is because the earth is like a womb getting progressively weaker, so of course those born later are inferior (10.45–46).

Ambrose's account is far from clear, but, since he expressly raises the question whether it is not unfair to keep people waiting so long for their reward, I take it that he is trying to offer some explanation, and that this explanation is to be found in what follows. Even before the judgment there is an anticipation of reward or punishment, and the anticipation of reward is, as it were, stratified and apparently progressive. There is a 'happiness broken up into several layers' (*per ordines quosdam digesta laetitia*), corresponding to the 'many mansions' referred to in John 14:2, and souls advance towards more complete bliss through these 'layers'. And seemingly not all souls will make the same progress, as even at the end there are different 'layers' or 'ranks' in glory, corresponding to different levels of merit and progress (11.48). Perhaps we should infer that the later comers, being a weaker generation, do not progress as far as earlier comers.

The final reward is to 'see the face of God', but who would dare to claim that he is able to endure such radiance? 'So let us not be afraid to be received by men.' That is the immediate promise proposed in IV Esdras 14.9, and it seems to be another reason for the delay imposed on souls; their interim reward is to be with Christ and with the saints (11.49–51). This is apparently what is meant by 'Abraham's bosom', though even there, it may be noticed, the 'radiance of God' replaces sunlight. There too Christ is the way to the Father (12.52–54).

Ambrose's exposition is not clear, and I may have misunderstood it, but it looks as if he is offering an account of post mortem progress up to the day of judgment, which certainly fills out the picture in such a way as to make sense of the delay between death and the final reward. But it seriously undermines the decisiveness of death – not surprisingly, in view of the Platonist inspiration. It therefore at least tends towards an abandonment of the basic christian principle that what is judged at the judgment is what we have done 'in the flesh', in favour of a judgment of what our souls have done before and after death.

It was no doubt at least partly the difficulty in giving any cogent sense to the period between death and judgment that led to the emphasis being shifted away from the last judgment to what was later called the 'particular judgment' at the time of death. In his sermons Caesarius of Arles effectively conflates the two. He can, if he wants to, give a traditional picture of the last judgment;[39] he can also talk as if the only important judgment occurs at the time of death: 'When the flesh begins to be eaten by worms in the tomb, the soul will be presented to God by the angels in heaven, and there, if it is good, it will be crowned, or, if it is evil, it will be cast into outer darkness.'[40] He is manifestly not interested in distinguishing between the particular and the general judgment, as we can see in Sermon 56, in which he exhorts his hearers constantly to bear in mind their own impending death and the judgment they will have to face, and proceeds to talk sometimes with reference to a single judgment of everyone and sometimes as if the time of death is the time of judgment; all that interests him is the fact that this life is the time in which we must repent, and after this life we shall be judged.

By the time we reach the *Dialogues* ascribed to St Gregory (and I have no desire to enter into the renewed controversy concerning their authorship),[41] it is clear that for most purposes it is assumed that people go to their reward at death. The disciple Peter asks whether the souls of the just can be received into heaven before the resurrection and Gregory replies that this cannot be affirmed or denied of all the just. Some lack perfect justice and so are separated from the kingdom of heaven by several stages (*mansionibus*), but 'it is clearer than daylight that the souls of the perfectly just are received in heaven as soon as they depart from the enclosure of this flesh.' Part of the evidence for this is provided by St Paul's desire to be dissolved and to be with Christ. Peter then asks what reward is left for the souls in heaven to receive on the day of judgment, and he is told that their increase at the judgment consists in the fact that their bodies too will then enjoy the bliss which their souls already enjoy. Now, as it says in Apocalypse 6.11, they have received a 'single stole'; at the judgment they will receive a second stole, because they will enjoy the glory of their souls and bodies together.[42] The doctrine enunciated here is borne out by the visionary material adduced, some of which makes it quite clear that both heaven and hell are already open to receive customers.[43]

In one sense the theory of the double judgment – an individual judgment at the time of death and a universal judgment at the end of time – was a great success. It established itself as the normal teaching of the western church. But as a way of actually making sense of the unclear inheritance of christian eschatology it rather petered out, since all competence was effectively transferred to the particular judgment, leaving nothing except the resurrection of the body and the consequent rewarding or punishing of the body to the general judgment. It is clear that, for the author of the Gregorian *Dialogues*, the only people who do not go immediately to heaven or hell are the people Augustine had identified as being good enough to benefit from our prayers, but not good enough to be beyond needing them,[44] the people who will later be identified as being in purgatory. And Augustine himself is explicit that such people cannot acquire any extra *merit* after their death, so there is not really anything new to be judged in them either at the last judgment. The problem we have already seen St Thomas almost helpless to deal with is already full constituted: what is left for the last judgment to judge?

I mentioned that there were two ways of dealing with the ambiguities of christian hope. The second way is found in an ancient prayer used in christian burial, and it is sufficiently opaque to have survived intact even in the twentieth century (it is still found, for instance, in the last Dominican Processionarium produced before the suppression of the Dominican rite).[45] I quote it, not quite in full, from what is probably its oldest form:

> O God, with whom all things that die are alive, for whom our bodies do not perish at death but are changed into something better, we beseech you in supplication to command the soul of your servant N. to be taken up by the hands of holy angels to be brought to the bosom of your friend, the patriarch Abraham, to be raised again on the last day of the great judgment . . .[46]

It is remarkable in this prayer that it is the soul which is to be raised again (*resuscitandam*), and that the body is said not to perish, in God's eyes, but to be changed. The underlying principle is clearly the one declared at the beginning of the prayer (perhaps derived from Luke 20:38): with God or for God (the prayer is found in both versions, *apud quem* and *cui*) nothing is dead, not even what is, on our terms, dead, so even the dead body is not dead in or for God. It is already changed into something better. The embarrassing time-lag between death and resurrection is thus bridged by putting the whole thing into God, so to speak. The thinking that lay behind the construction of this prayer cannot, of course, be retrieved now.[47] But we may surmise that the idea is that God is the God of the living, not the dead, so those who are alive in him in some way must be alive as real human beings, not disembodied souls. So the problematic is not one of a surviving soul waiting for its body to catch up with it, but of a person who is alive in God waiting to be brought back to life in himself and, so to speak, publicly. It is, if you like, a theological way of saying that we do not know what happens to the dead between now and the resurrection, but they are in God, so all is well.

It is presupposed that this applies only to those who 'die in the Lord'. The point is explicitly made in the oldest surviving prayer to use the formula we are considering: nothing perishes for God except what has perished for itself (*cui nihil perit nisi quod sibi deperit*).[48] Those whose continuity until the resurrection is guaranteed by their being alive to God are the just. If we want to press the theological point, we could say (though I do not know that this was ever said in antiquity) that they are the ones who always were in God's sight, so to speak, as his elect. As Psalm 1:6 says, the Lord knows the way of the just, but the way of the wicked shall perish; which seems to imply that perishing and not being known by the Lord are almost interchangeable notions.

In this context it is worth recalling that there is considerable ambiguity in early christian sources as to whether 'the resurrection' means a resurrection of all the dead, good and bad alike, to face judgment, or whether it means a resurrection of the saints to share in God's kingdom. It would probably be an exaggeration to say that there was ever a *doctrine* of selective resurrection; but where the emphasis is on the christians' hope of glory, it is natural that the resurrection should be mentioned specifically as part of that hope. Thus the apocalypse which concludes the *Didache* says, 'Then will appear the signs of truth: first the sign of stretching-out in heaven, then the sign of the sound of the trumpet, and thirdly the resurrection of the dead – but not of all. As it says, "The Lord will come and all his holy ones with him." '[49] Whether the original text then went on, as the corresponding passage in the *Apostolic Constitutions* does, with an account of the judgment of all the dead,[50] we have no way of knowing, since the text does not survive. But it would be quite wrong to infer that the *Didache* was formally denying the posthumous punishment of the dead. All it is doing is interpreting the word 'resurrection' as meaning the necessary precondition for the saints to come with the Lord when he appears in glory. Similarly the prayer we have been looking at is not concerned to propose a general eschatology, it is concerned to express a christian hope about those who die in the Lord.

It is, I think, in this kind of context that we must situate the widely attested liturgical memento of the dead, which, in its original form, made no distinction between saints (who might be supposed to be already in at least provisional bliss) and other dead christians (who might be supposed to need our prayers). In the Greek liturgies it is explicit that the memento is made for all the dead, beginning with the patriarchs and prophets,[51] and there can be little doubt that the memento in the Roman canon was meant to be similarly comprehensive. At any rate a similar embarrassment is attested in both Greeks and Latins at the apparent inclusion of saints in the church's prayer for the dead. Epiphanius explains that the memento has to be interpreted as a prayer for mercy with regard to sinners, but it is offered for the righteous ('the fathers, patriarchs, prophets, apostles, evangelists, martyrs, confessors, bishops and anchorites') as a way of affirming that, however righteous mere human beings are, the Lord Jesus Christ is in a class of his own.[52] Not totally convincing, perhaps. Similarly Augustine insists in one of his sermons that, when the dead are named at the altar of God, we are not praying for the martyrs, though we are praying for all the other dead. 'It is an insult to pray for a martyr, to whose prayers we should rather be commending ourselves.'[53]

It took the Latin church a surprisingly long time to disentangle the saints from its prayers for the dead. In 1202 Innocent III was asked by Jean aux Belles-Mains, former archbishop of Lyons, now a monk of Clairvaux, to explain why the prayer over the offering on the feast of St Leo (Leo II, that must be) had been changed.[54] In the older manuscripts the prayer went, 'Grant to us, Lord, that this oblation may benefit the soul of your servant, Leo, by the offering of which you bestowed remission of the sins of the whole world.' In the more modern manuscripts the text was found in a different form, asking God to grant that the oblation will benefit us at the intercession of St Leo. In fact both forms of the prayer are found in manuscripts from the ninth century,[55] but it is interesting that even in 1202 the issue could still be a live one. Innocent explained to the ex-archbishop, who had no doubt been scrutinising liturgical manuscripts while doing his homework before composing the prayers for the Mass of St Bernard, which he had sent to the pope earlier in the same year,[56] that the saints do not need our prayers, we need theirs; in support of this, he cites the sermon of Augustine I have just referred to. He says he does not know when or by whom the text of the prayer was altered. The unemended prayer was in fact simply a prayer from the mass for a dead bishop,[57] so clearly at some stage no necessary distinction was made between a dead bishop whom the church wished to honour as a saint and any other dead prelate the church merely wished to bury.

Once it is accepted that the dead cannot all be lumped together like this, then the rather promising line suggested by the old funeral prayer loses some of its viability, as it is not going to be enough, in the case of the saints, to say that they are alive to God. They must in some sense be alive in themselves, particularly if we wish to pray to them. So once again the emphasis shifts backwards from the last judgment to immediate post mortem glory. And the more this happens the harder it is to give any real sense to the last judgment, which should in principle be regarded as the dramatic conclusion to the whole story of the world, but which in practice becomes little more than a rather pointless epilogue, tidying up a few details after all the interesting stories are already completed. Even the resurrection of the dead ceases to be of any great interest, because the christian imagination (quite understandably) could never really believe in the glory of disembodied saints, and so habitually envisages them as already risen as fully fledged people, not as souls orphaned of their bodies. *Anima Petri non est Petrus*, as St Thomas very properly acknowledges,[58] and christian piety has never been interested in asking for the prayers of Peter's soul. It is Peter who is believed to be in heaven, whether or not that belief can be given a doctrinally accurate expression. And, if I am right to contend that the essential christian doctrine from the outset was not resurrection of the body versus immortality of the soul, but post mortem life of the person versus extinction of the person, and that the doctrinally significant point is not that there are three stages (ante mortem life, interim survival, resurrection), but that there is something marvellous in store for the saints when they are dead, then maybe the imagination of christian piety is not wholly mistaken in treating saints, and not just saints' souls, as being already in heaven.

NOTES

1 Origen, *Contra Celsum* 7.32.
2 Tertullian, *De Resurrectione* 1.
3 PG 46:13A.
4 PG 46:17.
5 PG 46:76–77.
6 PG 46:109.
7 PG 46:140B.
8 PH 46:77A. On this doctrine, cf. J. Daniélou, 'La résurrection des corps chez Grégoire de Nysse', *Vigiliae Christianae* 7 (1953) pp. 154–170, especially pp. 164–168.
9 *De Natura Hominis* 1, ed. Morani, Leipzig 1987, pp. 9–10.
10 Ibid. 2; for the last point, p. 38.5–7.
11 Ibid. p. 34.18–19.
12 Ibid. p. 35.
13 Ibid. 38, pp. 111–112.
14 *Corpus Praefationum* no. 767, first attested in the eighth century.
15 First Preface 'De Defunctis'. See *Corpus Praefationum* no. 505.
16 Op. cit. 1, pp. 6–7.
17 Ibid. pp. 9–10.
18 *Opera*, ed. W. Jaeger, vol. IX p. 40.
19 Cf. PG 46:45C.
20 PG 46:17A, 69B.
21 PG 46:136C.
22 *Corpus Praefationum* no. 225.
23 Bernard, *Sermo II in festo SS. Petri et Pauli* 5.
24 Seneca, *Consol. ad Marciam* 12.3.
25 *De Providentia* 5.7.
26 M. H. Laurent and F. Valli, eds, *I Miracoli di Caternina da Iacopo da Siena di Anonimo Fiorentino* (Fontes Vitae S. Catharinae Senensis Historici vol. IV), Florence 1936, pp. 19–20; M. H. Laurent, ed., *Il Processo Castellano* (Fontes vol. IX), Milan 1942, p. 42.
27 Rouët de Journel, *Enchiridion Patristicum*, Freiburg im Breisgau 1951, p. 783.
28 Lactantius, *Div. Inst.* 7.21.
29 *Adversus Anthropomorphitas* 16.
30 *Demonstratio* 8.19–20.
31 This is a point raised later on, against John XXII, by the Master of the Sacred Palace, Armand of Belvézer (the text is edited in *Archivum Franciscanum Historicum* 63 (1970) p. 306).
32 *Super Psalmos* 2.49.
33 *Enchiridion* 29.109; *In Io. Evang.* 49.10.
34 *De Genesi ad Litteram* 12.35.
35 *De Quantitate Animae* 33.76.
36 *Retractationes* 1.14.2.
37 *In Ioelem* II 1.11.
38 Ed. C. Schenkl, in Corpus Scriptorum Eccl. Latinorum vol. XXXII i (1896).

39 E.g. Sermon 57.4, in the Corpus Christianorum edition.
40 Sermon 5.5.
41 Francis Clark, *The Pseudo-Gregorian Dialogues*, Leiden 1987.
42 *Dial.* IV 25.2–26.4.
43 E.g. ibid. IV 17.1, 37.3–4.
44 Augustine, *Enchiridion* 29.110.
45 *Processionarium juxta ritum Sacri Ordinis Praedicatorum*, Rome 1930, pp. 192–193.
46 D. Sicard, *La Liturgie de la Mort dans l'Eglise latine des Origines à la Réforme Carolingienne*, Münster 1978, p. 89.
47 Sicard, op. cit. pp. 96–99, can suggest no sources except Luke 20.38 and can find no parallel for the idea that the bodies of the dead are changed, not lost, in the sight of God.
48 Sicard, op. cit. p. 98.
49 *Didache* 16.6–7.
50 *Apostolic Constitutions* 7.32.4–5.
51 Cf. Cyril of Jerusalem, *Cat. Myst.* 5.9.
52 Epiphanius, *Panarion* 75.8.
53 Sermon 159.1.1. (PL 38:868).
54 PL 214:1122C.
55 J. Deshusses, *Le Sacramentaire Grégorien* vol. 1, Fribourg 1971, p. 243.
56 PL 214:1032–1033.
57 Deshusses, op. cit. p. 346.
58 *Summa Theologiae* II.II. q.83 a.11 obi. 5.

8

Seneca thought that immortality was a fantasy encouraging foolish hopes. Lucretius thought it was a nightmare generating unwarranted anxieties. Christianity may or may not be foolish, but it certainly allows room for both post mortem hope and post mortem anxieties. If extinction seems an unsatisfactory prospect, christianity offers us the hope that we shall not simply be extinguished. If death is the denouement which permits us to make sense of life, christianity assures us that we shall be there, so to speak, to enjoy the denouement of our own lives. On the other hand, christianity also informs us in unambiguous terms that we shall all be judged. The denouement may, for some people, be an uncomfortable one. There is no reason why hope and anxiety should not both proceed from a single cause; dentists have a similar effect on most people. But the emotional ambiguity of the christian attitude to death does, I think, reinforce the doctrinal ambiguity we have been considering. Hope naturally focuses on the possibility of immediate benefit – it would have been surprising if the christian imagination had latched on to the idea of posthumous waiting-rooms, when it wished to give expression to its confidence in the hereafter. St Paul, wanting to be dissolved, and St Ignatius, hastening to his martyrdom, quite properly expect results at once. If even in this life we have died with Christ, albeit only symbolically in baptism, in order to live a new life with Christ, albeit only sacramentally and, with any luck, morally, it is surely reasonable to hope that when we have literally died with Christ we shall at once be raised with Christ. On the other hand it is equally natural that, when the christian imagination turns to the thought of judgment, it is the drama of the universal judgment that supplies its scenario. The publicity of it all is an essential element in the picture, whether we are thinking of our own embarrassment there or of the splendid spectacle of our favourite villains getting their just deserts. Sooner or later someone was bound to write the *Dies Irae*. Christian preaching and theology thus have to deal with two somewhat discordant requirements.

It was particularly in connection with martyrs that the early church tended to emphasise its confidence in their immediate reward. Clement of Rome says that, when Peter 'reached the limit appointed for his setting and bore witness (μαρτυρήσας) before rulers, he was snatched from the world and assumed to the holy place.'[1] Similarly Polycarp gives a whole list of martyrs including Ignatius and Paul, and affirms the confidence that we should have that 'all these did not run in vain, but in faith and righteousness' and that 'they are in the place which is their due, with the Lord with whom they also suffered.'[2] Ignatius himself, as we have seen, focused his own personal hope on his impending martyrdom: it was at martyrdom that he expected to acquire his own full reality as a human being and as a significant 'word of God'.

Ignatius in particular suggests a connection between 'setting from the world in order to rise in God' and the sense that there is something incomplete and indeed unconvincing about human life as we encounter it in the world,[3] and, although there is no reason to suppose that Ignatius was influenced by Platonism, there is an obvious affinity between his formulation of his hope and some of the concerns of Platonism, particularly its conviction that everything in this world is miserably blurred at the edges and can only be taken seriously on the assumption that there is something really real behind it.

Gregory of Nyssa was certainly influenced by Platonism, and he was probably not influenced by Ignatius, but in his sermon *De Mortuis* it is fascinating to see how he uses his Platonism to reaffirm a position which is strikingly close to that of Ignatius.

Gregory begins with some thoroughly Platonist remarks about this life not being an unambiguous good, from which he infers (and this is a recognisably Platonist gambit) that it cannot be a genuine good, so therefore it is a good thing to leave this life.[4] Death is a passage to a better life, which is intellectual and unbodily.[5] This bodily life that we have now rests on an unstable compound, held together by the tension between the contrary elements of which bodies are made. The other life is invulnerable and undisturbed, and is held together by the understanding of the divine nature.[6] The materiality of the body is alien to the soul's true character.[7] It is by death that we are born to a more genuine life. Babies show that they would have preferred to stay in the womb by crying as soon as they draw their first breath when they are born:

> Similarly people who make a fuss about leaving this present life seem to me to be in the same position as embryos, in wanting to live for ever in the domain of this material nastiness. When the pangs of death bring people to birth into another life, they emerge into its light and draw a breath of pure spirit, and then they know by experience the difference between that

life and the one we have now. But those who are left behind in this damp, soggy life are no more tham embryos. Not being really human, they feel sorry for the person who has gone on ahead out of this familiar domain which encloses us, as if he had lost something good, not realising that he is in the same situation as a baby that has come to birth: his eyes open, when he escapes from this present constraint (the eye of the soul, you must understand, by which people see the truth of reality), his sense of hearing is opened, enabling him to hear the ineffable utterances which the apostle says it is not possible for a man to speak. His mouth opens and he draws in the pure, immaterial breath of the Spirit, which attunes him to intellectual sound and the true Word, when he mingles with the noise of the feast in the chorus of the saints. So he becomes fit for the divine taste, by which he knows, as the Psalm says, that the Lord is good. Through the working of his sense of smell he perceives the good odour of Christ, and his soul acquires a power of touch, touching the truth and handling the Word, as John testifies.[8]

Death then, freeing us from the 'womb' of this bodily life, gives us access to true life, in which the true senses of the soul begin to operate, and in which we attain to a more authentic humanity. However we must not disdain this bodily life; it is the seed from which the crop grows.[9] But bodies are constantly changing, so bodily life is permeated by death;[10] we die daily, in a quite down to earth sense, and the nearest the body can get to immortality is this constant process of replacement.[11] But the body itself will be changed at the resurrection to become an adornment for the soul, once death has eliminated all that is of no value for the enjoyment of the life to come.[12] We are used to considerable changes in the body even in this life: our bodies are quite different when we are old from what they were when we were babies. But the change that occurs at the resurrection is incomparably greater, defeating our imagination.[13] At least, though, we can surmise that our risen appearance will be totally determined by our moral character, as even now to some extent our appearance reflects our mood. In the case of the resurrected body there can be no question of anyone being one thing and appearing to be another.[14]

Gregory, it seems to me, has admirably merged the Platonist aspiration towards a more real life than we have in this body with the primitive christian aspiration towards a more real life in which inner and outer will be completely at one. The sort of bodiliness we have now is at odds with itself and with us. Death, which frees us from this body, is paradoxically the means whereby we are born into a more integral and more fully personal way of being bodily.

In the sermon *De Mortuis* Gregory does not comment on the chronology of the resurrection. Elsewhere he certainly admits that the resurrection is a single event for the whole human race; in his Easter sermon he talks of the soul homing in unerringly on its own body even after an absence of thousands of years.[15] But in the *De Mortuis* it certainly sounds as if Gregory would be happier if the resurrection could be brought forward to coincide with death. The only delay that he alludes to is that some people are not ready for the full reality of the life to come when they die, so they need to be purged first in the fire.[16] Gregory's doctrine here, not surprisingly, attracted the attention of Latins looking for Greek evidence to support the doctrine of purgatory, but the Greeks at the Council of Florence were, alas, quite right to refuse his testimony. As they said, his doctrine is, on this point, pure Origenism. The fire in question is the fire of hell, but, like Origen, Gregory believed that hell was educational, and when its work was done everyone would sooner or later emerge from it into the life of bliss.[17]

Gregory certainly does not adopt the absolutely open-ended eschatology associated with Origenism, but his Origenistic perspective reinforces the tendency, which was already there for different reasons in Ignatius, to ignore (not necessarily to deny) the time-lag between death and resurrection.

Why not then go the whole way and make resurrection follow immediately after death? Such a doctrine would not necessarily fall foul of 2 Timothy 2:18, which is meant to exclude the belief (such as we have noted in some Gnostic texts) that the real resurrection can antedate death. It is intuitively correct to insist that if no death has occurred, no resurrection can be claimed either, any more than there can be a reconciliation without a previous quarrel or a reunion without a parting. The resurrection must always be the resurrection of the dead. As we have seen, St Thomas attests a general conviction in the schools that everyone must die before they can be resurrected, even the people alive at the end of the world. Similarly the Dominican collect for the feast of the Assumption makes it explicit that Mary died before being assumed into heaven.[18]

The real difficulty about immediate resurrection after death is the presence of the corpse, whether you wish to venerate it as relics (a practice already attested in connection with the remains of Polycarp)[19] or just to bury it decently. This must be one reason why Ignatius is so keen to disappear totally in death. If the beasts he is to face in Rome do their work properly, he hopes that absolutely nothing of his body will be left. This hope is mentioned in the immediate context of Ignatius' remarks about the disappearance of Christ at the ascension, though the nature of the connection is not explained. Ignatius' enthusiasm for total disappearance is surely not sufficiently accounted for by his explicit concern not to be a nuisance to anyone after he has 'fallen asleep'.[20] I doubt if he is really trying to spare the Roman church the trouble of burying him. It seems far more likely that he does not want his body to be still around when he is dead, because he wants to 'rise in the Lord', without the embarrassment of a spare body left behind in Rome.

Strictly speaking, maybe, the presence of a corpse ought not to exclude the possibility of immediate resurrection; such is presumably the conviction of modern theologians and exegetes who say that the resurrection of Christ would not be refuted by the discovery of Jesus' bones somewhere in Palestine. The resurrection would be but the most dramatic and total instance of something that goes on the whole time, as Gregory of Nyssa points out, namely the replacement of the body's discarded matter with new matter, a process that is not really impeded by the continuing availability of discarded teeth, hair, nails, not to mention dust and surgically removed organs. The resurrection would be a kind of whole body transplant.

Such a view might perhaps be philosophically defensible. All the same it is surely profoundly unnatural to think along these lines, and one is inclined to say that it would be misplaced zeal to attempt to force oneself to think along these lines. However correct it might be to rewrite the litany of the saints and say, 'Soul of St Peter, pray for us' and so on, it would be utterly foolish. Nobody really thinks that the soul of St Peter is in heaven; it is St Peter who is in heaven. Similarly we do not think that we have buried Aunt Matilda's corpse, we think that we have buried Aunt Matilda. And we are encouraged by liturgical rubrics to talk like that. The church has always provided services for burying clerics, friars, children, whatever. I doubt if there is any service book which contains a rite for the burial of the corpse of a cleric, the corpse of a friar, the corpse of a child. However proper it might be to say that neither Aunt Matilda's soul nor her body is the actual aunt, our original reason for generating such language in the first place about souls and bodies going to different places is that, when someone dies, we want to say two incompatible things about them: we want to say that they are in the graveyard, where we can take them flowers, and we also want to say that they are in heaven. Christians, from this point of view, are in exactly the same boat as the ancient Greeks. Whatever the philosophers may tell us, we want to say that both Aunt Matilda's soul and Aunt Matilda's body are Aunt Matilda. We need two ways of talking about her, because she is in two different places at once. The point is nicely illustrated in a prayer found in the funeral service in the thirteenth-century Roman pontifical: 'Bless this tomb of your servant, and make him rest here, and place him in the bosom of Abraham.'[21] Not logical maybe, but that is what we want to say.

This, I think, is the essential reason why immediate resurrection is not an acceptable doctrine. It is not religiously or humanly defensible. People go on pilgrimage to the tomb of a saint, because the saint *is there*, even if, to be of any use to his clients, the saint must also be in heaven. Having the body of a saint is not at all the same thing as being the proud possessor of Elvis Presley's T-shirt: it is to have *the saint*. Similarly with Aunt Matilda. We want to go and visit her grave and leave flowers there for her, and it would be vain to tell us that her mortal remains in the tomb are no more her than the exquisite doilies she crocheted, which we treasure in her memory. She is in the graveyard; she is not in the drawer where we keep her doilies.

Christian hope then, even though it tends to overlook the gap between death and resurrection, preferring to envisage people – people, not souls – going straight to their reward, has its own reasons, after all, for not entirely denying the futurity of the resurrection.

Judgment, on the other hand, for all the imaginative appeal possessed by an apocalyptic calling to account of all the nations, tended, at least in western christianity, to lose more and more of its business to the particular judgment, regarded as occurring at the time of each individual's death. Preachers like Caesarius of Arles may want to impress their hearers by giving a graphic account of the last judgment, or they may want to stress the urgency of the situation by insisting on the judgment that ensues immediately after death; what they are not likely to do is dwell on the in-between period which separates the two judgments, so that in practice, as we have already noticed in Caesarius, the two judgments coalesce and are felt to be one. And this is not just a matter of moralistic preachers wanting to fire their congregations with a sense of moral urgency. Nobody likes waiting for the results of an examination, whether medical or academic, longer than is necessary. We want to know how we have done.

There were also reasons for exempting some people entirely from the last judgment, not least Psalm 1:5, which says that the impious 'will not arise in the judgment, nor will sinners in the council of the just.' On this verse, Ambrose says that those who are worthy to share in the 'first resurrection' escape the judgment entirely, and arise, not 'in the judgment', but 'in the council of the just.' On the authority of John 3:18, Ambrose also says that the really wicked (*impii*) will not be judged, because they did not believe.[22] Caesarius of Arles similarly uses John 3:18 to support the contention that pagans, heretics and Jews will not come to judgment because of their unbelief.[23] By the time we get to Gregory there is a neat little scheme, waiting to be taken over by Peter Lombard, who uses it both in his Gloss on Psalm 1 and in his *Sentences*, thereby making it standard doctrine and posing considerable problems for the next generation of scholastics, who wanted to insist on the universality of the last judgment: 'Some are judged and perish, some are not judged and perish, some are judged and reign, some are not judged and reign.'[24] Thus moderately good and moderately bad believers are the only customers left for the last judgment. This is at best a compromise, and it sits ill with the traditional doctrine that all souls are kept in appropriate 'receptacles' until the judgment, though the Lombard duly cites Augustine, without comment, on the doctrine of receptacles.[25] Presumably the saints, at any rate, are not, on his view, confined to any such receptacles, since the Lombard himself bases the possibility of their hearing our prayers on the belief that they are already enjoying the vision of God.[26] Accordingly the author of the *Summa contra Haereticos* ascribed to Praepositinus of Cremona interprets the Lombard's doctrine as meaning that the receptacles are only for 'the moderately good and the moderately bad'. And these are the only ones who are actually judged at the last judgment.[27]

On this view the receptacles have become a kind of police cells attached to the court house, in which certain people await judgment. But in fact precisely the same people had already, by now, been assigned to purgatory, and no one maintained that there was no escape from purgatory before the judgment, so the whole thing was really quite unworkable. Effectively no one was left to be judged by the time the court was due to sit.

By the end of the twelfth century then, it is clear that there was one judgment too many, so we are not surprised to learn from Praepositinus that the heretics called Passagini deny that anyone goes to hell or to heaven before the day of judgment, precisely on the grounds that the Creed says that Christ is going to come to judge the living and the dead, and no one is judged twice.[28] What Praepositinus says about the Passagini gets taken up in the heresiological tradition and applied to the Catharists, rightly or wrongly.[29] It is probably easier to believe a different report, which declares that the Catharists only believe in the particular judgment at each individual's death and deny the last judgment.[30]

By the middle of the thirteenth century a Latin orthodoxy is well established, part of whose clarity may well be due to the pressure of the various heresies. Moneta of Cremona's chapters on the judgment are patently inspired by Praepositinus, but we notice at once that certain features of the anti-heretical position have changed. There is now no mention of any interim receptacles for souls before the judgment. Moneta clearly states that there are two judgments: one, which takes place at death, is a judgment of souls, the other is the last judgment of everyone, body and soul together. John 3:18 is no longer taken as indicating that some people are not judged then; they are 'already judged' only in the sense that they already have the grounds for judgment, that is, condemnation, in themselves. Everyone is therefore judged twice. And those who deserve it when they die, go straight to heaven or hell. The rest go to purgatory.[31]

Exactly the same doctrine is expounded by St Thomas in the closing chapters of book IV of the *Contra Gentiles*,[32] reinforced by the contention we have already noted, that everyone's will is fixed immutably at death. Thomas can clearly make no sense of any delay in giving the souls of the dead their just deserts, except in the case of those who have not completely been purged by penance when they die. If they were to be admitted into heaven immediately, he points out, that would give the slack an unfair advantage over the zealous. Otherwise there is nothing to prevent the souls of the dead going immediately to heaven or hell, as it is the soul which has essentially earned reward or punishment, not the body, and it would be odd if the God who insisted on prompt payment of wages in Leviticus 19:13 were himself to delay 'payment' gratuitously. On the other hand there is still room for a second judgment of body and soul together, because it is only then that the body too will be rewarded, after the resurrection, and any allocation of rewards involves an act of judgment.

All of this is quite cut and dried, and there is no evidence that anyone is bothered by the fact that the new Latin orthodoxy is not supported by the Latin fathers, such as Augustine. And the Latins are quite prepared to be dogmatic about their own new position, even though they are aware of a Greek tradition which does not believe in purgatory and still maintains that no one goes to heaven or hell before the last judgment. That tradition is dismissed by St Thomas as no more than 'the error of certain Greeks.'[33]

Since reunion with the Greeks was an important concern in the thirteenth century, any disagreement between Greeks and Latins on the fate of the soul had to be faced. On 4 March 1267 Clement IV sent the emperor Michael Palaeologus a profession of faith, in which it was clearly affirmed that the souls of those who had retained their innocence after baptism or who had completed their penance were quickly received into heaven (*in coelum mox recipi*) when they died. Penitents who were not yet entirely purged would enter heaven as soon as their purgation was completed. Those who died in a state of mortal sin or original sin would go quickly to hell (*mox in infernum descendere*). Nevertheless the document goes on, the holy Roman church also believes that everyone will appear before the tribunal of Christ after the resurrection, there to give an account of their deeds.[34] This credal formula remained classic thereafter; it was used at the second Council of Lyons in 1274 as a basis for reunion with the Greeks,[35] and it was thereafter sent to various orientals by various popes,[36] until it finally found its way, slightly adapted for reasons we shall see in a moment, into the Bull of Union promulgated at the Council of Florence,[37] even though Mark of Ephesus, on the Greek side at Florence, insisted that the Greek belief was that no souls went fully to their reward before the last judgment; in the interim they were kept in appropriately nice or nasty places.[38]

Latin orthodoxy seemed secure, but on All Saints day 1331 the eighty-six year old pope, John XXII, threw a very fierce cat among the pigeons. In his sermon in Avignon the pope chose to revive the doctrine which St Bernard had propounded in his All Saints sermons, that until the judgment the saints do not receive their proper reward, which is the vision of God; they are 'under the altar', as it says in Apoc. 6.9, which Bernard interprets as meaning that they are 'under the consolation and protection of the humanity of Christ'. It is appropriate that the complete reward should only be given to complete people, and souls are not complete people, so it is only after the resurrection that eternal life proper is imparted. This doctrine, the pope concludes, seems to be confirmed by the judgment story in Matthew 25:34. If it is only at the judgment that the blessed are told to take possession of the kingdom, it follows that they had not previously taken possession of it.[39]

What had got into the old man we can only conjecture, but the pope's sermon certainly started a furore, and that is perhaps what he intended.[40] He was in effect challenging the prevailing orthodoxy to produce its credentials, by showing that there was prima facie an overwhelming case on the other side. In a second sermon on 15 December he showed his hand rather more clearly, with an impressive dossier of scriptural and patristic authorities which seemed to deny the current doctrine that souls can go straight to their reward after death.[41] If people were shocked by what he was saying, he later commented, that was because they lacked first-hand experience of the patristic tradition, which they knew only indirectly, as it was filtered through the modern tradition of the schools.[42] The pope himself was not a university-trained theologian but he was an assiduous student, as we can see from his own annotated manuscripts, so in a way he could put himself in the position of the innocent outsider questioning the genuineness of the emperor's new clothes. The traditions we ourselves have been looking at confirm the legitimacy of the pope's challenge to what was essentially only an academic orthodoxy established in the thirteenth century.

For the next three years eschatology was the hot topic, eagerly debated in Paris and in Oxford, and of course in Avignon where John XXII insisted on a very thorough exploration of the whole issue.[43] How far anyone really wanted to take sides is unclear but several people were evidently convinced by the pope that a serious case could be made for denying the possibility of beatitude before the judgment. One such was John Lutterell, former chancellor of the University of Oxford.[44]

The strength of the pope's case lay in its appeal to tradition, which forced people to read Augustine, for instance, not just glosses culled from Augustine,[45] and so recaptured the possibility of seeing clearly the plain meaning of certain fundamental elements in the inherited language of the church. Thus the pope was surely right to be impressed by the Matthaean story of the judgment. It is undoubtedly a story about people going to their reward after the last judgment, and, as the pope said, if people are in fact rewarded or punished before their sentence is pronounced, everything is back to front.[46] Also it is quite clear – this is something the pope emphasised – that the reward is promised to people, not disembodied souls.[47] Also, as we have seen, the papal side was in line with tradition in wanting to attach the notion of immortality to the risen body or to the whole person, rather than to the soul.[48] The credal summaries of christian hope express the matter clearly and succinctly: in the Apostles' Creed, the Nicene Creed and the Athanasian Creed the resurrection comes *before* eternal life.[49]

The weakness of John XXII's case was that it was not and could not be radical enough to produce a convincing alternative to the prevailing orthodoxy. The forgotten tradition, of which the pope wanted to remind the church, was one which connected final bliss strictly with the resurrection; the corollary was that in the meantime the church held all her dead in hope, asking God to remember them – and the pope was, as a matter of history, quite right in maintaining that the memento for the dead in the Roman canon was not originally meant to exclude the saints.[50] But the pope could not simply propose a re-eschatologising of beatitude, because of the heresiological identification of the belief that there is no reward or punishment before the last judgment as heretical, and in particular because of the position the Latin church had been urging on the Greeks, insisting on purgatory for those who need it and on the immediate reception of everyone else into heaven or hell as soon as they die. John XXII himself had sent the standard Latin statement of belief to the king of Armenia in 1319,[51] and in 1326 he had written to the catholic hierarchy in Cyprus expressing his disapproval of certain Greeks who deny purgatory and 'falsely and temerariously assert that none of the saints is in paradise until after the general judgment, but they rest meanwhile without pain in a certain place.'[52]

John could challenge the academic orthodoxy prevailing among theologians, but he could hardly challenge the orthodoxy that had been formally presented by the church and by himself as pope against real or supposed heretics. His re-eschatologising of beatitude had to be tempered therefore, so as to allow for the saints to be in heaven already. St Bernard provided the ideal compromise, but the result was hardly traditional doctrine.[53]

A naive but telling objection was raised by king Robert of Anjou: it seems peculiar to propose the humanity of Christ as the interim object of beatitude for disembodied souls. Properly, no body can be the object of a disembodied soul's understanding.[54] The attempt by Durandus of St Pourçain to make the objection more rigorous by denying that disembodied souls *could even see* the humanity of Christ[55] was ruled to be erroneous by the University of Paris,[56] but the crucial point is not that disembodied souls cannot see the humanity of Christ, but that there is something essentially silly about the whole idea of disembodied souls making do with the humanity of Christ (which bodily eyes could see) until the judgment, at which point, when their bodies are restored to them, they will be allowed to move on to the vision of the Godhead (which a disembodied soul was all along equally well equipped, in principle, to contemplate).

The major difficulty in the papal position, though, is its need to lay great stress on an in-between state, which is not that of beatitude, but which is equally not that of this life. Lutterell in his letter on the beatific vision, draws attention to this 'second state',[57] and it was perhaps he who insisted on there being three states altogether in the debate reported by Durandus of Aurillac.[58]

The in-between state is of course already familiar to us in the form of interim receptacles, but, as we saw, this doctrine was essentially an attempt to resolve the ambiguity in the primitive tradition between an eschatology focused on death and an eschatology focused on judgment. What survived into the later western tradition from this attempt was the doctrine of purgatory. Otherwise the essentially binary eschatology of the main tradition reasserted itself. And there can be no doubt that the tradition is essentially binary.[59] Here, in the body, we walk by faith; hereafter we shall walk by vision (2 Cor. 5:6–7). This life is the time for meriting, hereafter is the time of reward. Here we are on the way (*in via*), hereafter we shall be at home (*in patria*). There are essentially two stages, not three.

Cardinal Ceccano tries to break down this binary structure, and argues that a false inference has been made from 2 Corinthians 5:6–7. St Paul says that 'while we are in the body, we are in exile from the Lord, for we walk by faith.' To infer from this that when we cease to be in the body, we are with the Lord by vision, is, Ceccano says, like arguing: 'While we are in the schools, we are not with the pope. Therefore, when we are out of the schools, we are with the pope.' There are plenty of other places we might be, and it is the same with the souls of the dead; they might be in purgatory, for instance.[60] But Ceccano's lesson in logic, however excellent in itself, is beside the point, as St Paul expressly says that we want 'to be in exile from the body and to be present to the Lord,' which makes it extremely difficult to believe that he envisaged any other possibilities than the two he actually mentions: being in the body in exile from the Lord, and being in exile from the body with the Lord.

The young patriarch of Alexandria, John of Aragon, puts his finger precisely on the difficulty,[61] as does Durandus of St Pourçain:[62] is the vision of Christ's humanity before the judgment meant to be seen as a reward or as something meritorious? It was the classic doctrine of the church that it is only this life in the flesh that constitutes the *locus merendi*, so it is awkward to treat the 'second state' as being part of the journey of faith, in which merit is won. But if there is already a reward in the interim state before the judgment, we are back precisely where the pope was concerned not to be, with rewards preceding judgment.

In fact the papal position tends unmistakably to assimilate the in-between stage more to this life than to final bliss. It regards us as *viatores* right up to the time of judgment (even for a short time after the resurrection, therefore), still, in some sense, working by faith and hope.[63] This ought to imply that we can go on meriting up to the time of judgment, which would seriously upset the traditional doctrine that it is what we do in the flesh that gets judged. It certainly undermines the decisiveness of death as setting the term to our progress and development. Though we may appreciate the concern of the papal position to affirm the integrity of the human person, body and soul, as the recipient of the reward of final bliss, we cannot help but notice that the logic of that same position drives it to negate the integrity of the human person in the run-up to that reward, since the process is not bounded by death nearly as much as it is bounded by the judgment. Even resurrection is not a decisive term because, as the papal view emphasises,[64] judgment comes after the resurrection and the reward comes after the judgment. So, whereas the standard scholastic view sees the decisive break as occurring at death, the papal view has us wandering on first with a body, then without a body, then with a body again, until the decisive break comes at the judgment.

What John XXII succeeded in doing was to discomfort the unduly bland assurance that the doctrine of the double judgment, particular and general, was satisfactory. He obliged people to reopen the question of what the general judgment was all about, if people's fate is essentially decided at the particular judgment.

In the perspective of a longer hindsight, we may say that the significance of his initiative is that he exposed the fundamental ambiguity there is in christian eschatology and showed up the need for a new theological engagement with the twin perspectives of what we may call personal and public eschatology. The prevailing academic orthodoxy of his time stressed the personal at the expense of the public, insisting on the rounding off of the story of each individual at death, but leaving little of any significance for the rounding off of the whole story at the last judgment. But fairness to the whole tradition is certainly not any better served by simply reversing the bias and stressing public eschatology at the expense of private eschatology, highlighting the drama of the universal judgment by playing down the decisiveness of the death of individuals.

The whole episode creates for us a crucial item on our theological agenda, and we must in due course try to deal with it.

In the short term John gave his successor, Benedict XII, something to think about. The old pope, on his deathbed, made a guarded submission to the prevailing orthodoxy. Cardinal Fournier, who had played an important role in the debates in Avignon and had compiled a monumental study of the whole dossier, became pope in his turn on 20 December 1334. After much thought and after a full discussion in the curia, the new pope decided to settle the essential dispute once and for all, and so on 29 January 1336 he issued a dogmatic definition in the Bull *Benedictus Deus*, and shortly afterwards he tried to publish his own dossier on the subject.

After the ascension of Christ, the pope declared, those who die in a state of grace go to heaven immediately or when they have been sufficiently purged in purgatory, and there they see 'the divine essence, with a direct, face to face, vision' without the mediation of any creature, even before the resumption of their bodies at the resurrection. They thereby enter into eternal life, in which faith and hope, as theological virtues, have no more part to play, and the vision of God which is begun thus, before the judgment, will be their joy for ever.[65]

In line with this definition the standard statement of faith used in dealings with the orientals was adapted, when it was reissued in 1338, to declare that the souls of those who are worthy are quickly received into heaven 'and enjoy the beatific vision of the divine essence'.[66] A similar addition was made, in slightly different words, when the statement was finally promulgated at the Council of Florence in 1439 in the Bull of Union.[67]

NOTES

1 1 Clement 5.7.
2 Polycarp, *Phil.* 9.1–2.
3 Ignatius, *Rom.* 2–3.
4 Ed. G. Heil in volume IX of Jaeger's edition of Gregory of Nyssa, pp. 31–34.
5 Ibid. p. 28.
6 Ibid. p. 35.
7 Ibid. pp. 42–43.
8 Ibid. pp. 46–47.
9 Ibid. pp. 48–49.
10 Ibid. p. 52.
11 Ibid. p. 58.
12 Ibid. pp. 59–60.
13 Ibid. pp. 62–64.
14 Ibid. pp. 64–65.
15 Edited in the same volume, p. 247.
16 Ibid. p. 54.
17 Gregory's *De Mortuis* is cited as evidence for purgatory in Nicholas of Cotrona and in St Thomas, *Contra Errores Graecorum* (Leonine ed. vol. XL pp. A 104 and A 149–150). At the Council of Florence it was cited, for instance, by Cesarini (Petit and Hofmann, *De Purgatorio Disputationes* pp. 9–10) and by Fantino Vallaresso, *Libellus de Ordine Generalium Conciliorum* 57 (ed. B. Schultze, Conc. Flor, II ii, Rome 1944, pp. 71–72). For the Greek rejoinder that Gregory was, on this point, Origenist, see Petit and Hofmann pp. 23–24. Gregory's Origenist eschatology is beyond doubt; cf., for instance, his *Catechetical Oration* 26.
18 Veneranda nobis domine huius diei festivitatem opem conferat salutarem, in qua sancta dei genitrix mortem subiit temporalem, nec tamen mortis nexibus deprimi potuit . . . (Humbert's Prototype of the Dominican liturgy, MS AGOP XIV L 1 f.48v). This text survived into the last edition of the Dominican breviary, Rome 1962, vol. II p. 694.
19 *Martyrium Polycarpi* 17–18.
20 Ignatius, *Rom.* 3.2–3, 4.2.
21 M. Andrieu, ed., *Le Pontifical de la Curie Romaine au XIIIe* siècle, Vatican City 1940, p. 509.
22 Ambrose, *In Ps. 1 Enarr.* 51–56 (PL 14:948–952).
23 Sermon 157.4.
24 Gregory, *Moralia* 26.27.50, cited by Lombard in his Gloss (PL 191:65A) and in IV *Sent.* 47.3. It is cited as a difficulty by Philip the Chancellor, *Summa de Bono*, ed. N. Wicki, Berne 1985, p. 642.
25 IV *Sent.* 45.1.

26 Ibid. 45.6.2.
27 Ed. J. C. Garvin and J. A. Corbett, Notre Dame 1958, p. 201.
28 Ibid, p. 200.
29 E. g. Moneta of Cremona, *Adversus Catharos et Valdenses*, Rome 1743, p. 376. Cf. M. Dykmans, *Revue d'Histoire Ecclésiastique* 68 (1973) pp. 30–34.
30 Alexander Nequam, *Speculum Speculationum* ed. R. M. Thompson, British Academy 1988. p. 21; MS Vatican lat. 4255 f.61, cited by Dykmans, art. cit. p. 34 note 3.
31 Moneta, ed. cit. pp. 375–381.
32 *Contra Gentiles* IV 91–96.
33 Ibid, IV 91.
34 Pontificia Commissio ad redigendum Codicem Iuris Canonici Orientalis, *Fontes* series III, vol V i, ed. A. L. Tautu, Vatican City 1953, p. 66.
35 Ibid, pp. 118–119.
36 Cf, ibid, vols, VII i p. 44 and VII ii pp. 37, 111, 140.
37 Alberigo pp. 527–528.
38 Petit and Hofmann, *De Purgatorio Disputationes* pp. 61–62.
39 M. Dykmans, ed., *Les Sermons de Jean XXII sur la Vision Béatifique*, Rome 1973, pp. 93–99. Cf. Bernard, *In Festo Omnium Sanctorum* sermons 3 and 4.
40 John XXII seems to have wanted to start a discussion, and he explicitly said he was not making any doctrinal decision in the matter (*Sermons* pp. 152, 156). For a discussion of his intentions, cf. Dykmans, *Sermons* pp. 58, 71–72.
41 *Sermons* pp. 100–143.
42 Ibid. pp. 149–150.
43 There is a useful outline of the course of the controversy in Dykmans, *Sermons* pp. 165–197.
44 Cf. his letter on the subject, edited in F. Hoffmann, *Die Schriften des Oxforder Kanzlers Iohannes Lutterell*, Leipzig 1959, pp. 103–119.
45 Cf. the comment of Cardinal Ceccano on the difference between the original text of Augustine and the Glosses derived from him: M. Dykmans, *Pour et contre Jean XXII en 1333: Deux Traités Avignonnais sur la Vision Béatifique*, Vatican City 1975, p. 139.
46 *Sermons* p.138.
47 Ibid. pp. 97, 104. Another text in *Recherches de Théologie Ancienne et Médiévale* 37 (1970) p. 239.
48 *Sermons* pp. 114–116. Other texts in *Archivum Franciscanum Historicum* 63 (1970) pp. 276, 304; *Pour et contre . . .* pp. 75–79; Lutterell, ed. cit. p. 103.
49 *Sermons* p.109.
50 *Revue d'Histoire Ecclés.* 66 (1971) p. 415. See Dykman's note in his edition of Robert of Anjou, *La Vision Bienheureuse*, Rome 1970, pp. 100–101. Cf. also *Sermons* pp. 111–112.
51 Tautu vol. VII ii p. 37. John sent similar letters to the Tartars in 1321 and the king of Serbia in 1323 (ibid. pp. 111, 140).
52 Ibid. p. 176.

53 On Bernard's doctrine and its sources see B. de Vrégille, 'L'attente des saints d'après S. Bernard', *Nouvelle Revue Théologique* 70 (1948) pp. 225–244.
54 Robert of Anjou, ed. cit. pp. 12, 20–21.
55 MS Vatican lat. 4006 f. 309rb.
56 H. Denifle, ed., *Chartularium Universitatis Parisiensis* vol. II, Paris 1891, p. 420.
57 See above, note 44.
58 For the text, ed. Dykmans, see *Rev. d'Hist, Ecclés.* 66 (1971) pp. 413–415; for Lutterell's role, see A. Meier, *Archivum Historiae Pontificiae* 9 (1971) p. 157.
59 In spite of his doctrine of receptacles, Augustine is quite clear that there are two 'times', not three. Cf. *Enarr, in Ps.* 148.1–2 (Corpus Christianorum vol. 40 pp. 2165–2166).
60 *Pour et contre . . .* p. 90.
61 Ed. Dykmans, *Analecta Sacra Tarraconensia* 42 (1969) p. 167.
62 MS Vatican lat. 4006 f.311[r].
63 Texts from John XXII in *Rev. d'Hist. Ecclés.* 66 (1971) p. 415, and *Rech. de Théol. Ancienne et Méd.* 37 (1970) pp. 240–244. The problem is noted, for instance, by Robert of Anjou, ed. cit. pp. 21–22.
64 Cf. *Archivum Franciscanum Historicum* 63 (1970) p. 275.
65 Tautu vol. VIII pp. 11–12.
66 Ibid. p. 46.
67 Alberigo p. 528.

9

The dogmatic definition issued by Benedict XII confirmed one aspect of traditional christian hope: those who are worthy go straight to heaven when they die. There is no break in the continuity of the beatific vision before, at or after the judgment. The obverse is also affirmed to be true: the damned go straight to hell when they die. The only interim condition which is recognised is that of purgatory for those who need it, but even they do not necessarily have to wait until the judgment before being admitted to heaven.

This is a reaffirmation, in more detail and with greater explicitness, of the position the Latins had been maintaining against some orientals, and it appears to leave the last judgment essentially unemployed, so that it is not surprising to find a certain embarrassment in the Latin documents on the subject of the judgment. They all stoutly maintain belief in the judgment, but they rather apologetically introduce the subject with a prefatory 'nevertheless'. This is already the case in the profession of faith sent to Michael Palaeologus by Clement IV, which says, after insisting that the dead go immediately to their reward, 'And nevertheless on the day of judgment all men will appear before the tribunal of Christ, with their bodies, to give an account of what they have done.'[1] A slightly expanded version of the same text appears in Benedict's definition too.[2]

Whatever else he may have achieved, John XXII certainly rubbed people's noses in this embarrassment, by suggesting a theory which would restore a real significance to the last judgment. And he was quite right to claim that the theory he was putting forward for discussion was well grounded in patristic tradition. His weakness, at least from a strategic point of view, was that he ignored the predominant ways in which that tradition had developed in the intervening centuries.

One very important development resulted in such an improvement in the conditions in the 'waiting-room' where the souls of the righteous were regarded as being kept until the judgment that the waiting-room effectively became part of heaven, with the necessary implication that they could be seen as already blessed even before the judgment, but not yet as having all the beatitude that is in store for them. In the context of this development both Bernard, who was one of John XXII's main sources, and Ambrose, who was one of Bernard's main sources, could be read as teaching, not that the saints are deprived of beatitude until the judgment, but that there is either a progress in beatitude until the judgment or at least that there is an increase in beatitude at the judgment.

The process is already beginning in Gennadius' classic *Liber Ecclesiasticorum Dogmatum*: 'After the Lord's ascension into heaven, the souls of the saints are with Christ, and when they depart from the body they go to Christ, waiting for the redemption of their bodies in order to be changed, together with their bodies, into entire and everlasting beatitude.'[3] Although Gennadius is probably intending to state the traditional doctrine of waiting-rooms, he has for all practical purposes let the saints into heaven before the judgment.

By the end of the eighth century the prevailing orthodoxy has changed so thoroughly that this text of Gennadius can be cited as evidence by the anonymous author of an indignant little pamphlet designed to refute the supposedly novel 'heresy' of denying that the saints enter the kingdom of heaven before the last judgment.[4] If Gennadius is reinterpreted like this as meaning simply that the saints are already in heaven, then inevitably his comment on 'entire beatitude' sounds as if what happens at the judgment is a passage from incomplete to complete beatitude.

Another eighth-century text makes this implication rather more explicit. In the commentary on Hosea which probably belongs either to Haimo or to Remigius of Auxerre, the three days alluded to in Hosea 6:2 are given various interpretations, two of which are relevant to our present inquiry. One identifies the first day as baptism, the second as 'the repose of souls', and the third as 'the general resurrection', which gives us the classic three-stage eschatology. But another interpretation identifies the first day as the first coming of Christ in the incarnation, the second as his second coming in glory, 'when he will be seen by everyone', and the third day, on this interpretation, is 'when, after the judgment is finished, he will show the elect a greater glory of his radiance' (*ampliorem gloriam suae demonstrabit claritatis*).[5]

This last suggestion was taken up into the Glossa Ordinaria, getting ascribed to St Jerome in the process, and from there it passed to the *Sentences* of Peter Lombard,[6] who cites it in support of his unhesitatingly affirmative answer to the question 'whether the beatitude of the saints is greater after the judgment'. The derivation of this question from the earlier theory of waiting-rooms is clear, as the Lombard's other evidence comes from Augustine and we are referred back precisely to an earlier distinction, where Augustine is quoted on the 'hidden receptacles' in which souls are kept until the judgment.[7] The other evidence cited from Augustine, not surprisingly, is the passage where he suggests that souls cannot enter fully into beatitude because they are distracted by their natural desire to be united to the body.

Thirteenth-century scholasticism had no use for posthumous waiting-rooms, so the Lombard's question about an increase of beatitude at the judgment effectively becomes a question about whether the resurrection, rather than the judgment, makes any essential difference to beatitude.

The Lombard's belief that perfect beatitude is not attained before the judgment seems to have passed uncontroversially into thirteenth-century theology, except that the resurrection is substituted for the judgment as the crucial factor in complete beatitude. Alexander Nequam seems to feel that he is on safe ground in asserting that 'the soul of Peter is not yet perfectly blessed, since it is deprived of the company of its former host' (*cum consortio hospitis pristini destituta sit*).[8]

In his commentary on the *Sentences* Bonaventure raises the question in a form possibly prompted by William of Auxerre: is the glory of the body part of the substance of beatitude?[9] He answers that it is, at least in the sense that it increases the joy of the saints in a way which is related to the essence of beatitude.

His exposition is a bit perfunctory, in that he does not actually discuss the precise points raised in the authorities he cites to support his conclusion, but it is reasonably clear what he is claiming. His authorities are mostly ones we are already familiar with: Peter Lombard contributes the assertion that after the judgment there will be 'greater joy and greater knowledge',[10] both of which are clearly related to the essence of beatitude. Bernard is adduced as claiming that the soul is so linked to the body that it cannot be brought to its final end (*consummari*) without it.[11] Augustine's suggestion is quoted, that desire for the body holds the soul back from the full enjoyment of the beatific vision.[12] Finally Bonaventure proposes an argument of his own, that perfect beatitude implies the satisfaction of all desires, so the soul cannot be perfectly blessed until its desire for union with the body is satisfied.

In the body of the article he rules out two ways in which, in general, one joy can be greater than another. All the saints enjoy an 'infinite good' (obviously God), so beatitude cannot be varied by any increase in the enjoyability of its object (*ex maiori obiecto*). It can be varied between different saints *ex maiori habitu*, but not in one and the same saint before and after the resurrection. This almost certainly refers to charity: Bonaventure is explicit elsewhere that charity does not increase any further in the blessed,[13] but there is naturally no problem about saying that one saint has greater charity than another and so enjoys the vision of God more.

This leaves us two other ways in which one joy can be greater than another. It may be greater because it is *latius et de pluribus*, a 'broader joy and an enjoyment of more things', or it may be greater because it is a more intense enjoyment of something that was already being enjoyed before. Bonaventure believes that beatitude can be said to be increased by the resurrection in both these ways, *quantum ad extensionem* and *quantum ad intensionem*. It is an enjoyment of more things, because after the resurrection the soul enjoys the glory of the body as well as its own, and also the glory of all those who are saved. How this is to be distinguished from the first kind of increase in beatitude, which Bonaventure ruled out, is not entirely clear. One of the objections raised is precisely that adding a finite good to an infinite good does not produce a greater good, so if the soul is already enjoying the infinite good of the vision of God, the addition of the finite good of the glorified body ought not to make any difference. In response to this objection Bonaventure replies that we are not talking about a greater good, but only about a greater enjoyment of the same good, but this obviously cannot make sense of the claim that beatitude is increased by becoming an enjoyment of more things. And Bonaventure apparently accepts the contention that desire for the body is a distinct desire, needing its own satisfaction if perfect bliss is to be achieved, so I cannot see how we can acquit him of leaving an unresolved muddle here.

The increase in the intensity with which the same object is enjoyed is less problematic. It does not fall foul of the exclusion of any increase *ex maiori habitu*. It seems to me to make sense to say that at a concert you might be thoroughly enjoying the music, while at the same time being distracted by an itchy leg. When the itch ceases your interest in the concert is not changed, but it is now unimpeded, so you can enjoy the music more than you did before.

If there is to be an increase in the intensity of beatitude on this basis at the resurrection, it must be the case that desire for the body constituted a real obstacle to full enjoyment of the beatific vision, so Bonaventure is clearly committed to recognising it as a distinct desire, so he must be taken seriously as meaning that beatitude is incomplete before the resurrection, even though he is careful to safeguard the belief that the essential object of beatitude, the beatific vision, is already definitively given before the resurrection, so that there is no change in the primary object of beatitude.

St Thomas, in his commentary on the *Sentences*,[14] argues along similar lines for a similar conclusion, that the resurrection produces an increase both in the intensity and in the extent of beatitude, but he adds a new argument, that the soul without the body is imperfect, since it is meant to be the form of the body, and as such it is incapable of producing a perfect act (*operatio*). So, since beatitude is an act (*operatio*), the act of the intellect grasping the very nature of God, as far as it can, this means that the soul without the body is incapable of perfect beatitude.

Much the same point is also made by Gerard of Abbeville in a Quodlibet, edited by Dykmans in his edition of the sermons of John XXII, because it was one of the works in John's library which may have influenced his thought.[15]

What John XXII shares with this theological tradition is the belief that the saints are already happy, though not yet perfectly beatified, before the judgment. But he is evidently dissatisfied with the way in which this belief had been expressed. He may in part have been influenced by St Thomas. We should not forget that he not only canonised Thomas, he also read his works fairly thoroughly. And Thomas came to be unhappy about the idea of incomplete beatitude, except with reference to this life. Beatitude proper must mean complete beatitude; anything short of that belongs only to *viatores*, people who have not yet arrived.[16]

Whether or not he was influenced here by St Thomas, John was certainly not satisfied by the current theory of an increase of beatitude at the resurrection. The only diversity he will acknowledge in beatitude is that different saints see God with differing degrees of clarity, but each one is 'perfectly blessed and entirely satisfied with his beatitude, so that he desires nothing more, nor will his degree of beatitude increase, once he has seen God.' And the resurrection cannot, in any case, make any difference to the beatitude of the soul, nor could any soul that was enjoying the vision of God have any concern about regaining its body.[17] Since he could see no way round the scriptural evidence that beatitude is consequent upon the judgment,[18] he concluded that even the saints in heaven are still *viatores* until the judgment.[19] He was also quite clear that the tradition connected beatitude with the judgment, not the resurrection, so he deflects the scholastics' question away from its preoccupation with the difference the glorified body makes to beatitude and brings it back closer to a much older problematic.

The situation facing Benedict XII was therefore rather different from that facing the thirteenth-century theologians. He felt it incumbent on him to insist that the saints do not have to wait until the judgment to enter into eternal life and commence their beatitude. But he seems to have been deeply impressed by John's concern to restore the last judgment to its proper place. So he too takes up and makes a highly original contribution to the question about the increase of beatitude which attends the judgment, and, unlike the earlier scholastics, he attempts to show that it is precisely the judgment, not the resurrection, which is the occasion for this increase.

As pope, he very properly confined his dogmatic definition to the essential minimum that needed official clarification. He was aware that considerable controversy surrounded the further question, whether there is an increase of beatitude at some stage after it is first acquired.[20] So, after publishing his official definition, he also prepared for publication a massive treatise he had compiled, as a cardinal, on the whole controversy about the beatific vision. In the outcome the treatise seems not to have been copied, so it probably never circulated at all widely, and to this day it has never been printed. But it is an extremely interesting attempt to respond to John XXII and well deserves our attention.[21]

Benedict develops his argument slowly and carefully in the third part of his treatise. First he reminds us that God's judgments are threefold: there was the judgment which resulted in the expulsion of Adam and Eve from paradise, there is the continual judgment of our deeds now, and finally there is the last judgment (I). The peculiarity of the last judgment is that only then shall we be able to see the propriety of God's judgments (II). Even the blessed do not yet know all people's merits and demerits, and indeed there are all sorts of things which even the angels do not yet know (III). They do not know the thoughts of men, which are at the source of their merits and demerits. Even we ourselves do not always know our own thoughts (IV). Chapter V underlines the hiddenness of God's judgments, particularly those involved in predestination. Until the judgment the angels do not even know the full list of the predestined (VI). Chapter VII explains on this basis why the last judgment is needed: it is the occasion when God will reveal publicly the reasons for the judgments that have until then remained hidden. It is then that God 'will show clearly to everyone why he judged the way he did in the first two judgments, and why he is judging the way he is in the third judgment, so that any room for complaint about God's judgment will be eliminated.' The next chapter, rather pedantically, unpacks this as meaning that at the last judgment everyone's merits and demerits will be known, so that the rightness of God's judgment will also become clear. Benedict then demonstrates that before the judgment the blessed do not have such knowledge, but they are entitled to want it, and the same goes for the angels too. Thus neither men nor angels will be completely perfect until the judgment, because they will not have all that they can legitimately desire. So until then beatitude is not entirely complete, on Augustine's principle that no one is blessed unless he has all that he wants (provided, of course, that he wants nothing improperly, which is presumably the case with regard to the saints in heaven, and anyway Benedict reiterates his conviction that it is quite proper for us to want to know our own and everyone else's merits).[22] So until the judgment:

> neither angels nor men will be fully blessed. Though they see the essence of God and are blessed, as far as that is concerned, because they already have the thing that is most important (*summum*) in beatitude, all the same, they do not have all that they legitimately want or could legitimately want, because they do not know the merits and demerits and the secrets of the hearts of angels and men, and so they are not yet fully blessed according to Augustine's definition of beatitude. And beatitude is also the condition which is complete with its collection of all goods,[23] and this collection of all goods does not exist where there is ignorance or lack of knowledge of things such as we have mentioned.(IX)

Chapter X assures us that after the judgment 'the book of God's foreknowledge and predestination' will be opened for the elect to see, which means that they will have a clearer and more perfect vision of God's essence than they have now and they will accordingly be more blessed than they are now. Merely seeing God's essence, without seeing in it the rationale of his will and particularly of predestination, is less satisfying than seeing God's essence and at the same time seeing in it his whole will and plan for creation and how he has brought his plan to fulfilment. A cause, as Benedict points out, is better known when it is known why it produces the effects it does, and an artist's art is better understood when his method of working and his purposes and intentions are known. So, Benedict triumphantly concludes in chapter XI, the angels and the blessed make a lot of progress in knowledge and in beatitude up to the day of judgment, and only after that do they make no more progress, because then they will have gained perfect knowledge of everything they can legitimately desire to know. The doctrine that the angels make progress up to the judgment is asserted on the authority of Peter Lombard,[24] and Benedict says that he sees no reason why the same should not apply to the souls of the blessed as well.

Chapter XII takes up Augustine's point about desire for the body preventing the saints from giving themselves fully to enjoying the beatific vision, and XIII argues, on this basis, that the saints will have a greater enjoyment of God in love after the resurrection, because until then their love is to some extent divided, as their love for their own bodies prevents a complete abandonment of themselves to loving God.

Chapter XIV ends the exposition with the claim that after the judgment God will reveal himself in far more ways than before, so that that is when the blessed will reap their full reward, and this is why the saints have written much more about beatitude after the judgment than they have about beatitude before the judgment – an argument which is, of course, designed to disarm the authorities cited by John XXII.

Like Bonaventure, Benedict is arguing for an increase in beatitude at the judgment both *extensive* and *intensive*, but he reserves far more for this second phase of beatitude than Bonaventure was prepared to do. Although theoretically he had committed himself to the identity of beatitude before and after the judgment, which is presumably meant to be secured by the doctrine that before and after the judgment alike the blessed have a direct vision of God's essence, according to Benedict's theory God greatly increases the clarity and the scope of his revelation of his own essence after the judgment, so that the increase in the blessedness of the saints can truly be regarded as deriving *ex maiori obiecto*, something which Bonaventure rejected out of hand, even at the cost of a certain confusion. And the expansion of the object of beatitude is, rather cleverly, associated with the judgment itself, inasmuch as it consists in the revelation of what had previously been the hidden judgments of God, or the hidden rationale of those judgments. So for Benedict, as for John XXII, the full revelation of God's essence is reserved till the judgment, and until then there is ample scope for the blessed to make progress, so that Benedict goes a long way towards conceding John's claim that the blessed are still *viatores* until the judgment.

Before the judgment then, the blessed still have to take a lot on trust and they still have much to hope for, which is why Benedict has to emphasise, in his dogmatic definition, that it is only faith and hope in their strict sense as theological virtues that lapse in the blessed.[25] The point is taken from Peter Lombard,[26] but unfortunately the text of the Lombard, which Benedict quotes and develops in chapter XIX of the first part of his treatise, rather undermines Benedict's own explanation of why there is still so much left to hope for at the judgment. The Lombard maintains that, even though the blessed are still hoping for the resurrection, they already have a very clear vision, in the Word of God, of both the resurrection and the judgment. Benedict rather labours this point: there is no room left for the theological virtue of hope precisely because the trust and expectation of the blessed are combined with such a clear vision of what is to come. How this clear anticipatory vision in the Word can be squared with the ignorance which is later postulated to secure a real role for the judgment as revealing much that people previously wanted to know, and did not know, is far from obvious.

Benedict's theory is not without some inherent difficulties, but it provides us with an unusually clear and extreme statement of the view that complete beatitude is not given until the judgment, and it connects the completeness far more seriously than previous theologians had done with the judgment rather than the resurrection. In a way which is somewhat reminiscent of Ambrose's position in the *De Bono Mortis* Benedict allows for continual progress up to the judgment, and he makes it quite clear that the incompleteness of beatitude until then concerns the very heart of beatitude, namely the vision of God's essence.

At the other extreme is the mature doctrine of St Thomas Aquinas.

St Thomas' basic instinct manifestly favours a two-stage rather than a three-stage eschatology. There is this life and the hereafter, not this life, the hereafter and then, as it were, the thereafter. Already in his commentary on book II of the *Sentences* he invokes this principle against the Lombard's belief that the angels continue to make progress in the knowlege of God until the judgment. Just as we are *viatores* only until the time of our death, so the angels were *viatores* only up to the time of their confirmation. At that point they arrived at their goal, so they attained 'the final perfection of beatitude, and no longer make further progress in the vision of God, in which their beatitude essentially consists.' To say anything else, in Thomas' view, smacks of the 'Greek error' of denying that human souls go to their reward before the judgment.[27]

In the first part of the *Compendium Theologiae*, dating probably from about the middle of Thomas' career, if not earlier, he gives a succinct account of his view of human destiny:

> The fulfilment (*consummatio*) of man consists in his attainment of his final end, which is perfect beatitude or happiness, consisting in the vision of God, as has already been demonstrated. The vision of God results in the immutability of both intellect and will: of intellect, because when it has reached the first cause, in which all things can be understood, the intellect's search comes to an end. The mobility of the will ceases, because, once the final end is reached, in which there is a fulness of all goodness, nothing remains to be desired. The will changes only because it desires something it does not yet have. So it is clear that the final fulfilment of man consists in perfect stillness (*quietatione*) or immobility, both with regard to the intellect and with regard to the will.
>
> It has already been shown that immobility brings us under the rubric of eternity. Time, with its before and after, is caused by movement, so when movement is eliminated, before and

> after cease, so we are left with eternity, which exists all together (*quae est tota simul*). So in his final fulfilment man attains to eternity of life, not only in the sense that he lives immortally with regard to his soul, which is natural to the rational soul, but also in the sense that he is brought to perfect immobility.[28]

The only fly in the ointment, at this stage in the development of Thomas' thought, is the difficulty of reconciling this perfect immobility with the need to recognise that, until the resurrection, there is still unfinished business. In the *Compendium*, as in the commentary on the *Sentences*, Thomas still feels obliged to say that beatitude is incomplete until the soul is reunited with the body. As he argues in the *Compendium*:

> There cannot be a complete immobility of the will unless its natural desire is totally fulfilled; and things that were born to be naturally united naturally desire to be united with one another . . . So, since the human soul is naturally united with the body, it has a natural desire to be united with the body, so the will will not be able to be entirely still until the soul is joined to the body, that is, until the resurrection of man from death.

Thomas also proposes a development of the argument found in the commentary on the *Sentences*: final perfection presupposes the 'first perfection' of being complete according to the nature of what you are, and, in the case of human beings, that means being bodily, since a disembodied human soul is not a complete human being. So man's final beatitude requires that the soul should be reunited with the body. Thirdly it is unnatural for the soul to exist on its own without the body, and nothing unnatural can endure for ever. So, since the soul itself is incorruptible, it must be reunited with the body.[29]

It is clear that this concession goes against the basic thrust of Thomas' position, which is to say that, once the vision of God is attained, there is nothing more to be desired, and in the *Summa* Thomas tries to find another way of dealing with the resurrection. In I.II q.4 a.5 we find all the arguments Thomas had previously used featuring now as objections, which alerts us at once to the fact that Thomas has changed his mind fairly radically about what he wants to say. Objection 1 is the argument from the *Compendium* about natural perfection being presupposed by beatitude. Objection 2 is the argument from the commentary on the *Sentences* on the impossibility of a perfect *operatio* proceeding from something that exists imperfectly. Objection 3 makes the same point more epigrammatically: beatitude is the perfection of a human being, and a disembodied soul is not a human being. So beatitude cannot exist in a soul which is not in the body. Objection 4 is the familiar point from Augustine about natural desire for the body impeding the soul from enjoying heaven fully. Objection 5 is another familiar argument, that beatitude involves the satisfaction of every desire, so cannot be present unless the desire for union with the body is satisfied. Objection 6 takes up a detail from the Augustinian point adduced in objection 4, which we need not bother ourselves with here.

It is a pity that Thomas had not changed his mind sooner and thought through the implications in a more leisurely way. Most of the *Summa* was written at high speed, and this may explain why there is a certain wobbliness in the article we are presently considering, in which the body of the article appears to concede an important point, which the answers to the objections do not concede. But we must surely interpret the article in the light of the objections and the answers to them. And in these answers Thomas argues: (1) beatitude is an intellectual perfection, and the intellect transcends the body, and so a disembodied soul lacks no perfection which is required for beatitude. (2) The soul is not just the form of the body, it exists in its own right, so it can exist perfectly on its own and produce its own operations perfectly. (3) Beatitude is in the intellect, and so can continue to be there as long as the intellect remains, and on this basis the human being whose intellect it is can be said to be blessed. Thomas illustrates this claim with the remarkably silly example of a black man who is white, inasmuch as his teeth are white, which remains true even if his teeth are all pulled out. They are still his teeth, and so, in their regard, he is still white. The response to the fourth and fifth objections tries to clarify exactly in what sense the blessed soul desires reunion with the body and in what sense this desire can be said to hamper beatitude. Thomas excludes the possibility of anything actually interfering with the soul's enjoyment of bliss, but the lack of the body prevents beatitude from being perfect in every way. The soul is not held back from its own enjoyment of God, but it would like the body to share in that enjoyment. The desire of the soul is entirely satisfied *ex parte appetibilis*: there is nothing left to be desired. But it is not entirely at rest *ex parte appetentis*. The soul does not yet enjoy bliss in every way it would like to. This is not totally coherent, but one can see what Thomas is trying to get at. I can be perfectly happy admiring the scenery, even if I am conscious of wishing that Mary Jane was there to enjoy it too. But strictly speaking Thomas has ruled out even this kind of wish, if there is really nothing left to be desired *ex parte appetibilis*. So it cannot be a matter of my wishing Mary Jane were there too, but of knowing that she too would have enjoyed the view. Thomas ought, in all rigour, to have said that there is nothing more to be desired, but there is something else which is still desiring it (*ex parte appetentis*). But it would be awkward to ascribe desires directly to dead bodies, so the desire has to be ascribed to the soul in some way. It is clear that Thomas is at least trying to minimise the damage done by this admission.

In the body of the article, Thomas distinguishes between perfect and imperfect beatitude. The latter is all that is possible in this life, and it is impossible without the body. Perfect beatitude is reserved to the hereafter and it does not require the body, except in a very reduced sense. Thomas makes a distinction between what is necessary for something to exist and what is necessary for its *bene esse*. A soul is necessary for a human being to exist at all; it is necessary in the first sense. Good looks and quick wits are not necessary in this sense, but they do contribute to human *bene esse*. It is only in this weaker sense that the body is necessary for beatitude. And here Thomas apparently concedes what he denies in the answers to the objections: the soul will possess its own operation more perfectly the more perfect it is in its own nature, and the perfection of its nature requires union with the body.

Assuming that Thomas is not intending to contradict himself, we must take this apparent contradiction as minimally as possible. The absence of the body, he has said, means that beatitude does not have every conceivable kind of perfection. But he is clearly arguing that even the disembodied soul lacks no perfection which is strictly necessary even for complete beatitude, so the body can only contribute an accidental or incidental kind of perfection, such as might be contributed by having a brilliant soprano who was also dazzlingly good-looking.

In the later article on the last judgment (III q.59 a.5), which we have already looked at, Thomas argues that the soul has already achieved its definitive beatitude at the particular judgment; what is left for the last judgment concerns essentially the role of any individual life in the story of the whole world. As part of this public dimension, it is appropriate that bodies should at last receive their reward (ad 3). It is not clear that anything actually happens which can make any real difference to the souls which are already blessed, especially as such souls have already been able to see, in God, all that concerns them including, apparently, future contingents, which would presumably include such things as the resurrection and the judgment.[30]

Thomas' basic conviction remains that, once beatitude is reached, as soon after death as the soul is ready for it, there is nothing more to be desired. The resurrection thus inevitably appears as rather an embarrassment. The story is already complete before the resurrection, and Thomas is very insistent on this aspect of decisive arrival. Once it is attained, there is no more change. Beatitude is a participation in eternity.[31] Similarly the whole world will reach a definitive and unchanging condition. In St Paul's words, 'The figure of this world passes' (1 Cor. 7:31). The present world order is set up to sustain the life of human beings who have not yet reached their goal, and all the movement that goes on in it is in view of this goal. After the judgment the human race will have reached its final goal, so there will be no further need for any movement, as Thomas argues. The whole world, in the new creation, will therefore be immobile. The renewed heavenly bodies, which constitute our present index of time, will stop moving, so, as it says in Apoc. 10.6, 'There will be no more time'. With the cessation of the movement of the heavenly bodies, all other movement will cease.[32]

The only exception to this final immobility will be the resurrected bodies of the saints. Thomas' view of the significance of these resurrected bodies is not unlike that of Gregory of Nyssa. The saints will have no need to move, since their every desire is already satisfied. But they will move simply to express the well-being of their souls.[33] So we have the rather surrealistic picture of a renewed creation, in which nothing at all is moving except the saints, who move, as it were, simply for the fun of it.[34]

Once again the resurrection constitutes an embarrassment in an otherwise simple picture of individual lives, and then the whole creation, arriving at a definitive end and therefore stopping. The end of time leaves eternity in full possession of the field, and in eternity there is no successiveness, no before and after. According to Boethius' classic definition, it is a complete possession of life *all at once* (*tota simul*).[35] Inasmuch as it sees everything in God, the soul can see everything at once.[36] Similarly it does not need the variety of external goods, because it can enjoy all that such goods could provide by enjoying them in God, who is the 'supreme source of goods'.[37]

This last point acts as an antidote to the impression one could get that Thomas' idea of beatitude is rather narrow. He is not saying that we shall see God and that must suffice, he is saying that we shall see God and, in seeing God, enjoy all that we are capable of enjoying, but doing so all at once in him. It is a comprehensive, not an exclusive, beatitude.

We also need to bear in mind the standard procedures of negative theology. To say that beatitude is eternal and therefore non-successive does not mean that all the richness of time is lost, it means that it is retained, but without the concomitant impoverishment which is inseparable from successiveness. We can get some idea of what this means (though inevitably not much) by considering what it means to hear a whole symphony. At what point do you hear a whole symphony? To hear it all at once within time would, of course, mean the most appalling cacophony. But even in time it is possible to hear a whole symphony, not just to hear a sequence of bits of symphony. The bits add up to a whole. Eternity is this sort of *tota simul possessio* enhanced far beyond our present comprehension.

To say that beatitude is eternal and therefore not, in any ordinary sense, in time, is to claim for it all the intensity which we sometimes find in peculiarly rich moments of enjoyment, but in such a way that there is no longer any inevitable decline from that intensity, as there must always be in time. It is to suggest that, though such moments cannot in any way be prolonged – duration can only be the death of them – they can still be kept.

Thomas' account of beatitude, as the triumphant and definitive arrival of a human story at its proper and blissful conclusion, apart from his manifest embarrassment about the resurrection, seems to me to make far more sense than the picture given by Benedict XII. Thomas retains what I take to be the basic christian tradition that the end of the human story has to be situated at death; and this is also in line with the human problematic we were looking at earlier, with the help of various classical texts.

It must also be right – this is something John XXII saw – to assign the bestowal of the essential reward to the end of a human story, not to its middle. There is a basic flaw in Benedict XII's story line. It is just silly to envisage souls reaching the beatific vision of the divine essence and then fussing about their bodies or about why Aunt Jane is in heaven and Uncle Tom is not. If Benedict's theory were right, the human story would be like a love story in which the happy couple fall into each other's arms about two thirds of the way through the book, but cannot live happily ever after just yet because she has lost her shopping list. The rest of the book then describes how she eventually finds her shopping list and *then* they can all live happily ever after.

The presence of the body must either matter totally or not at all. It makes perfectly good sense to say, as John XXII wanted to, that without the body the soul is simply not a fit subject for beatitude. Or you can say, as I suspect Thomas wanted to say, that the soul can get on perfectly well without the body, in which case it can simply ignore the fact of its own disembodiment. But I doubt whether it makes sense to say that the body matters a little, so that the soul can be quite happy without it, enjoying the vision of God, but all the same the absence of the body niggles it.

However, if it is right to say that beatitude essentially belongs to human beings, not to human souls, we cannot leave the resurrection out of the picture entirely. So what are we going to make of it? That, in the immortal words of the bard, is the question.

NOTES

1 Tautu vol. V i p. 66.
2 Ibid. vol. VIII p. 12.
3 *Lib. Eccl. Dog.* 45; ed. C. H. Turner, *Journal of Theological Studies* 7 (1906) p. 97.
4 PL 96:1384B.
5 PL 117:48A.
6 IV *Sent.* d.49 c.4.
7 IV *Sent.* d.45 c.1.
8 *Speculum Speculationum*, ed. cit. p. 22.
9 Bonaventure, IV *Sent.* d.49, Quaracchi 1889, pp. 1012–1013. William of Auxerre maintains that the glorification of the body is not, properly, part of beatitude, though he appears to take it for granted that the soul is 'more blessed' after the resurrection: *Summa Aurea* III, ed. J. Ribaillier, Grottaferrata 1986, pp. 93, 249.
10 IV *Sent.* d.49 c.4.2.
11 *De Diligendo Deo* 11.30.
12 *De Gen. ad Litt.* 12.35.
13 I *Sent.* d.17, p. 317.
14 IV *Sent.* d.49 q.1 a.4 q.1.
15 *Sermons* pp. 45–50.
16 Cf. *Summa Theol.* I.II q.4 a.5, q.5 a.4, III q.59 a.5.
17 *Sermons* pp. 137–138.
18 Cf. ibid. p. 152.
19 See the text edited in *Rech. de Théol. Anc. et Méd.* 37 (1970) p. 244. An unidentified critic pointed out the awkwardness of maintaining that the saints before the judgment are both *viatores* and *in patria* (*Pour et contre* . . . p. 212).
20 Cf. the preface edited by A. Meier in *Archivum Hist. Pont.* 7 (1969) pp. 147–158, especially p. 151.
21 The only known copy of the work is in MS Vatican lat. 4006. The third tractate, on the increase of beatitude, which is what will chiefly concern us here, occupies fols. 33^{v}–66^{r}. Since the tractate is clearly structured, I shall give references to its chapter numbers, not to individual folios.
22 Benedict refers to Augustine, *De Trinitate* 13.5.8.
23 This is Boethius' classic definition, *Cons. Phil.* III prose 2.
24 II *Sent.* d.11 c.2.
25 Tautu vol. VIII p. 12: Actus fidei et spei in eis evacuant, prout fides et spes proprie theologicae sunt virtutes.
26 III *Sent.* d.26 c.4.
27 II *Sent.* d.11 q.2 a.1.
28 *Compendium Theologiae* 149–150.

29 Ibid. 151.
30 Cf. C. J. Peter, *Participated Eternity in the Vision of God*, Rome 1964, pp. 54–67.
31 *Summa Theol.* I.II q.5 a.4 ad 1.
32 *Contra Gentiles* IV 97.
33 Ibid. IV 86.
34 Cf. *Compendium Theologiae* 171.
35 *Cons. Phil.* V prose 6. Cf. Augustine, *Ep.* 130.8.15 (commenting on *omnes dies* in Ps. 26:4), 'There "all the days" do not happen by coming and going, nor is the beginning of one day the end of another; they are all endlessly all at once (*omnes sine fine simul sunt*).'
36 *Summa Theol.* I q.12 a.10.
37 Ibid. I.II q.4 a.7 ad 2.

10

All is not yet clear. Nevertheless before probing further into the darkness let us review where we have got to so far. Are we in sight of a plausible account of christian eschatology, which will do justice both to the data of revelation and to the human requirements we have identified?

I have suggested that there are certain difficulties involved in the idea of human immortality, not least the risk that it will leave human life shapeless and that it will tend to trivialise our story by trivialising its ending, which is death. The christian doctrine of eternal life, understood as meaning a participation in eternity, beyond time, certainly avoids the problem of leaving life shapeless: it secures a decisive end to the story, a point of arrival beyond which, in a sense, nothing more 'happens'. And if eternal life is seen as enfolding, not just as superseding, the life lived in time, it cannot be accused of trivialising life.

The envisaged end is a genuine dénouement of the story. This is assured both by the traditional insistence that it is this mortal life and the whole of this mortal life that is judged, even if it is judged on the basis of how it ends (to cater for last-minute conversions or defections), and by the Augustinian doctrine of merit, which makes glory the culmination and fulfilment of the whole process of grace working in this life. And the triumphant outcome does not blot out all the ambiguities and upsets that have gone before. This is the point of Benedict XII's view that we shall all finally know the rationale of God's judgments, and of the scholastic belief that the saints remember their past sins and that such remembrance is part of their bliss.[1] Redemption would not make sense without an awareness of the mess that needed redemption. Julian of Norwich is only giving a more dramatic expression to this sober scholastic doctrine when she says that in the hereafter sin shall be no longer shame to man, but rather worship. It is an essential part of the glory of the saints that they are saints with a shady past.[2]

Prescinding, for the moment, from the problems posed by damnation, there seems to be a good chance that the christian doctrine of eternal life does provide a viable way of shaping and understanding human lives.

It is sometimes objected that christianity offers pie in the sky as a basically irrelevant consolation for a uselessly miserable life. It is not enough in response to say that the risen Christ bears the marks of his passion, just as dead heroes in the Homeric Hades bear the traces of their dying,[3] though this does support the essential minimum claim that the risen life is stamped by at least some of the tragedy that characterises this life. But if the same pie could be had by the same person in the same sky without all the antecedent pains, the happy ending would still be basically irrelevant to the rest of the story, in the same way that the immortalising of Peleus at the end of Euripides' *Andromache* is.

One aspect of the question can be formulated quite precisely: if the new life, typified by the risen Christ, is what human existence was all along meant to be about, why were human beings not simply created like the risen Christ at the outset? This is the question Irenaeus is raising, when he asks why Adam was not created perfect. His answer is surely the right one: human beings are intrinsically such that they grow to maturity over a period of time. Being a fully developed human being is, in this regard, like knowing how to ride a bicycle or speak French. We would not know what to make of a claim that some newly discovered drug could impart instantaneously the ability to ride a bicycle or speak French. Such skills result from the acquisition of certain bodily and mental habits and are therefore necessarily skills with a history behind them. Similarly, if Adam had been created perfect at the outset, he would have been an entirely different sort of being.

Redemption means the redemption of particular people with particular histories, and the eternal life they finally enjoy is *their* eternal life because it is the eternal life given to people with these histories. They are what they are in their eternal bliss because of what they have done and been through in this mortal life.

There seems to be no objection to saying, following Irenaeus' hint, that all the works of God throughout the whole of time constitute the *plasmatio hominis*, the fashioning of man. Eternal life is the taking possession, all at once, of a whole lifetime, including all its details, in a final perfection which makes such a lifetime precisely a whole.

So what is the difference between the christian enjoying his pie in the sky, precisely as the person he has become as the result of all he has gone through, and Peleus enjoying his immortality with Thetis precisely as the person he has become as the result of all he has gone through? One crucial difference is that Thetis is not claimed to have been responsible for the whole previous career of

Peleus, so the connection between the happy ending and the painful story is fortuitous. This is essentially the point raised by Irenaeus against the Gnostics: he can tell a more plausible tale than they can, because he believes that the whole human story is governed by a single divine will, whereas they do not.

Peleus could well ask Thetis why she did not intervene sooner, before all the disasters struck, and it would make a lot of difference if it transpired that she had been keeping a watchful eye on the situation the whole way through and had chosen exactly the right moment to come and make him immortal; if it turned out that she had not given him a thought for years, he could reasonably complain that the whole thing had been thoroughly badly managed. The christian doctrine of creation and providence allows for a strong claim that the whole thing has been excellently managed, even if at times it appeared to have got out of hand. A good author can afford to let us think he has lost control of his own tale, so long as he has not really lost control and can bring the whole story to a proper conclusion in the last chapter.

It also makes a considerable difference to the story that Peleus was not in any way aiming at the denouement effected at the last minute by Thetis. The conclusion of his story is therefore not in any real sense the fulfilment of his story. Christians, by contrast, hope for an eternal life which will be the fulfilment of their own most serious aspirations. It may be very nice to be offered pie in the sky, when all you wanted was a cup of tea on earth, but it cannot help but be an essentially irrelevant, even if welcome, boon, like boarding a boat to go to Boulogne and arriving in Dieppe and discovering that Dieppe is really a much nicer place. Where we are talking about the final goal of a whole human life, this is a very serious difficulty.

The specifically christian doctrine of redemption allows us to develop this point further. There is continuity and discontinuity involved. The ante mortem story does not simply carry on into the post mortem situation. Christian belief teaches, not just that a mortal life reaches its triumphant conclusion in immortality, but that a human life that fails is recreated gloriously by the God who created and moulded that life, and whose continuity of creative purpose guarantees that the final glory is not just the denouement of the story, but also the remedy for its failures.

This may look like cheating, but is it? Suppose I struggle for years to ride a bicycle and die without ever having succeeded. In the resurrection I find I am able to ride a bicycle. That is surely quite different from, say, a tone-deaf, hoarse-voiced Philistine, who had never given a thought to music in his life, being resurrected with the voice and musical skills of Maria Callas. That would be cheating.

The doctrine of redemption allows us to say that glory is not the crowning of a successful life, nor is it the completion of a steady process of development. It is rather the imparting of success as a gift to people who had been struggling and often failing to lead an adequately human life. Death can thus be seen as the final failure of a failing life, but it is redeemed, so that its finality becomes the fulfilment of a process of divine creating instead of being the last petering out of a series of failures. Life is authentically fulfilled in a glory of which it was not intrinsically capable on its own. Its fulfilment, that is, is 'supernatural'.

If we are puzzled as to how failure can be fulfilled in glory, it is a familiar puzzle. Much of the time involved in learning how to ride a bicycle is spent falling off bicycles and falling off bicycles does not, on the face of it, lead naturally to staying on bicycles. Yet the eventual ability to stay on the bicycle is the legitimate consequence of all the failures to stay on the bicycle.

It is the doctrine of redemption, not just that of the resurrection, which raises questions about identity. We may certainly wonder whether the healthy thirty-year old[4] we meet at the resurrection is the same person as the one whose decline into senility and decrepitude had so distressed us in this world. We may even more emphatically wonder whether the athletic thirty-year old in front of us is really the same person as the baby we buried at the age of two months. This is where it is tempting to invoke the immortality of the soul, as Gregory of Nyssa and Nemesius did, to guarantee the identity of the person who died with the person who is resurrected. But there is just the same problem about the identity of the soul. Is this soul basking in the radiant clarity of eternal truth really Uncle Jack, whom we last saw pottering aimlessly round the geriatric ward? Is this other illumined soul really Aunt Mabel, who died convinced (wrongly) that she was the empress Josephine?

If the soul is to be the guarantee of identity at the resurrection, it rather looks as if Aunt Mabel may have to be resurrected as the empress Josephine, which would pose interesting legal problems for the last judgment to sort out. Unless, of course, we are going to appeal to the soul as meaning something other than the actual contents of someone's mental life – the Real Person lurking in the depths beneath the vagaries of consciousness, like the Real Insect that sustains the continuity of identity between the caterpillar, the chrysalis and the butterfly. I am not convinced that such talk of Real Persons and Real Insects is anything more than a confusing way of simply postulating that there is continuity of identity.

There is no need for christians to quarrel with Derek Parfit (or the Buddhists) and insist that identity is vested in some 'Deep Fact', which exists apart from the patterns of continuity and connectedness which compose what we normally mean by a person and the life of a person,[5] though christians (and Buddhists) might disagree with Parfit about where such stories end. Nor need we be unduly bothered by tricky cases, such as Parfit devises for the discomfiture of people who want to insist on some 'Deep Fact'. If Tom, Dick or Harry are three identical triplets and, at a certain juncture, for good medical reasons, Tom's brain is cut in two and Dick and Harry receive half each instead of their own brains, I should not be thrown into any particular quandary if I were their parish priest. If Dick and Harry want to claim Tom's property, on the grounds that they are Tom, I shall not support them; they must inherit his property in the normal way. If they are all good christians, I shall presume that they will be resurrected as a glorified Tom, Dick and Harry, not as Tom, Tom and Tom. But that does not mean that there is some deep Dickness and Harriness there, which is unaffected by the two brothers' change of brain. All I would say is that the story which culminates in their resurrection poses some unusual problems of integration, which I am happy to leave God to sort out at the last judgment.

If we do not appeal to some 'Deep Fact' to guarantee continuity of identity, how are we going to formulate our confidence that the redeemed person is the same as the person who died? We cannot have heaven full of people wondering who they are, like the unfortunate ghost in Diana Wynne Jones' book, *The Time of the Ghost*, who spends most of the book trying to work out who she is.

The prayer, *Deus cui omnia mortalia vivunt*, suggests that we can simply refer the matter to God: the continuity between ante and post mortem existence resides in the fact that what is dead is always alive to God. As it says in the limerick, the tree in the quad will continue to be 'since observed by yours faithfully, God'. This appeal to the creator to guarantee the identity of the resurrected has not been noticeably popular with philosophers,[6] but perhaps it deserves another run for its money.

Imagine you find me, one day, engaged in drawing what appears to be a giraffe. Later on you find me tinkering with it so that it begins to look less like a giraffe. After I have tinkered with it for some weeks it does not look like a giraffe at all, it looks much more like a winged rhinoceros. I assure you that that was what I was really working towards all along. In a sense you have to take my word for it that I have been working on a single drawing all these weeks, not on a succession of different drawings. Nor would it make any significant difference if, instead of tinkering with the original drawing, I threw away one draft after another and started again.

In the case of a human artist, we should probably say that he spent all those weeks *trying* to produce the drawing he wanted, and naturally we cannot say this about God; it does not make sense to talk of God *trying* to do something. But if both my drawing and my waste-paper basket survive, art historians may see how much light is shed on the famous winged rhinoceros by all the earlier drafts, and, if they are prudent, they will confine themselves to telling the story of the drawing without presuming to reconstruct the story of what was going on in the artist's mind. And that would give us a tolerably good analogy to use in speaking about the story of the artefact which is a human life, whose artist is God. The history is part of the reality of the artefact, and it is the history of a single artefact, even if the end-product is quite unlike what was there to start with. We are back with Irenaeus' explanation of why Adam was not created perfect.

Does this analogy suffice to secure the right sort of identity, though? Unlike a drawing of a winged rhinoceros, human beings are expected to have a certain awareness of themselves. Does the intention of the creator suffice to establish my identity in my own eyes?

I do not see why it should not, provided that the creator succeeds the whole way through in creating *me*; and there are problems in supposing that he might fail to do that, if that is what he intends to do. Something must have gone very wrong if I disagree with my creator about who I am – Adam, as it were, insisting that he is really Eve. Maybe hell is like that. Presumably part of what it means for God to create me is that I *am* me, with whatever self-awareness that entails, and I do not think we need, for our present purposes, to go into difficult philosophical questions about what it means for me to know that I am me. If God creates or recreates a life-story designated by the name 'Tugwell', and identifies me as the person whose story it is, I do not quite see what it would mean for me to challenge the identification. Even if there is a considerable difference between the resurrected me and the sorry specimen I am now, I do not see why I should not happily say at the resurrection, 'So that's what I was meant to be!'

Obviously some memory of what I was is required, but no more than could be produced by God creating certain memories in me afresh, as he would presumably have to do anyway if I died in a state of total amnesia. The only problem would be if the memories I have at the resurrection do not actually correspond to anything that happened. But that would mean either that God was mistaken in his identification of me, or that he was lying when he declared me to be the resurrected Tugwell. And that would be suspiciously like God saying, 'Let there be light', while actually creating a banana. And that cannot mean anything.

What God creates and what exists must coincide. Since, ex hypothesi, we are talking about a continuity of creative purpose in the creator, there must be a corresponding continuity of identity in the creature. And if, as is generally supposed, the blessed see creatures in God, they must see creatures as God sees them. If he says that a particular sequence is the story of a single life, the blessed will all *see* it as such.

This seems to me an acceptable, if perhaps not terribly informative, scenario. But we can without detriment, I think, back down a bit and admit that what we are really saying is that we do not know what happens to the dead, except that they disappear from our view and we believe them to be alive to God in some sense, so that what we perceive as a break in the continuity of their existence is not an interrruption of their existence in the sight of God, whatever that may mean for them. As the old prayer has it, even their bodies do not perish in his sight, but are changed into something better.

There would certainly be something very odd about a doctrine of resurrection ex nihilo, without any kind of continuity of existence between the person who died and the person who was resurrected. That would smack very much of the production of a replica of the dead person, rather than a genuine resurrection of the same person. This is the main reason, at least until a relatively recent period, why christians have appealed to the immortality of the soul. As Nequam rather engagingly remarks, there would be no point in the soul surviving except in order to receive the fulness of glory in a resurrected body.[7] Apart from its usefulness in interpreting and reinforcing belief in the resurrection, christian tradition is remarkably uninterested in claiming immortality for the soul by right, and the language of the Bible and the liturgy is, if anything, inimical to such a claim, treating immortality rather as something belonging only to God by right and then, by God's gift, to the risen Christ and those who are saved in him as a result of the resurrection. It is a hope proposed to the believer, not a property inherent in the human soul. The only formal appearance of immortality by right in christian doctrine is, as we have seen, in the ill-conceived Bull of Leo X, which was intended to settle a philosophical, not a doctrinal, dispute.

All that christian orthodoxy is concerned to secure can surely be adequately safeguarded without appealing to any sort of 'hybrid' view of human nature. The coincidence of mortality and immortality, of life and death, in the believer rests on the coincidence of divinity and humanity in Christ. Christian belief does not require the ascription of immortality or even life to the soul on its own.[8] If there is a life which the believer has, which is not reducible to the life of the psychosomatic person, it is the supernatural life which belongs essentially and by right to Christ, which the believer shares by grace. Such dogmatic authority as has been given to the phrase 'the immortality of the soul' can be squared with the mainstream of christian tradition most simply by interpreting it as insisting on the immortality of the human person, and that can be taken as meaning essentially the belief that, by the act of God, there is something there even after death which can be judged by God and awarded either eternal life or everlasting damnation.

The dificulty, as we have seen, is to combine a doctrine of immediate post mortem beatitude with a doctrine of the resurrection of the body and the last judgment. John XXII's attempt to postpone beatitude until after the judgment, which eliminates the suggestion that something less than a full human person can enjoy beatitude, was ruled to be unacceptable. So we seem to be left either with Benedict's picture of essentially, but incompletely, happy souls, enjoying the vision of God, but still fussing over little details until the judgment, or Thomas' picture of completely happy souls, which appear to have no need at all for any resurrection of the body or any further judgment, and which cannot in any case be waiting for the resurrection, since they are not in time.

If we start with Thomas' conviction that the blessed, if they are that at all, must be entirely blessed, we must conclude that the resurrection and the judgment are either not future to them or that they do not matter to them. After the attainment of entire beatitude, it is inconceivable that there is more to come which is of any concern.

The suggestion that the resurrection, at any rate, may not be future to the blessed is, on the face of it, supported by *Deus cui omnia mortalia vivunt*, with its statement that bodies do not perish, but are changed into something better. And, if we take up the Lombard's point that the blessed already have a clear vision, in God's Word, of the resurrection and the judgment, it becomes even more tempting to say that, from the point of view of the blessed, there really is nothing more to happen. And Thomas does in fact come clean and admit that, for the blessed, nothing is future.[9]

Christian eschatology, as we have seen, comes in two-stage and three-stage varieties, but I have suggested that the three-stage varieties are all attempts to harmonise two apparently divergent two-stage eschatologies, and I have also argued that they are all unsatisfactory. The essential tradition is a two-stage doctrine, and whatever theory we end up with ought, I submit, to retain this basic form.

Rather than trying to merge the two different two-stage eschatologies, we should say that the second stage, the one that concerns the hereafter, calls for a sort of split screen, just as Homeric eschatology did. Homer's dead heroes are both in Hades and lying on the battlefield, and christian eschatology similarly supports the propriety of saying both that the dead are in heaven and that they are in their tombs. Both Wordsworth and his little maid are right, she in insisting that 'Two of us in the churchyard lie' and he in trying to persuade her that 'they two are in heaven.'[10]

The reason why the resurrection has to be regarded as future is that we find ourselves in possession of corpses. People who go to heaven without leaving their corpses behind them are treated as having anticipated the resurrection by translation or assumption, people like Enoch and Elijah and the Virgin Mary and, on a more generous view, Moses and St John too, not to mention the motley crew who came out of their tombs at the time of Christ's resurrection. This is not an invitation to us to speculate on how they all get on in heaven, with Christ and his mother, a patriarch and an apostle and a motley crew sporting bodies, while the rest of the saints do not. It is a statement about what we apparently do not have in our possession on earth. We do not possess relics of Mary's body, whereas, if the archaeologists are right, we do possess the relics of St Peter.

It is from our point of view, not that of the blessed, that the resurrection is future. From our point of view, the life of the saints is hidden in God. What we have is, so to speak, what they have left behind in time, their bones and their influence and so on. In that sense they are still part of *our* story, part of the temporal story of the world. According to St Thomas it is from this point of view that the dead are judged at the last judgment. As far as they are concerned, their story came to its conclusion and was judged at the time of their death. At the last judgment the split screen becomes single: the temporal process comes to an end and all that is hidden in God is revealed. The whole story is 'published'. When Christ is revealed, the saints will be revealed with him. It would, no doubt, be a fascinating spectacle for a conveniently placed observer belonging to a different world-order, which was not brought to an end at the same time. Within our own world-order, though, in one sense, the judgment cannot make any difference to anyone, since none of us will be left to observe it. At the end of the story the spectators have all become players. It is surely absurd to imagine souls suddenly discovering with a jolt that they have got their bodies back; the most that could be said is that bodies suddenly discover that they are no longer left behind. But it is saner to say that what the resurrection and the judgment means is that there are no longer two perspectives, one eternal and one temporal.

If, from the point of view of the blessed, the resurrection is not future, this does not mean that they have two bodies at the same time, one resurrected and one lying in the tomb, because there is no 'same time' between time and eternity. In eternity there is no before and after, so it cannot be said that the bodies of the blessed are resurrected 'before' some general resurrection which is to come 'after'. However tricky it may be to work out the logic of the relationship between eternity and time, we must at least be on our guard against attempting to set up false temporal relationships between them.[11]

The embarrassment of the time-lag between death and resurrection, on this hypothesis, is dispelled by recognising that it is a time-lag only from our point of view in time, not from the point of view of the blessed. They are beyond time. Indeed the resolution of the time-lag problem can be seen as an argument in favour of the traditional doctrine of beatitude as a participation in eternity.

The relationship between us and the saints thus falls within the problematic of the relationship between time and eternity. In spite of the gulf there must always be between God and creatures, the saints 'share in the divine nature' (2 Peter 1:4) and there is no reason a priori why we should not expect to run into the same problem in their regard that we inevitably run into when we try to make sense of the relationship between God's timelessness and our temporal world.

However puzzling timelessness may be, it is worth noting that it impinges on us in connection with very basic and familiar religious practices, such as prayer. Imagine that I am waiting at Reading for the Bristol train to come in. It is natural that I should, if I am a believer, pray that it will arrive on time. But such a prayer inevitably entails the prayer that the train has already left Paddington on time, so that I am effectively praying for something to have come about already in the past, which cannot possibly make sense if God's existence is sequential in the same way as mine is, or that of British Rail. A great deal of our praying is manifestly of this kind, and it must at least be recognised that it can only be made intelligible on the assumption that God is not bound by temporality in the same way that his creatures are.

This allows us to retrieve much of the old practice of praying for the saints. There is an easily identifiable reason why it seems odd to pray for canonised saints, and it is related to Parfit's comments on the legitimacy of having desires about the past.[12] It does not make sense to have desires about a past that is already known, but it makes perfectly good sense to have desires about a past that is not yet known. If a friend of mine is working in Beirut and I hear on the news that three more people have been kidnapped there, it is perfectly intelligible for me to desire (and therefore to pray) that my friend is not one of them. Such a desire (and such a prayer) become meaningless only when I have discovered whether or not my friend is one of them. Similarly it is odd to pray for canonised saints, whom we believe to be in heaven, but there is nothing odd about desiring or praying that any of the uncanonised dead should be in heaven, however many of them are in fact already there.

We are deeply familiar then with the interaction between our own temporal world and the domain of eternity which is beyond time, however impossible it may be to provide a satisfactory conceptual analysis of it. Inevitably we talk as if God, or the saints, are still in time, and it is quite right for us to do so, so long as we remind ourselves periodically that we are talking in the only way we can, but that we are really out of our depth. St Thomas, for all his belief that the blessed are beyond time, can still talk, without jibbing, of them learning from God about 'what has to be done' (*agenda*) to further the good order of this world.[13]

A more serious problem is posed by the resurrected body. It is hard to imagine bodies existing timelessly. As we have seen, Thomas exempts the bodies of the saints from the universal immobility which will characterise the new creation,[14] though it is clear that the saints can have no further reason to move their bodies, if they have arrived definitively at their goal and so have no further purpose to fulfil, and it is not at all evident how a soul, whose will is immutable, is to produce movement in the body. In addition, it is difficult to see how, if time is the measure of movement,[15] it is possible for there to be movement in the new creation, without there also being time.

One possible way forward is suggested by Proclus' dictum that souls have eternal substance, but their operation is in time.[16] In an otherwise immobile universe 'time' could not mean time as we know it now, but there is perhaps no reason why we should not appeal to that other sort of time which medieval thinkers ascribed to angels and which they called *aevum*, which allows for successiveness but is not measured by the movement of the heavenly bodies. The bodies of the resurrected saints, on this basis, could be allowed to move in their own kind of time, even while the soul was, in itself, beyond time.

This is not a suggestion that would have found much favour with St Thomas. After the translation of Proclus' *Elements of Theology* in 1262 he was certainly interested in this work, and made much use of it in his commentary on the *Liber de Causis*, but the only sense he can see in the proposition we are considering here is to apply it to the heavenly bodies, to which he had already ascribed an immutable substance and a capacity to move.[17] The blessed, however, like the angels, are eternal in their operation as well as in their being,[18] and Thomas seems quickly to have gone off the idea that the angels operate both in eternity and in *aevum*. In his disputed question *De Potentia*, probably dating from his first year in Rome (1265–1266), he ascribes to the angels simultaneously a knowledge and vision of God, which is unchanging and is 'measured by participated eternity', and a self-knowledge which is unchanging and 'is measured by *aevum*' and a knowledge of other creatures which is not unchanging.[19] In the corresponding passage in the first part of the *Summa Theologiae*, written probably only a year or so later, he carefully avoids any such combination of eternity and *aevum*.[20] In fact he has rather a problem, since he believes that the angels are in perfect beatitude ever since their confirmation, after their first act of choice, yet at the same time he allows that they can grow in the incidental joy that is caused by such things as their success in helping our salvation,[21] and he clearly needs to keep angels in *aevum*, at least for the duration of this world.[22] It is probably quite deliberately that Thomas refrained, in the *Summa*, from explicitly ascribing participated eternity to the angels, in spite of their possession of beatitude.

It is probably best simply to say that we cannot, from our present vantage point, expect to understand what it is like being resurrected. If it is necessary to postulate some sort of temporality for resurrected bodies, then we must say that their temporality does not affect the essential non-temporality of the blessed any more than the temporality of creation affects God. And that is hardly any more illuminating than admitting that we are out of our depth.

Another difficulty is posed by people who die without ever having really lived a human life. If beatitude involves the redemption and glorification and the gathering up into timeless simultaneity of a whole human life, what can beatitude mean for someone who died as a foetus? Peter Lombard quotes Augustine as maintaining that any being that can count as human and as alive is a candidate both for death and for resurrection, including at least formed foetuses.[23] He offers no explanation of what their resurrected life might be like, though presumably even foetuses are included in the standard scholastic belief that everyone is resurrected at the age of thirty, which must entail equipping them with suitably mature personalities as well as mature bodies, and this would seem to go entirely against Irenaeus' explanation of why Adam was not created perfect. They would be a case of human maturity achieved without the proper process of coming to maturity.

Prudentius accommodates the Holy Innocents in heaven by imagining them playing with their crowns before the altar,[24] which is a pleasing conceit, but it does not really help very much.

A Molinist might always say that God knows what dead foetuses would have been like, if they had grown up, but there are difficulties about this. If it means that, in some possible world, these foetuses would have grown up in such and such a way, it does not alter the fact that these actual foetuses did not grow up in any way. If it means that God had a plan for their growing up, but it was thwarted, we can only wonder what had the power to thwart omnipotence.

I doubt very much whether we can do more than plead that we know so little of what glory means for any of the elect, that it would be foolhardy to exclude the possibility of even such limited experience as foetuses have being glorified. If there can be such a thing as glorified inexperience, maybe the Victorians were not being totally stupid in treating dead children as angels.

Before we conclude, there are obviously still several items on the agenda, on which a few words ought to be said, and, first, hell. Hell functions in christian doctrine, as it does in other religions, as the final guarantee that what we do matters. There is a way of comporting ourselves in life which does not lead to a glorious conclusion in the hereafter. And, however squeamish modern sentimentality may be about such things, it is proper that a life devoted to serious wickedness should end up getting what it deserves. Christianity has always allowed for last-minute conversions, but even these have to be real conversions, which means that the ex-sinner must have a genuine intention to try and undo the harm he has done and to change his way of life to the best of his ability, even if in fact he dies before he can achieve very much. Anything less than this would be a failure to take human beings and their deeds seriously.

If we want to say more about hell than that it is a real possibility we have to proceed with caution because, as Julian of Norwich reminds us, we lack reliable information.[25] But if eternal life is the reward given to the elect, we can infer that the damned do not have eternal life, even if they endure for ever. The scholastics certainly thought that they remain in time, on the basis of Psalm 80:16, 'The enemies of God have lied to him and their time will be for ever.'[26] This is why, according to St Thomas, the damned are still capable of fear, because they still have a future to anticipate, whereas the blessed, having no future to wait for, are in no further need of hope.[27] Whereas eternal life takes up and glorifies the finality of death, on the model of Christ who 'always lives slain', damnation is a death which never succeeds in dying. As St Bernard says, 'This is the second death, which is always slaying, without ever completing the slaughter (*quae numquam peroccidit, sed semper occidit*);

would that they could die once and not go on dying for ever!'[28] Death is the end for the damned, as it is for everyone else; their will thereafter is immutable. But it is an end which is not a conclusion. To quote St Bernard again, in hell 'they will be finished without finishing, they will die without dying' (*sine fine finientur, sine morte morientur*).[29]

If hell means that certain life-stories never arrive at a proper conclusion, maybe we can invoke an old moral commonplace to suggest a reason why this may be appropriate. If you make money your objective, it is not clear that you can ever declare yourself satisfied that you have realised your objective; however much money you have, you can always want more. St Bernard appeals to this principle of the insatiability of wrong desires to suggest that the wicked:

> naturally want some way of bringing their desire to a conclusion (*unde finiant appetitum*), but at the same time they stupidly reject the way in which they could approach a conclusion – conclusion, I mean, in the sense of achievement, not exhaustion (*non consumptioni sed consummationi*). So they hasten, not to be fulfilled in a happy conclusion, but to be worn out by futile toil (*non beato fine consummari, sed consumi vacuo labore accelerant*).[30]

Where heaven, then, draws all time together into a wholeness in which even failures and disappointments become glorious, hell is the apotheosis of frustration, going on and on and on, without ever reaching any sort of consummation, in such a way that nothing can really count as success.

On purgatory there is little more to report, but there are problems which must be faced. The official doctrine of purgatory is emphatically not a way of giving people a second chance, nor does it envisage any sort of posthumous finishing school or mental hospital, nor is it concerned to provide a nursery where dead infants can grow to maturity. It is strictly for people with unfinished penance. According to the little catechism sent by Innocent IV to his legate among the Greeks in 1254, what is purged there is sins, not souls.[31] The word 'purge' is used here in the same sense as when we talk of 'purging' debts. It is probably not easy for most of us today to make anything very much of this notion of the dead having to complete their penance before they can be admitted to heaven, but perhaps our belatedly converted malefactor can help us a little. Even without appealing to the idea of unfinished penance, we can surely see a sense in saying that it is unseemly for him to go straight to heaven, just as if he had spent years trying to lead a decent christian life. As St Thomas points out, it seems unfair to the person who has in fact spent years trying to be a decent christian.[32]

At first sight this rather prickly refusal to make too many concessions sits ill with the instinct to revel in the apparent 'unfairness' with which God seems to give the most splendid gifts to the most unworthy recipients. The Middle English *Pearl*, for instance, is an extended meditation on the way in which God seems to bestow greater gifts on those who toil less.[33] Ephrem, reflecting on the 'good thief', appears to enjoy the fact that 'it is a robber, then, who opened up paradise again, not anyone righteous,'[34] and there is a splendid anonymous Syriac poem about this same thief presenting himself at the gates of paradise and being denied entry by the angel on duty, who gets more and more indignant at the suggestion that a robber should be allowed in, when no one else is ever allowed in.[35]

Scholastic theology does not in fact deny such extravagances of mercy. It recognises that there can be an influx of grace resulting in such a fervour of charity that a converted sinner is freed in one fell swoop both from his sins and from any need to do penance for them.[36] The point is, surely, that there are different kinds of human story involved, and it is not implausible to suggest that, even subjectively, some sorts of story cry out for purgatory. According to St Catherine of Genoa:

> When the soul is separated from the body, if it does not find itself as pure as it was when it was created, it flings itself into purgatory of its own accord, seeing itself hindered in a way that cannot be remedied by any other means. If it did not find such provision made for removing the hindrance, a hell far worse than purgatory would come into being for it in that instant . . .
>
> I see well, that the divine essence is so pure, so spotless, much more than anyone can imagine, that any soul which has in it an imperfection, no greater than the tiniest speck, would fling itself into hell, into a thousand hells, rather than find itself in his presence with such a blemish, however small. Seeing purgatory provided for the removal of this blemish, it flings itself in it, as we have already said several times, and it feels that it finds a great mercy there, in being able to remove this hindrance there.[37]

This hesitancy of the unready soul is reminiscent of Peter saying, 'Depart from me, Lord, I am a sinful man' (Luke 5:8), and it echoes Ambrose's question, who is now ready for the unmediated company of God. The mood is admirably caught in Herbert's famous poem, 'Love bade me welcome, but my soul drew back,' where the poet is reluctant to accept the divine invitation, saying, 'Let my shame go where it doth deserve.'

Underlying both the delight in the good thief going straight to paradise and this sense of hesitancy is the same basic conviction that there is something inescapably odd about any of us going to heaven at all, and some such feeling of oddness is probably an intrinsic part of human beatitude. Part of the fun of heaven, so to speak, is that we have no business to be there. Belief in purgatory underlines one aspect of this feeling.

The problem is how to reintroduce in the case of purgatory the time-lag we have been trying to escape from in connection with beatitude. If we accept the traditional 'geography' and locate purgatory at the top of hell, there is perhaps no problem, as purgatory can be supposed to share in the temporality of hell. As described by patristic and medieval writers, the torments of purgatory make hell an eminently suitable place for it to be. But it is not clear that the torments are an essential part of the doctrine, and it is misleading to identify purgatory too closely with hell, because it lacks just that pointless definitiveness which makes hell so appalling.

It is tempting to recall that belief in purgatory grew out of the earlier belief in posthumous waiting-rooms and to suggest that waiting is the essential characteristic of purgatory. If this suggestion is accepted, purgatory would then involve a situation similar to that of the Old Testament saints before the coming of Christ. It would be a place of death rather than punishment, a state of waiting for the coming of the Saviour, just as on earth we can still be said to await his coming (Phil. 3:20; Tit. 2:13). What sort of temporality can be ascribed to it it is difficult to say. Certainly not eternity or the infernal travesty of eternity. Popular stories about souls being freed from purgatory at identifiable points in our time are not concerned to answer speculative questions about its own temporality, but maybe the answer they imply is as good as any we are likely to get. Alternatively we might resort to science fiction and imagine purgatory as existing in a kind of time bubble, in which people are quite unable to help themselves, though they can still be helped. Their helplessness is certainly something which particularly impressed medieval piety.[38]

I have tried to flesh out the claim made in Chapter 5, that christian doctrine contains the wherewithal to construct an eschatology which is humanly and speculatively viable, even if it cannot answer all our questions. I have suggested that it does offer us a real hope, without degenerating into the irresponsible daydreaming feared by Seneca or the sort of irrelevant happy ending satirised by Euripides. On the basis of this hope, we can find a way of dealing with this life, including its tragedies and upsets, that is less cramped than the genteel hedonism of Epicurus or the highmindedness of the Stoics. And, unlike Homer's heroes, christians not only hope that their lives, tragic as they may be, will be gathered up into an artistically satisfying whole, they also hope to be present to enjoy the songs that are sung of them. But christians also believe that, finally, all the songs are but facets of one song, a song of God's making, a song sung all at once in the Word which was in the beginning with God, and which became man and becomes words to enable us to find our true identity and our true fulfilment in being ourselves words of God in the one Word.

NOTES

1 Peter Lombard, IV *Sent.* d.43 c.5; Bonaventure, IV *Sent.* d.43 dub. III, ed. cit. p. 903; Thomas, *Summa Theologiae* Suppl. q.87 a.1.
2 Long Text, chapter 38.
3 *Odyssey* 11.40–41; cf. Bremmer, op. cit. pp. 83–84.
4 It was believed that everyone will be resurrected in the prime of life, about thirty years old, corresponding roughly to the age at which Christ was resurrected: cf. Peter Lombard, IV *Sent.* d.44 c.1; Thomas, *Contra Gentiles* IV 88; *Summa Theologiae* Suppl. q.81 a.1.
5 Cf. D. Parfit, *Reasons and Persons*, Oxford 1984.
6 It is suggested by R. T. Herbert, *Paradox and Identity in Theology*, Ithaca 1979, pp. 149–155; cf. R. W. Perrett, *Death and Immortality*, Dordrecht 1987, pp. 136–139.
7 *Speculum Speculationum*, ed. cit. p. 22.
8 This does not, of course, settle either way the quite separate question whether there can be any mental activity in human beings which is not necessarily accompanied by or dependent on some bodily process.
9 *Quaestio Disputata de Spe* a.4 ad 3; *Summa Theol.* II.II q.18 a.2 ad 2.
10 William Wordsworth, 'We are seven'.
11 Cf. Thomas, *Summa Theol.* I q.10 a.4 ad 1: time and eternity are not the same kind of measure. They are therefore presumably incommensurable.
12 Parfit, op. cit. pp. 171–172.
13 *Summa Theol.* II.II q.52 a.3.
14 *Compendium Theol.* 171.
15 *Summa Theol.* I q.10 a.6.
16 *Elements of Theology* 191.
17 *Summa Theol.* I q.10 a.5; *Super De Causis*, ed. H. D. Saffrey, Fribourg/ Louvain 1954, pp. 15–16.
18 *Summa Theol.* I q.10 a.3.
19 *De Potentia* q.4 a.2 ad 19.
20 *Summa Theol.* I q.58 a.6 and 7.
21 Ibid. q.62 a.9.
22 This is required, for instance, for the movement Thomas recognises in angels (I q.53).

23 IV *Sent.* d.44 c.8.
24 Prudentius, *Cathimerinon* 12.131–132.
25 Long Text chapters 32–33, 36. This last chapter suggests that it is 'folly' to turn our minds to the subject of the damned; the Lord wants us to attend gladly to himself as our Saviour and to the salvation he provides. What the gospel is about is redemption (Long Text ch. 30); it is not intended to answer our questions about damnation, except in so far as they are directly pertinent to the understanding of salvation.
26 E.g. Philip the Chancellor, ed. cit. p. 669; William of Auxerre, *Summa Aurea* III, ed. cit. p. 250.
27 *Summa Theol.* I.II q.67 a.4; II.II q.18 a.2.
28 *De Consideratione* 5.12.26.
29 *De Diversis* 42.6.
30 *De Diligendo Deo* 7.19.
31 Pont. Comm. ad redigendum CIC Orientalis, *Fontes* III vol. IV i, ed. T. T. Haluscynskyj and M. M. Wojnar, Rome 1962, p. 175.
32 *Contra Gentiles* IV 91.
33 Cf. *Pearl* 597–600. Cf. the introduction in the edition by E. V. Gordon, Oxford 1953, pp. xxi-xxiii.
34 Ephrem, *Commentary on the Diatessaron*, French trans. by L. Leloir (Sources Chrétiennes 121), Paris 1966, p. 361.
35 S. Brock, ed. *Sogiatha, Syriac Dialogue Hymns*, Kottayam 1987, pp. 28–35. I am grateful to Dr Brock for drawing my attention to this hymn.
36 E.g. *Contra Gentiles* III 158.
37 Catherine of Genoa, ed. U. Bonzi, *S. Caterina Fieschi Adorno*, vol. II, Turin 1962, pp. 334–335.
38 Cf. Gerald de Frachet, *Vitae Fratrum*, ed. B. M. Reichert, Louvain 1896, pp. 287–288.

Appendix

The 1979 Letter from the Sacred Congregation for the Doctrine of the Faith

The most recent official document on eschatology is a letter addressed by the Sacred Congregation to the Presidents of Episcopal Conferences 'on certain matters pertaining to eschatology', published on the pope's authority on 17 May 1979.

This short declaration lists seven points which Catholic theologians are expected to bear in mind:

(1) The resurrection of the dead.
(2) This resurrection applies to 'the whole man' (*totus homo*), and is an extension to the elect of the resurrection of Christ.
(3) 'The church affirms the continuation and subsistence, after death, of a spiritual element, endowed with consciousness and will, in such a way that the human "I" subsists, though for the moment lacking its body.'[1] This spiritual element is conveniently called 'the soul'.
(4) Ways of thinking and talking are to be shunned, which would make nonsense of the prayers and rites offered for the dead.
(5) The church looks forward to 'the glorious manifestation of our Lord Jesus Christ', but this is imparted differently, and not necessarily immediately, depending on the state of each individual immediately after death.
(6) No explanation of what happens after death can be accepted which would eliminate the significance of the Assumption as a unique privilege of Mary, in the sense that her bodily glorification anticipates that which is in store for the rest of the elect.
(7) The church believes in the beatitude of the righteous and the eternal punishment of sinners, 'who will be deprived of the vision of God, and this punishment will have repercussions on the whole being of sinners.' There can be a purification, in the case of the elect, before they come to the vision of God, which is quite distinct from the punishment of the damned. 'This is what the church means, when she speaks of Hell and Purgatory.'

It is striking how very restrained the claims are which the Sacred

Congregation wants to insist on. There is no mention of the immortality of the soul, for instance, but only of its 'continuation and subsistence', which reflects, probably unconsciously, the hesitation we have noticed in the older christian tradition with regard to 'immortality' in this sense.

Item (3) postulates an 'interim' condition in which the soul 'subsists' without the body. The word 'soul' is retained chiefly, it seems, because it would be more trouble than it is worth to try to do without it. I am inclined to agree. I do not think that the Sacred Congregation is necessarily excluding the sort of analysis I have offered of why we find ourselves, sometimes (and probably not very often), needing to talk in terms of the soul going on existing independently of the body. What is important, I have argued, is in fact the continuing existence of the corpse or relics of the dead; if we are to avoid denying the significance of the corpse, while at the same time maintaining that there is more to the dead than their mortal remains, it is likely enough that we shall end up talking about their souls. What we must not do, I submit, is imagine that such talk adequately describes the situation of the dead saints *as it appears to them.*

The Sacred Congregation seems to be well aware of this problem. After its list of essential items of belief, it goes on to warn us (a) not to be beguiled by images, which, it says, are often the cause of great difficulties for the faith, though we must respect the images contained in the Bible and not water them down to such an extent that they become meaningless; (b) we must be aware that 'neither the Bible nor the theologians give us sufficient light to enable us to give a proper description of the life which is to come after death.' What is essential is that we believe, first, in the 'fundamental continuity that there is, by virtue of the Holy Spirit, between our present life in Christ and the life that is to come', and, secondly, that we appreciate the serious difference there is between the economy of faith, by which we live now, and the 'dispensation of full light', when we shall be with Christ and see God. It is to that fulness of light that we are drawn spontaneously by our hearts, 'even if it is beyond the reach of our imagination'.

Item (6) draws attention to the need to safeguard the special prerogatives of Our Lady. My proposed eschatology might seem to entail a playing down of these prerogatives, but I do not think that it raises any more problems than any other eschatology. If we simply say, rather naively, that our Lady's prerogative is that she is in heaven with her body, and the other saints have to wait for their bodies, we will have to hush up or otherwise dispose of Enoch, Elijah and the saints who came out of their tombs at the time of Christ's resurrection. If we take due note of them, we cannot just say that Our Lady's privilege consists in her anticipation of the resurrection. Her unique privilege is her role in the universal story of salvation, as the Mother of God. Her essential bliss, of course, is the same as everyone else's, namely the vision of God; but her 'public' glory, so to speak, is unique. No other saint can claim to be so intimately involved in the salvation of all the elect. If their converts are the glory of the apostles, as St Gregory maintained,[2] we must say that all those who are saved are her 'clients'. It is this uniquely close association with the universal salvific work of her Son which gives a special radiance to her anticipated resurrection, her assumption. But, once again, we must remind ourselves that it is *from our point of view* that her resurrection is brought about in advance of that of nearly everyone else. And, if that is a special glory, it is surely sufficient that it should be so from our point of view. Christian doctrine is not concerned to give us gossip about the details of what life in heaven is like for those who are there. We could not understand it if we were to be given such gossip. It is surely a splendid enough fact for us to be getting on with that Our Lady's corpse was no more available for burial than was that of her Son after his resurrection. We cannot describe her life after death any more than we can describe anyone else's. Christian imagination can certainly revel in marvellous pictures of her enthronement as Queen of Heaven. I defy it to imagine her as the only saint there with a body. And why should it try? That is not the point of the doctrine of the Assumption.

NOTE

1 It is alleged in J. Neuner and J. Dupois, eds, *The Christian Faith in the Doctrinal Documents of the Catholic Church*, London 1983, p. 691, that there is a discrepancy between the text of the document published in *Acta Apostolicae Sedis* and the text published in *L'Osservatore Romano*, the latter missing out the phrase 'though for the moment lacking its body'. The discrepancy, however, is not between two different official versions of the Latin text (which would indeed be startling), but merely between the official Latin text and the English translation published in the weekly English edition of *L'Osservatore* (which must be the edition used by Neuner and Dupois, since their citation of '23 July 1979, pp. 7–8' only makes sense with reference to this edition). The Latin text published in the daily edition (16–17 July 1979, p. 2) is identical with that published in *Acta Apostolicae Sedis*, except for a change in the word-order which in no way affects the meaning.

2 Gregory, *Hom. Ev.* 1.17.17 (PL 76:1148B).

Notes and Bibliography on the Sources

Aeschylus (*c*. 525–456 BC). Greek tragedian. Editions of his surviving works in the main series of classical texts. The major collection of fragments is now S. Radt, *Tragicorum Graecorum Fragmenta* vol. III, Göttingen 1985.

Aethiopis. One of the post-Homeric Greek epics. Fragments in T. W. Allen, *Homeri Opera* vol. V, Oxford 1912 and often reprinted.

Albert the Great, St (*c*. 1193–1280). Dominican philosopher and theologian; teacher of St Thomas Aquinas. For a study of his life, see S. Tugwell, *Albert and Thomas*, New York 1988, pp. 3–39. A critical edition of his works, published in Cologne, is in progress.

Albinus (mid-2nd cent. AD). Middle Platonist philosopher. Edition of his *Didaskalikos* by P. Louis in the Budé series, Paris 1945.

Ambrose, St (*c*. 339–397). Bishop of Milan. Critical edition of his works in the Corpus Scriptorum Ecclesiasticorum Latinorum.

Anacreon (*c*. 570–*c*. 485 BC). Greek lyric poet. Edition of surviving fragments in D. L. Page, *Poetae Melici Graeci*, Oxford 1962.

Anselm, St. (*c*. 1033–1109). Archbishop of Canterbury. Critical edition of his works by F. S. Schmitt, Edinburgh 1946–1961.

Aphrahat (died after AD 345). A Persian christian writer. His *Demonstrations* were composed, in Syriac, in 336–337 and 344–345. Edited by J. Parisot, with Latin translation, in *Patrologia Syriaca* vols I-II, Paris 1894, 1907.

Apollodorus (1st or 2nd cent.). Writer on Greek mythology. Edition by J. G. Frazer, Loeb Classical Library 1921 and often reprinted.

Apostolic Constitutions (latter half of 4th cent.). A collection of church law, probably of Syrian origin. Edition by F. X. Funk, Paderborn 1905; also in Sources Chrétiennes.

Apostolic Fathers. A collection of early christian writings, from between the middle of the 1st cent. and the middle of the 2nd. Among the many editions there are two useful ones, with English translations: J. B. Lightfoot, London 1893; Kirsopp Lake, Loeb Classical Library

1912–1913 and often reprinted. For an introduction to their thought, see S. Tugwell, *The Apostolic Fathers*, London 1989.

Aristophanes (*c*. 445–*c*. 385 BC). The greatest writer of Greek Old Comedy. Editions of his works in the main series of classical texts. I have made much use of the edition of the *Frogs* (produced in 405) by W. B. Stanford, 2nd edn, London 1963.

Aristotle (384–322 BC). One of the greatest Greek philosophers. There are many editions of his works, but references are given in the standard way, according to the pagination in the edition by I. Bekker, Berlin 1831–1870. There is a complete English translation of the surviving works and major fragments, ed. Jonathan Barnes, Princeton 1984.

Armand of Belvézer (first half of 14th cent.). Dominican theologian. Master of the Sacred Palace (1328–1334). His comments on the controversy about the beatific vision under John XXII are contained in MS Cambridge University Library Ii 3.10.

Atticus (fl AD 176). Middle Platonist philosopher. Edition of the surviving fragments by E. des Places, Paris 1977.

Augustine, St (354–430). For a study of his life, see Peter Brown, *Augustine of Hippo*, London 1967. Many editions of his works.

Barnabas. See Apostolic Fathers. Edition of the *Letter of Barnabas* by P. Prigent and R. A. Kraft, Sources Chrétiennes no. 172, Paris 1971. The date is disputed but the letter probably comes from the AD 70s.

Benedict XII (pope 1334–1342). Cardinal Jacques Fournier. His dossier on the beatific vision controversy is contained in MS Vatican Library lat. 4006.

Bernard of Clairvaux, St (1090–1153). Cistercian abbot. Critical edition of his works by J. Leclercq, C. H. Talbot and H. M. Rochais, Rome 1957ff.

Bessarion (1403–1472). One of the Greek prelates at the Council of Florence; he remained in communion with Rome after the collapse of the union, and was made a cardinal in 1439.

Boethius (*c*. 480–*c*. 524). Christian philosopher. There are many editions of his most famous work, *De Consolatione Philosophiae*.

Bonaventure, St (*c*. 1217–1274). Franciscan theologian. Critical edition of his works by the Franciscans of Quaracchi, 1882–1902.

Caesarius of Arles, St (*c*. 470–542). Archbishop of Arles. Critical edition of his sermons in Corpus Christianorum Series Latina.

Cajetan, Thomas de Vio (1469–1534). Dominican theologian, important in the revival of Thomism. Master of the Dominican Order 1508–1518. Appointed bishop of Gaeta in 1519. He was made a cardinal in 1517.

Callimachus (first half of 3rd cent. BC). Hellenistic Greek lyric poet. Critical edition by R. Pfeiffer, Oxford 1949. Edition, with English translation, by A. W. Mair, revised by C. Trypanis, and by C. Trypanis himself in Loeb Classical Library, 1955 and 1958.

Catechism of the Council of Trent (Roman Catechism). A summary of christian doctrine, produced on the authority of the Council of Trent, largely by Dominican theologians, and published in 1566. See R. Rodríguez and R. Lanzetti, *El Catecismo Romano: Fuentes y Historia del Texto y de la Redacción*, Pamplona 1982.

Catherine of Genoa, St (1447–1510). Her spiritual doctrine was written up after her death, but there is no reason to doubt the accuracy of the reporting. Critical edition in U. Bonzi, *S. Caterina Fieschi Adorno*, Turin 1961–1962, which also contains an important study of her life. Several translations into English are available.

Catherine of Siena, St (1347–1380). Sister of the Dominican Order of Penance. For an introduction and selection from her writings, see K. Foster and M. J. Ronayne, *I, Catherine*, London 1980. The projected *Fontes Vitae S. Catharinae Senensis Historici*, ed. M. H. Laurent and others, never reached completion, but several volumes were published.

Catullus (84–54 BC). Latin poet. Editions of the text in the major series of classical authors.

Ceccano, Annibaldo di, Cardinal (*c.* 1282–1350). In 1333 he composed a treatise in support of John XXII's views on the beatific vision; edited by M. Dykmans, *Pour et contre Jean XXII en 1333*, Vatican City 1975.

Celsus (late 2nd cent. AD). Pagan philosopher, who wrote the first extended criticism of christianity *c.* 176–180. His work is known through the massive response of Origen, of which the best edition is that by M. Borret, Sources Chrétiennes nos 132, 136, 147, 150 and 227, Paris 1967–1976. There is an important English translation by H. Chadwick, Cambridge 1953.

Chrysippus (*c.* 280–*c.* 206 BC). Leading Stoic philosopher. The fragments of his voluminous writings are edited in J. von Arnim, *Stoicorum Veterum Fragmenta*.

Chrysostom, St John (*c.* 347–407). Bishop of Constantinople. Apart from editions of all his works, including PG, his *Homilies on Matthew* have been edited by D. Ruiz Bueno, Madrid 1955–1956.

Cicero (106–43 BC). Republican Latin writer. His essay on the dream of Scipio is contained in *De Republica* VI. Editions of his works in the major series of classical authors.

Clement IV (pope 1265–1268).

Clement of Alexandria (*c.* 150–*c.* 215). Alexandrian christian theologian. Critical edition of his works by O. Stählin in Die Griechischen Christlichen Schriftsteller.

Clement of Rome, St (1st cent.). Traditionally identified as the second or third pope. '1 Clement' is the letter sent from the Roman church to the Corinthians either in the 70s or in the 90s. Critical edition by A. Jaubert, Sources Chrétiennes no. 167, Paris 1971. For other editions, see Apostolic Fathers. '2 Clement' is not by Clement, and its provenance and date are not known, but it probably belongs approximately to the middle of the 2nd century. Critical edition in K. Bihlmeyer's revision of the edition by F. X. Funk, *Die Apostolischen Väter*, Tübingen 1970.

Councils. For the texts of church Councils, see Alberigo in the bibliography of modern works. There is an important series of publications concerning the proceedings of the Council of Florence, published by the Pontifical Institute of Oriental Studies: *Concilium Florentinum, Documenta et Scriptores.*

Corpus Praefationum, ed. E. Moeller, Corpus Christianorum Series Latina vol. 161, is a very important collection of liturgical Prefaces in Latin, from the oldest known texts up to the present day.

Cypria. A post-Homeric Greek epic. Fragments edited in Allen, *Homeri Opera* vol. V.

Cyril of Alexandria, St (died 444). Patriarch of Alexandria, and an important Alexandrian theologian. The most complete edition of his works is still that in PG.

Cyril of Jerusalem, St (*c.* 315–386). Bishop of Jerusalem. Author of a set of doctrinal and liturgical catecheses. Critical edition of the latter by A. Piédagnel, Sources Chrétiennes no. 126, Paris 1966.

Damascene, St John (*c.* 675–*c.* 749). Important Greek theologian. Critical edition of his *Expositio Fidei* by B. Kotter, Berlin 1973.

Damascius (*c.* 462–538 or later). One of the last significant pagan Neoplatonists, who played an important role in the revival of the Academy in Athens. Edition of his commentary on the *Phaedo*, with English translation, in L. G. Westerink, ed., *The Greek Commentaries on Plato's Phaedo* vol. II, Amsterdam 1977.

Didache. One of the earliest known christian writings, perhaps from as early as the middle of the 1st century. See Apostolic Fathers. Among many editions, there is a valuable one by W. Rordorf and A. Tuilier, Sources Chrétiennes no. 248, Paris 1978.

Diogenes Laertius (probably early 3rd cent. AD). Compiler of lives and teaching of Greek philosophers. There is a convenient edition, with English translation, by R. D. Hicks, Loeb Classical Library 1925 and often reprinted; also an Oxford Classical Text, ed. H. S. Long, Oxford 1964.

Durandus of Aurillac (mid-14th cent.). Dominical theologian. In 1334 he took part in the discussions in the University of Paris on the beatific vision controversy.

Durandus of St Pourçain (*c.* 1270–1334). Dominican theologian, regarded with suspicion in some circles. Bishop of Limoux in 1317, he was translated to several other sees and died as bishop of Meaux. A short treatise on the beatific vision is contained in MS Vatican Library lat. 4006 ff. 307–312.

Ephrem, St (*c.* 306–373). Syriac christian poet and theologian; doctor of the church.

Epicharmus (early 5th cent. BC). Greek comic poet, with philosophical leanings.

Epictetus (*c.* 55–*c.* 135). Stoic philosopher. There is a convenient edition, with English translation, by W. A. Oldfather, Loeb Classical Library 1926–1928 and often reprinted.

Epicurus (341–271 BC). Greek philosopher. Editions of surviving texts and fragments in C. Bailey, *Epicurus, The Extant Remains*, Oxford 1926 (with English translation); H. Usener, *Epicurea*, Leipzig 1887; P. von der Muehll, Leipzig 1922; G. Arrighetti, *Epicuro, Opere*, 2nd edn, Turin 1973.

Epiphanius (*c.* 315–403). Bishop of Salamis; dedicated opponent of heresies. His *Panarion* is edited by K. Holl in Die Griechischen Christlichen Schriftsteller.

Euripides (*c.* 485–*c.* 406 BC). Greek tragedian. A new critical edition by J. Diggle is in progress in the Oxford Classical Texts. There are many important commentaries on individual plays published by Oxford University Press, some of which are cited in the notes.

Fantino Vallaresso (*c.* 1392–1443). Venetian aristocrat. Elected bishop of Parenzo in 1415, he became archbishop of Crete in 1425.

Gennadius (fl. AD 470). Church historian. Edition of his *Liber Ecclesiasticorum Dogmatum* by C. H. Turner in *Journal of Theological Studies* 7 (1905–1906) pp. 78–99.

Gerald de Frachet (1205–1271). Dominican writer. On the orders of Humbert of Romans he compiled a collection of edifying tales about St Dominic and other early Dominicans, known as the 'Lives of the Brethren'; ed. B. M. Reichert in vol. I of Monumenta Ordinis Praedicatorum Historica, Louvain 1896.

Gerard of Abbeville (*c.* 1220–1272). Parisian theologian, and a fierce opponent of the friars.

Gesta Romanorum. A very popular 14th-century collection of anecdotes. Edition of the Latin text by W. Dick, Erlangen/Leipzig 1980. I have used the Middle English verison, ed. S. J. H. Herrtage, Early English Text Society ES 33, 1879.

Glossa Ordinaria. The commentary of the whole Bible, which had become standard by the end of the 12th century. The text is printed with the commentary of Nicholas of Lyra, Venice 1588.

Gospel of the Egyptians. An apocryphal gospel, probably written in the first half of the 2nd century.

Gospel of Philip. A Gnostic apocryphal gospel, probably from the 2nd or 3rd century. See the translation and commentary by R. McL. Wilson, London 1962. There is also a translation in J. M. Robinson, ed., *The Nag Hammadi Library in English.*

Gospel of Thomas. An apocryphal gospel, possibly of Encratite origins, adapted by Gnostics for their own use. The earliest portions of the text probably go back to the middle of the 2nd century. Edited, with English translation, by A. Guillaumont and others, *The Gospel according to Thomas*, Leiden/London 1959.

Gospel of Truth. A Gnostic apocryphal gospel, dating from about the middle of the second century. English translation by K. Grobel, London 1960; also in Robinson.

Gratian (first half of 12 cent.). Compiler of the *Decretum*, which became the first standard collection of church law in the medieval western church. Edited by E. Friedberg in vol. I of his *Corpus Iuris Canonici*, Leipzig 1879.

Gregory I, St (pope 590–604). Doctor of the church. There is a modern edition of the *Dialogues* ascribed to him, by A. de Vogüé, in Sources Chrétiennes (in progress).

Gregory of Nyssa, St (*c.* 330–*c.* 395). One of the Cappadocian fathers of the church. There is an edition of his works in progress, launched by W. Jaeger. There is a new edition of his *Life of Moses* by M. Simonetti, Milan 1984; there is an edition of the *Catechetical Oration* by J. H. Srawley, Cambridge 1903.

Haimo of Auxerre (died *c.* 865). Monk of St Germain, Auxerre; writer and biblical commentator.

Heraclitus (fl. *c.* 500–480 BC). Greek philosopher. Fragments are cited according to the numbering in DK. There are several important editions (most of which renumber the fragments): M. Marcovich, Merida 1967; C. H. Kahn, *The Art and Thought of Heraclitus*, Cambridge 1979; C. Diano and G. Serra, Milan 1980; T. M. Robinson, Toronto 1987.

Herbert, George (1593–1633). Anglican divine and poet.

Hermas (1st cent.). See Apostolic Fathers. There is a separate edition by R. Joly, Sources Chrétiennes 53, Paris 1968.

Herodotus (*c.* 485–*c.* 425 BC). Greek historian. The standard edition is the one by C. Hude in the Oxford Classical Texts, 1927.

Hesiod (8th cent.?). Greek poet. Important editions of his main works by M. L. West: *Theogony*, Oxford 1966; *Works and Days*, Oxford 1978.

Hilary of Poitiers, St (*c.* 315–367). Doctor of the church. Edition of his *Super Psalmos* by A. Zingerle, Corpus Scriptorum Ecclesiasticorum Latinorum vol. 22 (1891).

Hippocratic Writings. A motley collection of medical writings, probably dating from the 5th century BC. There is a convenient edition, with English translation, by W. H. S. Jones, Loeb Classical Library 1923–1931 and often reprinted.

Hippolytus (*c.* 170–*c.* 236). An important Roman theologian. Edition of his *Refutatio omnium Haeresium* by M. Marcovich, Berlin 1986; of the *Contra Noetum*, ascribed to Hippolytus, by R. Butterworth, London 1977.

Homer (8th cent.). The greatest Greek epic poems, the *Iliad* and the *Odyssey* are ascribed to Homer, though they may not be by the same poet. Various hymns, from different periods, are also ascribed to Homer. There is a standard edition of all this, and the remains of the post-Homeric epic, in 5 volumes in the Oxford Classical Texts, edited by D. M. Monro and T. W. Allen (*Iliad* 1920) or just by T. W. Allen (*Odyssey* 1917–1919; volume V, 1912). There is an important edition of the *Homeric Hymn to Demeter* by N. J. Richardson, Oxford 1974.

Homilies, Anglican. A collection of Homilies issued by the Church of England in 1571. The first book dates from 1543, including the 'Exhortation against the Fear of Death', which is probably by Cranmer. The second book was added during the reign of Queen Elizabeth.

Horace (65–8 BC). Roman lyric and satirical poet. Editions of the text in the main series of classical authors.

Hugh of St Cher (died 1263). Dominican theologian and biblical scholar. The first Dominican to be made a cardinal (in 1244). He composed, or at least edited, a commentary on the whole Bible, of which there are many editions.

Humbert of Romans (died 1277). Master of the Dominican Order 1254–1263. His work 'On the Formation of Preachers' is being edited by S. Tugwell. A translation of a substantial part of the work is included in S. Tugwell, *Early Dominicans*, New York 1982.

Iamblichus (*c.* 250–325). Neoplatonist philosopher.

Ibycus (6th cent. BC). Greek lyric poet. The surviving fragments are edited in D. L. Page, *Poetae Melici Graeci.*

Ignatius (martyred early in the 2nd cent.). Bishop of Antioch. His letters were written on the way to his martyrdom in Rome. See Apostolic Fathers. There is a separate edition by P. T. Camelot, Sources Chrétiennes 10, Paris 1969.

Innocent III (pope 1198–1216). His works are contained in PL 214–217.

Innocent IV (pope 1243–1254). An important canon lawyer.

Irenaeus, St (*c.* 130–*c.* 200). Bishop of Lyons, and one of the most systematic of the early christian theologians; he developed his theology in response to the challenge of heterodox Gnosticism. Important edition of his *Adversus Haereses* by A. Rousseau and others, Sources Chrétiennes, Paris 1965–1982.

Jean aux Belles-Mains (*c.* 1120–1204). Born in Canterbury, he was a friend of Thomas Becket. In 1162 he became bishop of Poitiers, then archbishop of Lyons 1182–1193.

Jerome, St (*c.* 342–420). Doctor of the church. Edition of his letters by J. Labourt in the Budé collection, Paris 1949–1963. Edition of his commentary on Matthew in Corpus Christianorum Series Latina vol. 77.

John XXII (pope 1316–1334). Edition of his sermons on the beatific vision by M. Dykmans, Rome 1973. Other texts by John XXII are edited by Dykmans in *Revue d'Histoire Ecclésiastique* 66 (1971) pp. 401–417, and *Recherches de Théologie Ancienne et Médiévale* 37 (1970) pp. 232–253.

John of Aragon (1302–1334). Son of James II of Aragon, nephew of Robert of Anjou, king of Jerusalem. Archbishop of Toledo in 1319, patriarch of Alexandria in 1328. Edition of his letter on the beatific vision by M. Dykmans, *Analecta Sacra Taccaconensia* 42 (1969) pp. 156–168.

Julian of Norwich (*c.* 1342–*c.* 1416). Anchoress and theologian. Edition by E. Colledge and J. Walsh, Toronto 1978.

Justin Martyr, St (*c.* 100–*c.* 165). Christian apologist. There is a workable edition by D. Ruiz Bueno, *Padres Apologistas Griegos*, Madrid 1954.

Lactantius (*c.* 240–*c.* 320). Latin theologian and apologist. Edition by S. Brandt and G. Laubmann in Corpus Scriptorum Ecclesiasticorum Latinorum vols 9 and 27.

Leo X (pope 1513–1521).

Liber de Causis. An anonymous Arabic work, based on Proclus' *Elements of Theology*, translated into Latin by Gerard of Cremona (died 1187). During the 13th century it acquired considerable importance in Latin philosophy and theology, and was commented on by St Thomas near the end of his life; it was he who first recognised its dependence on Proclus.

Lucian (*c.* 120–after 180). Greek prose writer. Edition of his works by M. D. Macleod in the Oxford Classical Texts, 1972–1987.

Lucretius (*c.* 98–55 BC). Roman philosophical poet, a fervent disciple of Epicurus. Edition, with translation and commentary, by C. Bailey, Oxford 1950.

Luther, Martin (1483–1546). Pioneer of the German Protestant reformation.

Lutterell, John (died 1335). Chancellor of Oxford University 1317–1322. He went to the papal court at Avignon in 1323 and thereafter spent much of his time there.

Mark of Ephesus (*c.* 1391–1444). Metropolitan of Ephesus. Greek theologian at the Council of Florence, and leader of the opponents of reunion with the Latins.

Menander (342–*c.* 292 BC). Leading exponent of the Greek 'New Comedy'. Edition, together with some other fragments of New Comedy, by F. H. Sandbach in the Oxford Classical Texts, 1976. Commentary by A. W. Gomme and F. H. Sandbach, Oxford 1973.

Metrodorus (*c.* 331–278 BC). A close associate of Epicurus.

Moneta of Cremona (died *c.* 1250). Dominican theologian. There is an edition of his massive *Summa contra Catharos et Valdenses*, written about 1241, Rome 1743.

Nemesius (fl. *c.* 390). Bishop of Emesa and a philosopher. Critical edition of his *De Natura Hominis* by M. Morani, Leipzig 1987, and of the influential Latin translation made by Burgundio in 1165, by G. Verbeke and J. R. Moncho, Leiden 1975, with an important study of his doctrine.

Nequam, Alexander (1157–1217). English theologian, who became an Augustinian canon *c.* 1200 at Cirencester. Edition of his *Speculum Speculationum*, which he wrote towards the end of his life, by R. M. Thomson (Auctores Britannici Medii Aevi vol. XI), Oxford 1988.

Nigel of Canterbury (*c.* 1130–*c.* 1200). Monk of Canterbury. Edition of his *Miracula Sancte Dei Genitricis* by Jan Ziolkowski, Toronto 1986.

Noetus (*c.* 200). Christian heretic, who denied the distinction of Persons in the Trinity. He was condemned at Smyrna *c.* 200.

Origen (*c.* 185–*c.* 254). The greatest of the Alexandrian theologians and exegetes. For an introduction to his life and works, see J. W. Trigg, *Origen*, Atlanta 1983 and London 1985. Important editions of his works in Die Griechischen Christlichen Schriftsteller and Sources Chrétiennes.

Pausanias (fl. *c.* 150 AD). Author of an important survey of Greece and its monuments. Convenient edition, with English translation, by W. H. S. Jones, H. A. Ormerod and R. E. Wycherley, Loeb Classical Library 1918–1935. Modern translation in Penguin Classics by Peter Levi, 1971.

Pearl. Late 14th-century English poem, in north-west Midland dialect, probably by the author of *Sir Gawain and the Green Knight*. Edition by E. V. Gordon, Oxford 1953; editions, with the other poems from the same manuscript, by M. Andrew and R. Waldron, Berkeley 1979, and by A. C. Cawley and J. J. Anderson, London 1976.

Peter Lombard (*c.* 1100–1160). His *Sentences* became the standard theological textbook in the 13th century; edited by the Franciscan fathers at Grottaferrata, 1971, 1981. For his commentary on the Psalms, which also became a standard work, the edition in PL 191 must still be used.

Philip the Chancellor (died 1236). Became Chancellor of Notre Dame, Paris, in 1217. An important theologian in the University of Paris. Edition of his *Summa de Bono* by N. Wicki, Berne 1985.

Philo (*c.* 30 BC–AD 45). Alexandrian Jewish philosopher and writer. There is a convenient edition, with English translation, by E. H. Colson and others, Loeb Classical Library 1929–1962.

Pindar (*c.* 520–after 446 BC). Greek poet. There is a standard edition by C. M. Bowra in the Oxford Classical Texts, 1947.

Plato (427–348 BC). Founder of the Academy in Athens, and one of the most influential philosophers of all time. Standard edition by J. Burnet in the Oxford Classical Texts, 1903–1915. There is a one-volume translation of all his works, ed. E. Hamilton and H. Cairns, Princeton 1961.

Plutarch (*c.* 47–*c.* 123). Greek philosopher and historian. An edition of his works is in progress in the Teubner series and there is an edition, with English translation, by B. Perrin and others in the Loeb Classical Library, 1914–1976.

Polycarp, St (*c.* 69–155). Bishop of Smyrna, martyr. Edition of his letter and the contemporary report of his martyrdom by P. T. Camelot, Sources Chrétiennes 10, Paris 1969.

Porphyry (3rd cent.). Philosopher and disciple of Plotinus, whose writings he edited. Edition of some of his works, including *De Antro Nympharum*, ed. A. Nauck, Leipzig 1886.

Praepositinus of Cremona (*c.* 1140–*c.* 1210). Parisian theologian. Edition of the *Summa contra Haereticos* by J. N. Garvin and J. A. Corbett, Notre Dame 1958; the ascription of this work to Praepositinus has been questioned, perhaps wrongly.

Proclus (*c.* 410–485). One of the last pagan Neoplatonists, holder of the chair in the Academy in Athens. Edition of his *Elements of Theology* by E. R. Dodds, with English translation and commentary, Oxford 1963. Editions of some of his other works are appearing in the Budé classics.

Prudentius (348–*c.* 410). Spanish-born christian poet. Of the many editions, two deserve mention: M. P. Cunningham, Corpus Christianorum Series Latina vol. 126 (1966), and I. Rodríguez, Madrid 1981.

Pseudo-Clementines. A variety of Jewish–Christian writings, essentially from the 3rd century. Critical edition of the *Clementine Homilies* and the *Clementine Recognitions* by B. Rehm and F. Paschke in Die Griechischen Christlichen Schriftsteller vols 41 and 51 (1953, 1965).

Ptolemy (2nd cent.). Disciple of Valentinus, the Gnostic. Edition of his *Letter to Flora* by G. Quispel, Sources Chrétiennes no. 24, Paris 1966.

Remigius of Auxerre (*c.* 841–*c.* 908). Student at St Germain, Auxerre, he later taught there and then at Rheims and Paris.

Rheginos, Letter to. Gnostic text, datable to the 2nd century. Translation and commentary by M. L. Peel, *The Epistle to Rheginos*, London 1969.

Robert of Anjou (1278–1343). King of Jerusalem and Sicily from 1309, since his older brother, St Louis, had been allowed to become a Franciscan. He was a talented amateur theologian. His intervention in the beatific vision controversy is edited by M. Dykmans, *Robert d'Anjou, La Vision Bienheureuse*, Rome 1970.

Seneca (*c.* 4 BC–AD 65). Stoic philosopher and playwright. Edition of his philosophical letters and some of his treatises by L. D. Reynolds in the Oxford Classical Texts, 1965 and 1977.

Sophocles (*c.* 496–406 BC). Greek tragedian. Standard edition by A. C. Pearson in the Oxford Classical Texts, 1928.

Stoics. One of the main Hellenistic schools of philosophy, founded by Zeno (334–262 BC). For surviving texts and testimonies, see J. von Arnim, *Stoicorum Veterum Fragmenta*, Leipzig 1905–1924.

Strato (3rd cent. BC). Aristotelian philosopher, head of the Peripatetic School *c.* 287–*c.* 269.

Swedenborg, Emanuel (1688–1772). Swedish scientiest and religious thinker, of a theosophical kind.

Tertullian (*c.* 160–*c.* 225). The first major Latin theologian. Edition, with English translation, of *De Resurrectione Carnis* by E. Evans, London 1960.

Theognis (6th cent. BC). Greek elegiac poet and moralist. Edition by M. L. West in *Iambi et Elegi Graeci* vol. I, Oxford 1971.

Thomas Aquinas, St (1226–1274). Dominican theologian. For a study of his life and works, see S. Tugwell, *Albert and Thomas*, New York 1988. A critical edition of his works is in progress, by the Leonine Commission. Otherwise the most complete edition available is found in the volume pubished by Marietti, Turin. For the *Summa Theologiae* there is a useful edition, with English translation, in the 60-volume 'Blackfriars Summa', London 1964–1981. For the *Catena Aurea* I have used vols 11–12 of the Parma edition (1860–1862). There is a good edition of the commentary on the *Liber de Causis* by H. D. Saffrey, Fribourg/Louvain 1954. The edition of the commentary on the *Sentences* by P. Mandonnet and M. F. Moos (Paris 1929–1947) is incomplete, so for the last part of book IV recourse must be had to older editions; I have used vol. 11 of the Vivès edition, Paris 1874.

Timon of Phlius (*c.* 320–*c.* 230 BC). Sophist and (mainly comic) poet.

Vergil (70–19 BC). Rome's greatest epic poet. There are many editions and versions of his *Aeneid*. There is a useful edition, with commentary, of the whole *Aeneid*, by R. D. Williams, London 1972, 1973.

Waleys, Thomas (*c.* 1288–*c.* 1350). English Dominician theologian, whose firmly expressed opposition to John XXII on the subject of the beatific vision resulted in his imprisonment in Avignon, though he was released probably in 1334, before the death of John XXII. For his part in the controversy, see T. Kaeppeli, *Le Procès contre Thomas Waleys OP*, Rome 1936; M. Dykmans, 'A propos de Jean XXII et Benoît XII: La Libération de Thomas Waleys', *Archivum Historiae Pontificiae* 7 (1969) pp. 115–130.

Wesley, John (1703–1791). Anglican priest, who became founder of

Methodism. There is an edition of his works in progress, published initially at Oxford, then at Nashville, Tennessee.

William of Auxerre (died 1231). Influential Parisian theologian. Edition of his *Summa Aurea* by J. Ribaillier, Grottaferrata 1980–1986.

Xenophanes (late 6th cent. BC). Greek poet and philosopher. Edition of the surviving fragments in DK.

Xenophon (*c.* 428–*c.* 354 BC). Greek prose writer and historian. Standard edition of his works by E. C. Marchant in the Oxford Classical Texts, 1900–1910.

ABBREVIATIONS AND MODERN WORKS

Alberigo, J., and others, *Conciliorum Oecumenicorum Decreta*, 3rd edn, Bologna 1973.
Andrieu, M., ed., *Le Pontifical Romain au Moyen Age*, Rome 1938–1941.
Barnard, L. W., *Justin Martyr*, Cambridge 1967.
Bollack, J., and A. Laks, *Etudes sur l'Epicurisme Antique* (Cahiers de Philologie 1), Lille 1976.
Bostock, D., *Plato's Phaedo*, Oxford 1986.
Bremmer, J., *The Early Greek Concept of the Soul*, Princeton 1983.
Brock, S., *Sogiatha: Syriac Dialogue Hymns*, Kottayam 1987.
Burkert, W., *Lore and Science in Ancient Pythagoreanism*, trans. E. L. Minar, Cambridge Mass. 1972.
Cullmann, O., *Immortality of the Soul or Resurrection of the Dead?*, London 1958.
Denifle, H., with E. Chatelain, *Chartularium Universitatis Parisiensis*, Paris 1889–1897.
Denzinger, H., *Enchiridion Symbolorum, Definitionum et Declarationum de Rebus Fidei et Morum*, 32nd edn, enlarged and revised by A. Schönmetzer, Herder 1963.
Deshusses, J., *Le Sacrementaire Grégorien* vol. I, Fribourg 1971.
Diano, C., *Scritti Epicurei*, Florence 1974.
Dillon, J., *The Middle Platonists*, London 1977.
DK =Diels, H., *Die Fragmente der Vorsokratiker*, 9th edn, revised by W. Kranz, Berlin 1960.
Dodds, E. R., *The Greeks and the Irrational*, Berkeley 1971.
Dover, K. J., *Greek Homosexuality*, London 1978.
Fränkel, H., *Dichtung und Philosophie des frühen Griechentums*, Munich 1976.
Garland, R., *The Greek Way of Death*, London 1985.
Gibson, E. C. S., *The Thirty-Nine Articles of the Church of England*, London 1906.
Griffin, J., *Homer on Life and Death*, Oxford 1980.
Grillmeier, A., *Christ and Christian Tradition*, rev. edn vol. I, London 1975.
Guthrie, W. K. C., *History of Greek Philosophy*, Cambridge 1962–1981.
Hänggi, A., and I. Pahl, *Prex Eucharistica*, Fribourg 1968.

Harder, R., *Über Ciceros Somnium Scipionis*, Halle 1929.
Heidegger, M., *Being and Time*, trans. J. Macquarrie and E. Robinson, Oxford 1962.
Hick, J., *Death and Eternal Life*, London 1985.
Journel, R. de, *Enchiridion Patristicum*, Freiburg i.Br. 1951.
Kahn, C. H., *The Art and Thought of Heraclitus*, Cambridge 1979.
Kelly, J. N. D., *Early Christian Creeds*, 2nd edn, London 1960.
Krell, D. F., *Intimations of Mortality: Time, Truth and Finitude in Heidegger's Thinking of Being*, University Park, Pennsylvania 1986.
Le Guin, U., *The Farthest Shore*, London 1973.
Lewis, C. S., *The Great Divorce*, Fontana edn, London 1972.
Lloyd-Jones, H., *The Justice of Zeus*, Berkeley 1971.
Long, A. A., and D. N. Sedley, *The Hellenistic Philosophers*, Cambridge 1987 (cited by individual text, since the references are the same in both volumes, vol. I containing translations and comments, vol. II containing original texts).
McDannell, C., and B. Lang, *Heaven, A History*, New Haven/London 1988.
Macdonald, G., *Complete Fairy Tales*, New York 1977.
Macleod, C. W., *Homer, Iliad book XXIV*, Cambridge 1982.
Nagel, T., *Mortal Questions*, Cambridge 1979.
Nauck, A., *Tragicorum Graecorum Fragmenta*, ed. with supplement by B. Snell, Hildesheim 1983.
Osborne, C., *Rethinking Early Greek Philosophy: Hippolytus of Rome and the Presocratics*, London 1987.
Parfit, D., *Reasons and Persons*, Oxford 1984.
Perrett, R. W., *Death and Immortality*, Dordrecht 1987.
Peter, C. J., *Participated Eternity in the Vision of God*, Rome 1964.
Petit, L., and G. Hofmann, *De Purgatorio Disputationes in Concilio Florentino habitae* (Concilium Florentinum, Series A, vol. VIII fasc. II), Rome 1969.
PG = Migne, *Patrologia Graeca*.
PL = Migne, *Patrologia Latina*.
Rist, J. M., *Stoic Philosophy*, Cambridge, 1969.
Robinson, J. M., ed., *The Nag Hammadi Library in English*, San Francisco 1977.
Sacred Congregation for the Doctrine of the Faith, *Epistula ad Venerabiles Praesules Conferentiarum Episcopalium de quibusdam Quaestionibus ad Eschatologiam spectantibus*, in *Acta Apostolicae Sedis* 71 (1979) pp. 939–943.
Sicard, D., *La Liturgie de la Mort dans l'Eglise Latine des Origines à la Réforme Carolingienne*, Münster 1978.
Swinburne, R., *Faith and Reason*, Oxford 1981.
Taplin, O., *Greek Tragedy in Action*, London 1978.
Tod, M. N., *Selection of Greek Historical Inscriptions* vol. I, Oxford 1933.
Tugwell, S., *Albert and Thomas*, New York 1988.
Tugwell, S., *The Apostolic Fathers*, London 1989.
Tugwell, S., *Early Dominicans*, New York 1982.
Usener, H., *Epicurea*, Leipzig 1887.
Van Eijk, T. H. C., *La Résurrection des Morts chez les Pères Apostoliques*, Paris 1974.

Vellacott, P., *Ironic Drama, A Study of Euripides' Method and Meaning*, Cambridge 1975.
Vermeule, E., *Aspects of Death in Early Greek Art and Poetry*, Berkeley 1979.
Von Arnim, J., *Stoicorum Veterum Fragmenta*, Leipzig 1905–1924.
Wilde, Oscar, *Complete Shorter Fiction*, ed. I. Murray, Oxford 1980.
Williams, Charles, *Descent into Hell*, London 1949 (first publ. 1937).
Williams, Charles, *Shadows of Ecstasy*, London 1965 (first publ. 1931).

Index

(a) Biblical references

(b) Index of sources